A WOMAN'S PLACE IN EDUCATION

A Woman's Place in Education

Historical and sociological perspectives on gender and education

SARA DELAMONT

Avebury

Aldershot • Brookfield USA • Hong Kong • Singapore • Sydney

Published by
Avebury
Ashgate Publishing Limited
Gower House
Croft Road
Aldershot
Hants GU11 3HR
England

Ashgate Publishing Company
Old Post Road
Brookfield
Vermont 05036
USA

British Library Cataloguing in Publication Data

Delamont, Sara
    Woman's Place in Education: Historical
    and Sociological Perspectives on Gender
    and Education. – (Cardiff Papers in
    Qualitative Research)
    I. Title II. Series
    376

    ISBN 1 85628 583 9

Library of Congress Catalog Card Number: 95-80521

Printed in Great Britain by
Antony Rowe Ltd, Chippenham, Wiltshire

Contents

List of tables

List of figures

Acknowledgements

The research reported in these papers was supported by the ESRC, SCRE, and the Welsh Education Office.

All the opinions expressed are entirely my own. Lesley Pugsley read the manuscript and worked extensively on the bibliography. Elizabeth Renton typed the original drafts, Jackie Swift prepared the final, camera ready version.

Paul Atkinson commented on many of these pieces at some stage, and made invaluable comments.

1. Introduction: A woman's place in education: myths, monsters and misapprehensions

Preface

This introductory essay is based on two public lectures given in the mid-1980s. In 1984 I was the President of the British Educational Research Assocation, and my presidential address was called 'A Woman's Place in Education'. In 1985 I gave an invited lecture called 'Fighting Familiarity: Focusing on Gender as a Strategy and a Tactic in Qualitative Research' to a summer school on qualitative methods at Warwick University. This chapter combines the central features of these two lectures.

In 1887 a book was published called *Forbidden Fruit for Young Men*. It consisted of questions put by men on relations between the sexes answered by a doctor. One query was as follows:

> Should the girl who wishes to fulfil her maternal duties avoid the influence of education? And should the educated woman remain celibate?

The expert answered firmly YES

> Girls who are natural, and would like to be (well) married, would do well to avoid education, remembering that the personal advantage to the highly educated woman impairs her usefulness as a mother. Those who overtax their vital energies by an intellectual strain likely to produce ill effects on their offspring, ought to accept a voluntary celibacy.

They are self-made invalids and must accept the penalties of the position.

> (Macdonald, 1981:16)

This idea did not die with Queen Victoria. In 1920 a woman doctor, Arabella Kenealy wrote that:

> The woman of average brain attains the intellectual standards of the man of average brain only at the cost of her health, of her emotions, or of her morale. (p.155)

Kenealy argued that the girls' secondary schools established since the 1870's were producing in 1920, girls who had lost "every womanly characteristic", and who had lapsed "to the biological grade not of cultured, but of rough working men". Kenealy believed that schools like Wycombe Abbey, St.Leonards and Bedford High School for Girls were making girls more masculine in physique, so they became "more like colts or smaller bullocks!" They also became masculine in their mental processes, so that:

> ...male mental proclivities develop: obsessions to wear trousers, to smoke, to stride, to kill.

By despising cookery, needlework and child care and excluding them from the curriculum, the state schools for girls had:

> ...engendered the race of stunted, precocious, bold-eyed, cigarette-smoking, free-living working girls who fill our streets, many tricked out like cocottes, eyes roving after men, impudence upon their tongues, their poor brains vitiated by vulgar rag-tunes and cinema scenes of vice and suggestiveness.

Kenealy blamed the feminist movement for the schooling of girls, and for leading Britain (and the whole Anglo-Saxon race) into Prussianism, socialism, Bolshevism and Anarchism! (We should be so lucky!)

It is easy to laugh at such wild statements, and ridicule such bizarre views. Anyone can be wise after the event. In this chapter I propose to make four points about woman's place in education which will lead us to see Arabella Kenealy in a different light. These four points are:

1. The views held by experts (e.g. doctors, clergyman, judges) on woman's place in education during the period 1850-1945 now seem to us quaint, illogical and even lunatic.

2. **But**, it is very easy for us to look back and mock both the opponents of womens' education (and their supporters) while ignoring the facts that our views today may well be founded on equally shaky, unexamined premises.

3. **Consequently** it is the task of educational researchers to scrutinise the unexamined assumptions, the take-for-granted, commonsense 'reality' of educational institutions and practices - and this includes the roles played by schools and colleges in reproducing sexual divisions in society. By researchers I mean men **and** women scholars, because single-sex research will not scrutinise and make problematic every day reality.

4. Finally, I discuss what woman's place in education **is** - once we have challenged the myths, dispelled the misapprehensions, and learnt to avoid the monsters. It will come as no surprise that my view is that woman's place in education is wherever the action is - not at the margins and in the backwaters.

The debate and the cause 1850-1950

Both sides of the struggle to gain women's entry to academic secondary education, university degrees and the liberal professions during the 1850-1950 period appear absurd today.

Opponents of women's education believed that the female reproductive system made her health so precarious that she could not study Greek or Algebra without the risk of brain fever or sterility. Such dangers to the health and welfare of ladies (because no one really expected working class females to learn Latin or go to university) were not just serious for the individuals. The lady might become sterile and thus threaten the survival of their class and race. If the 'best' women did not have babies, their class and race would either die out, or have to mix in inferior stock.

We find such ideas absurd today. We believe that the feminist educational pioneers, who held that regular exercise without tight corsets would ensure good health in female scholars, were closer to scientific truth. Yet when we hear about how pioneers like Ada Benson ran their schools and colleges many of *their* ideas seem bizarre. For example, when Bedford High School for Girls (founded in 1882) opened its playing fields in 1900 the girls had to walk there in silence, and could only walk beside a friend if written permission had been granted by both sets of parents and the headmistress. Gloves, of course, had to be worn on the walk, and hats were *de rigeur* (Godber and Hutchins, 1982:211).

The reasons for these rules has been explicated elsewhere (Delamont and Duffin, 1978, Delamont 1989, 1993b) and is not repeated here. My point is that it is all too easy to mock such beliefs and practices, while ignoring the social context in which they were held; and to assume that we are not too wise to hold any mistaken notions, and all our beliefs are grounded in scientific fact. Our beliefs about sex roles and education today may be just as mistaken as Kenealy's. We need to be very, very careful to study the basis for our beliefs and not accept, passively, the things that our culture takes for granted. Our job is to scrutinise, to challenge, to dig deeply into what non-researchers take for granted.

This is not an easy strategy. Michael F.D.Young (1971) told us two decades ago that we should 'make' problems, rather than 'take' them from educators. This is easier said than done, especially when we want to scrutinise the reproduction of sex roles in education. It is hard to remember that when a teacher says "I want four boys to carry these boxes", or a pupil announces that "drama is for sissies" or a parent decides that her son is not going to learn cookery, these are only late 20th Century versions of the myth that giving women the vote would produce a pacifist, temperance-introducing government.

In the main body of this chapter the need to 'make' research problems is explored, using qualitative research on everyday life in schools, and the schooling of girls and boys as interrelated illustrations.

Gender and familiarity

This section brings together two issues that concern me when I consider the current state of qualitative research in education: the familiarity problem and the boom in 'women's studies'. I have written about both issues before: familiarity in Delamont (1981, 1983c) and Galton and Delamont (1985) and gender issues in Delamont (1980, 1983a, 1983b, 1984a). However the relationships between the two themes have not been fully explored, although the results are of interest both to qualitative researchers uninterested in gender, and to those concerned to study gender as a topic. My argument is that few qualitative researchers have lived up to the standard set by Becker (1971) and Young (1971), and that focusing on gender can help us deal with the familiarity problem *and* provide important data. Focusing on gender is characterised both as a strategy and as a topic.

Before considering these two topics, it is necessary to exemplify what I mean by qualitative research. It is not a term with which I feel particularly happy - I would normally write about 'ethnography'. For the purposes of this paper qualitative research is taken as synonymous with what Cohen and Manion (1985: 41) call interpretive methodologies. Included within qualitative research would be participant and non-participant observation, unstructured/open-ended interviewing, life-history and oral-history elucidation, and certain kinds of documentary research. Sampling is likely to be theoretical, and rigour, reliability and validity are more a matter of reflexivity than statistical probabilities and correlations. Theorizing and generalising will be done via generic problems and the use of formal concepts.

In educational research qualitative methods have been much more intensively used on some topics than others. Research on school ethos, on classroom processes, and on teachers' attitudes has been done with both qualitative *and* quantitative methods - but there is a very little qualitative research on social mobility. My own research in education has been mainly qualitative, and focused on interaction in schools and classrooms, the evaluation of CA1, the training of chemistry teachers, and the problems of research students in education. (Delamont, 1983c and 1983d; Delamont and Howe, 1973; Galton and Delamont, 1976; Eggleston and Delamont, 1983) Most of what follows is based on school and classroom ethnography, but the general principles would apply to other empirical topics, so I have used examples from others areas where possible. With these preliminaries in mind, let us turn to the familiarity problem.

The familiarity problem

In 1971 Howard Becker went into print saying that one of the most serious problems facing the contemporary classroom and school observer was that

> it is first and foremost a matter of it all being so familiar that it becomes impossible to single out events

He said that when he talked to educational researchers 'who have sat around in classrooms trying to observe' he found that

> it is like pulling teeth to get them to see or write anything beyond what 'everyone' knows

Becker's comment appeared in an American 'anthropology of education' collection, while M.F.D. Young (1971) was issuing his similar clarion call to British sociologists. Although there are significant differences between British and American researchers in their use of qualitative methods

(Delamont and Atkinson, 1980) it is clear that, in 1971, on both sides of the Atlantic there were similar feelings about researchers taking too many features of schooling for granted. It is fifteen years now since those diagnoses were made, and in this paper I want to show that neither has been heeded sufficiently, suggest why this might be so, and then move to consider gender as one focusing device for tackling the problem.

The central argument in Young's (1971) piece was, of course, that sociologists had focused so much on structures that they had neglected to study the *content* of education and who had power over it. Young did offer a solution for sociologists, instead of taking the problems of teachers, to make the curriculum problematic. Becker (1971) did not offer any solution to the familiarity problem, although he and Blanche Geer did a project on learning in non-educational setting such as barbers' shops (Geer, 1972). It is my contention, however, that the Becker/Young diagnosis was correct, and that little has changed since. Our task now is to devise strategies to deal with the familiarity problem.

Harry Wolcott (1981) was making a similar point, when he wrote that it took a colleague from outside educational research:

> to jolt me into realizing that the kinds of data teachers gather 'on' and 'for' each other so admiringly reflect dominant society and its educator subculture.

This colleague was 'particularly intrigued' by the research about 'Time on Task' [Denham and Liberman, 1980], and commented:

> How incredible...that teachers would measure classroom effectiveness by whether pupils appear to be busy. How like teachers to confuse "busy-ness" and learning.

Wolcott then pointed out that he and his educational research colleagues

> have not systematically encouraged our students...to go and look at something else for a while. We keep sending them back to the classroom. The only doctoral student I have sent off to do fieldwork in a hospital was a nurse-educator who returned to her faculty position in a school of nursing!

There were, therefore, some pieces of evidence that most ethnographers were trapped by the familiarity of their research setting. I do not intend here to examine subsequent research to see if there has been any change, but to argue that many of the people currently doing research are still having the problem. Accordingly, it is useful to run through the strategies I suggested to combat the familiarity problem:

1.   Studying unusual classrooms in our own culture.
2.   Studying schools and classrooms in other cultures.
3.   Study non-educational settings.
4.   Adopt gender as the main focus.

I will only deal with 1-3 briefly here, with an example of a study that 'works' because of its employment.

1)   *'Unusual' settings in our culture*

A great deal of insight into ordinary schools and classrooms can be gained by studying unusual ones. Apart from Atkinson's (1981, 1984) work on a medical school, we can see ordinary schooling better when we have read about the Newsom Department in a Catholic School (Burgess, 1983), a men's cookery class in an adult education centre (Coxon, 1983), an industrial training unit of slow learners (Shone and Atkinson, 1981), or the Harvard Business School (Cohen, 1973).

2)   *'Other cultures'*

The most interesting school ethnography I've ever read is Bullivant's (1978) research in an Orthodox Jewish Boys' School in Australia which is particularly fascinating because the study shows culture-clash between schools and home, among very clever, very scholarly, boys rather than among failures. Equally fascinating are Singleton's (1979) study of *Nichu*, a Japanese school; Kleinfeld's (1971) research among Eskimo teenagers in a Catholic Boarding School in Canada, and Dale Eickleman's (1978) work on how Islamic scholars learn in Koranic schools and universities.

3)   *Non-educational settings*

My favourite example here is a particularly exotic one - research on urban Brazilian *Umbanda* (Leacock and Leacock, 1975). I have argued elsewhere that their data on how Brazilians learn to receive spirits, and take part in ceremonial dancing offer fascinating parallels for teacher training. Paul Atkinson (1981, 1985) has drawn on equally intriguing parallel between Homer's *Iliad* and the street *argot* of Labov's inner city blacks. Harry

7

Wolcott (1977) used the Australian kinship organizational device of opposed moieties to illuminate the relationship between teachers and educational administrators and innovators. An analysis of icon painting (Kenna, 1985) would throw light on the ways in which infant school teachers expect paintings to be constructed (King, 1978 p.36). Howard Newby's (1977) work on deference and paternalistic authority in farming areas offers illuminating parallels for studying relationships between parents and teachers, ancillaries and staff, and between the head and his staff.

4)   *Adopt gender as the focus*

Many school and classroom ethnographies have not treated gender as an issue at all. For example David Hamilton's (1977) study of an open-plan infants class hardly mentions that the teachers were not only working in a type of building quite new to them, but were also teaching mixed classes for the first time. David Marsland's (1982) essay on 'The sociology of adolescence and youth' focuses on studies of male adolescents, and never even *mentions* that all work on females, or criticisms of the field by feminists, are being ignored. Leaving aside for the moment the inaccuracies and lacunae that arise when researchers ignore gender, or focus on males only, let us consider first the *power* that resides in focusing on gender as a strategy for illuminating otherwise taken-for-granted situations.

If we accept that most of us find educational institutions and the interactions in them too familiar too much of the time, how does focusing on gender help? It can act as a new lens through which to view the previously taken-for-granted, as in Carol Joffe's (1974) research in a 'progressive' nursery school in San Francisco. This pre-school was run by a group of parents on self-consciously 'progressive' lines, yet Joffe, by concentrating on gender, was able to raise our consciousness about schooling. Joffe reports that one aspect of the school buildings which disturbed parents was that the lavatories were uni-sex. The fact that this school did not sex-segregate its lavatories is a salutary reminder that we do not 'see' many of the organizational devices which separate males and females in our schools.

Similarly, Joffe noted that when the teachers commented on the clothes and appearance of pupils, girls got such compliments not boys - but girls only got compliments when wearing skirts and dresses. Girls in trousers, like boys, received no favourable remarks on their clothes or appearance. This finding, which needs to be replicated in other educational settings, raises very interesting questions about sex role socialization, and about how teachers interact with children. Similar challenges to what we take for granted about children's toy and play preferences can be seen in the work of Serbin (1978). Serbin's work not only revealed that teachers were unaware of the ways in which they reinforced the very 'clinging' behaviour in girls they disliked, but also focused our attention on proxemics and object - use in the classroom. Both these are topics which, if studied closely, can provide novel analyses of important classroom dimensions. It took Serbin to make the cliche 'boys play with cars, girls with dolls' problematic and study *why* they did so.

Two pieces of research on gender differences in school which revealed important aspects of pupil culture are those of Sussman (1977) and Guttentag and Bray (1976). Guttentag and Bray were working on an action-research project to reduce sex differentiation in schooling, and found a fascinating feature of pupils' playground culture. They report that ten year old boys avoided the girls because of a belief that if they touched a girl they became polluted with a mysterious contagion, called 'cooties' or 'girl-touch', which needed to be cured by a ritual. Sussman's ethnography of American progressive primary schools revealed that the more 'pupil-centred' the regime, the more sex-segregating the pupils engaged in. This is an important hypothesis about 'progressive' classrooms which deserves careful research attention.

In Britain we have two pieces of research on infant and primary pupils (King, 1978; Clarricoates, 1980, 1983) where, because both class and sex are highlighted, a fuller and more rounded picture of school life emerges than from studies which pay attention only to class, ignoring sex (Sharp and Green, 1976; Nash,1973). At secondary level the insights of Buswell (1981, 1984) into everyday life in a mixed comprehensive school are sharpened by her attention to the constant gender differentiation compared to, for example, Larkin's (1979) essentially familiar study of a surburban American high school.

Wolcott (1981) is concerned about the way in which features of schooling taken for granted by educationalists are built-in to educational research rather than scrutinized. Precisely because schools are imbued with unthinking sexism, focusing upon gender differentiation is a powerful strategy for making the familiar strange, and challenging the taken-for-granted realities of educational institutions.

So far I have concentrated on using gender as a strategy for tackling the familiarity problem, but for the remainder of the chapter I want to address the importance of gender as a topic in its own right.

Gender as a topic

When we turn to educational research which focuses on gender as a topic we immediately confront four paradoxes. First, we have a boom in research on women and girls in nearly all sectors of the education system which has had little or no impact on the mainstream of the subject. Second, we have several assertions and assumptions being made about gender and education on the basis of what, on inspection, is a rather shaky data base by the very people who have attacked the extant research for being grounded on inadequate samples and methods. Third we have a serious shortage of research on boys and men *as males*, rather than studies which treat them as typical/normal representatives of the whole of humanity, because all-male samples are now only feasible among those who choose to ignore gender as an issue. Fourth we have the call for 'feminist' methodology which, if heeded, would prevent any research by or on females being taken seriously by mainstream educational circles. Each of these is examined in turn.

The booming ghetto

There is no doubt that research on women and girls, in education has grown rapidly with the rise of the new women's movement since the late 1960s. An American bibliography (Wilkins, 1979) has 1134 items; Coates (1983) lists 224 items from Britain and Europe published since 1970; and the bibliography by Riddell (1984) is 25 pages of very small print packed with references. There is plenty of research being done now on a range of topics, in nearly every sector of the education system. However, as Acker (1982, 1984) has pointed out, much of it is in books, journals and research reports which are only read by those interested in 'women's studies', and its impact on the mainstream disciplines of educational research have feminist critiques and new bodies of research, but the material is presented and represented as a separate appendix to the 'real work' of the discipline.

The houses built on sand?

Much of the force of feminist critiques of existing educational research has come from pointing out that only half the story is being told. Thus Brian Simon's four volume history of education in Britain fails to deal with women's education at all (Simon, 1965, 1974a, 1974b, 1990); the philosophy (Martin, 1984) psychology (Sayers, 1984) and sociolinguistics (French and French, 1984) of education have all been criticised on similar grounds; while sociology of education has been particularly censured

(Acker, 1981). There is no doubt that women and girls have been neglected, and that the accounts offered by the various disciplines are thereby impoverished. However, there is also no doubt that some of the supposed 'findings' on women and education rest on some inadequate basis. Some of the studies are methodologically suspect, others draw on tiny samples which may well be unrepresentative.

Dale Spender's (1982: 57) dramatic claims about language use in secondary classrooms is a good example of this. Spender argues that in co-educational secondary comprehensive schools there is a grossly unjust division of classroom talk. Boys take an unfair share of the pupil talk time available, and receive an unfair proportion of the teacher's talk, time and attention. If a teacher tries to reduce the boys' contributions below 70% of the pupil talk, or devote attention to girls, boys react violently. She summarises her findings as follows:

> in a sexist society boys assume that two-thirds of the teacher's attention constitutes a fair deal and if this ratio is altered so that they receive less than two-thirds of the teachers' attention they feel they are being discriminated against.

Now, if this is a real finding, it is one to which we should all pay attention. However, Spender bases it on an unspecified number of lessons (sometimes 'many' and sometimes 'ten'), and any classroom researcher would be vehement that such sweeping statements should not be based on such a small, personalised, and unrepresentative sample of lessons. Flanders (1970) proposed six hours as a *minimum* sampling period to categorize a teacher's style; Croll (1980) points out that the ORACLE project draws on 47,000 observations of 58 teachers and 85,000 observations of 489 pupils. Spender's researcher is patently inadequate. A more thorough review of the literature on sex differences in teacher-pupil interaction by Bossert (1982) concludes, more accurately if less dramatically:

> These results leave us in a muddle. Teachers do treat girls and boys differently, but the extensiveness of this differential treatment, whether it is perceived by students, and how it might affect their sex-role behaviour and attitudes in unknown.

It ill behoves critics of existing research for ignoring women's experiences to set in its place studies which are equally badly done purely because the results are ideologically exciting.

The irony of the absent male

Research on boys and men in education has now become a paradoxical topic. On one hand we have a plethora of research on all male samples in all areas of educational research from social mobility (Halsey et al., 1980), history (Simon, 1974a and 1974b), grammar school streaming (Lacey, 1970), delinquency and school ethos (Rutter et al., 1979) medical student socialization (Becker et al., 1961) urban street gangs (Parker, 1974) and public school parental choice (Fox, 1985). Yet in all these projects the male samples are not studied *as males* who might have different perspectives from females, but as representatives of the UK Population, the rise of the working class, the inhumanity of the grammar school, the importance of a good ethos, the learning environment of medical school, life in an inner-city slum, and the social role of private schooling in modern Britain.

When we need to know something about men's different experiences compared to women's, we typically have no available data. In a society where most people live in mixed world, and where most educational institutions are mixed, this is distinctly odd. There are at least three areas of research where data on males *as males* would be of considerable educational value: the stigmatised clever woman, sexuality in adolescent life, and subject-choice at secondary school.

Long ago Komorovsky (1946) found that female undergraduates in the USA believed that men did not like clever women, and therefore 'played dumb'. She repeated the research in 1972 and found that the next generation of college women still felt constrained by male prejudice, *and*, by studying men, showed that they were correct. College men did indeed feel threatened by clever women. In the UK we have a study of Scottish women students (Galloway, 1973) which found they believed men disliked clever women. We still do not have any research on men to see if it is true in Britain!

As Morgan (1981) has pointed out 'taking gender seriously' is not a simple operation as research on sexuality, in particular, shows. The sexual double standard is a second example. Deidre Wilson (1978) and Lesley Smith (1978) show clearly that teenage girls do not necessarily believe that all females can be easily divided into 'slags' and 'virgins', but they *are* convinced that boys believe this. Lesley Smith's sample of fourteen to sixteen year olds in Bristol were quite clear about where they stood. For example:

> Liz: Look I don't believe there should be one standard for a boy and another for a girl. But there just is round here and there's not much you can do about it. A chap's going to look for someone who hasn't had it off with every bloke. So as soon as you let them put a leg over you, you've got a bad name.

Because boys believe it, and the boys' definition of the situation is the determining one, girls have to abide and live by it. Girls have to guard their own behaviour, and choose their friends carefully, because a slag's friends are contaminated by her. Some researchers have shown boys hold this simplistic view of girls (e.g. Parker, (1974; Willis, 1977) but no detailed work has been done. Yet it is an important area for social policy. Adolescent girls believe that boys think that only slags use contraception - and therefore to be known as knowledgeable about it or to be 'on the pill' brands one as promiscuous. If boys really believe this, then the implications for health education are clear - it has to be directed at boys, and it has to challenge their simplistic views of females' 'virtue'. Directing homilies at girls to use contraception is unlikely to be effective in dealing with teenage pregnancies because they see themselves as powerless against male ideology. The social consequences of being labelled a slag by local boys are seen as more serious than risking pregnancy by unprotected sexual relations.

The third area where attention has been focused on females and not on males is that of co-education and subject choice at secondary school. Shaw (1976) was one of the first of the recent group of scholars to raise doubts about the effects of co-education on girls. Since Shaw other authors have questioned the benefits of co-education (e.g. Deem, 1984), alongside a continuing anxiety about the small number of girls studying maths, sciences and heavy craft subjects (Kelly, 1981). It is now clear from the reviews by Bone (1983) and Steedman (1983) that it is not possible to disentangle the relative importance of single-sex schooling compared with social class and initial ability, when the specialisation patterns and exam success of girls are considered. Upper and middle class females, and those of higher ability, are more likely to be in single-sex schools than working class and lower ability ones, so the three factors are confounded. However, we have seen projects designed to encourage more girls into science and craft subjects, as well as research into exactly what it is about science, maths and craft which repels this. Such enterprises are based on clear ideas that sex equality demands numerate women who can make a dovetail joint and understand electricity. If so, it is equally clear that sex equality demands boys who can order a meal in rural Austria, cook a Christmas pudding and sew on a button. Yet we have not seen publications or research on how to attract and retain boys in needlework, German or cooking. Powell and Littlewood (1982) have expressed concern about the failure of foreign languages to retain boys, but we lack detailed data on classroom interaction, boys' perception of the subject and so on. The data from the ORACLE transfer studies (Galton and Willcocks, 1983; Galton and Delamont, 1985) suggest that boys particularly resent the oral methods used to start French, but that project did not study how this related to their sense of masculinity. Measor and Woods (1984) have made some moves to focus on these issues, but we are a long way from understanding the role of masculinity in education.

Feminist methodology or good methodology?

The second edition of Cohen and Manion's (1985) excellent book of educational research methods points out that there have been developments in methodology since 1980, and that the new version includes expansions and revisions. One development which they have excluded is feminist methodology and it is that topic and its exclusion from standard handbooks that forms my last point.

Sue Clegg (1985) has produced an excellent over-view of the debates on feminist methodology, and it is not necessary to recapitulate all aspects of it here. Let me just say that two ideas frequently found in the debates over feminist methodology worry me a great deal. These are the equation of feminist research with qualitative methods only, and the argument that sound scholarship can be judged by the criterion of personal authenticity.

Arguing that quantitative methods are unsuitable for, or unacceptable, for feminist research seems to me to insult researchers who use them; ignore the fact that policy makers are often more influenced by numbers than accounts; and make unduly optimistic assumptions about qualitative research. (The first two arguments can be followed up in Jayaratne, 1983; the last in Lofland, 1985).

Arguing for personal authenticity is superficially appealing, but seems to me to be quite erroneous. Not only does it reinforce stereotypes that women are:

irrational
ruled by their emotions
unable to generalize

14

liable to personalize everything

but it can lead to absurdities. Dorothy Smith (1976), a scholar I much admire - her work on women under capitalism seems to me the best thing on the topic (Smith, 1977) - has written a paper on creating a sociology for women, which illustrates my problem with the authenticity criterion. Smith argues that Talcott Parson's sociology, in which she was trained, is built upon the model of a rational man planning his life in a rational, rule-governed world. She offers as a challenge to this school of sociology her own biography:

> I think I would be by no means alone in seeing in my past not so much a *career* as a series of contingencies, of accidents, so I seem to have become who I am almost by chance.

Smith argues that this is true of other women for females

have little opportunity for the exercise of mastery or control

So, Smith argues, if women had built modern sociology it would *not* have taken the form it did under Parson's influence. Moreover women in social sciences (as opposed to those in the arts) have not learnt how to build social science from their experience.

Smith's critique of Talcott Parsons is devastating and certainly shared by this author. However, I cannot accept her base for it. Any socially deprived, powerless group could be used to show how Parsons' supposed theory of mankind is actually a theory of WASP middle class urban males. For example the work of Liebow (1967) on Afro-Americans would serve just as well to challenge the supposed universality of Parsons's ideas.

Dorothy Smith's own experiences have given her a valuable *insight* but it cannot be said to prove or disprove anything. There is no evidence that all women are like those she pictures - drifting through a series of accidents. If I apply Smith's criterion to my own biography, I find that her description of 'women' lacks personal authenticity. My own experience is of planning a rational career in which occupational values have always taken precedence over personal ones. My biography fits Talcott Parsons's model of man better than Smith's model of woman. On Smith's own account I should therefore be a Parsonian.

Obviously that is silly. Because of my scholarly knowledge of the lives of the powerless I know that Parsons's model is inadequate. My personal experience (like Dorothy Smith's) is only useful *to make things problematic*, not as a criterion of academic soundness. If a theory 'feels' wrong about oneself, or about 'women in general' then it probably is wrong or inadequate, but personal authenticity should not be our criterion of falsification. We should use our academic authority and skills to challenge it, and rebuild it. Good feminism will not be built on bad social science.

The research agenda

So far I have been loosely talking about 'we'. Many men will have assumed that 'we' meant women researchers. However I do not mean women researchers. I mean all of us. Sex roles are too important to become a ghetto area in educational research. This is not just because sex roles are an important research topic, it is also because when researchers focus on how sex roles are reproduced in educational institutions they gain excellent leverage on many other aspects of these institutions. For example, once we begin to examine the introduction of needlework to boys, we can begin to think clearly about what needlework is doing in the school curriculum as a whole. Once women entered Yale, certain previously unconsidered aspects of Yale life became visible, problematic, and were open to scrutiny.

So, I believe that the payoff from research on sex roles is considerable for both sexes. I am also cynical enough to fear that if only women work on the subject, the results will be 'written off', and not believed. If a woman discovers that 20% of all biology teachers never address an open question to girls in their classes, it can be written off as feminist (even hysterical) propaganda. When a man decides that sex roles in questioning in biology is worth researching, does a project, and finds that 20% of teachers never address an open question to girls, it will be believed.

This is not, of course, a state of affairs I condone - an ideal world would judge all results on their merits, not the sex of their author - but it is a recognition of contemporary research politics that if Neville Bennett, Maurice Galton, or A.H.Halsey produced a research report demonstrating sexual inequalities it would be received as objective. If I did it, it would be feminist propaganda.

So men and women need to work on sex roles, not just women. It is also important that educational research ignore the calls for 'feminist methodology'. There is no such thing! There are research projects carried out according to scientific standards, and there are projects which have strayed from them. The latter may have built sexist assumptions into their research instruments, but that makes them badly done, not male metholodology. An empirical example will demonstrate what I mean here.

Irene Jones, a research student at Leicester, reanalysed the data (published and unpublished) from the Murdock and Phelps (1973) study *Mass Media and the Secondary School*. She found that the research instruments had sexist assumptions built into them affecting boys and girls. One section offered pupils role models, such as 'leader' and tomboy'. Murdoch and Phelps found that girls and boys had different preferred roles - but they had not, as Irene Jones shows, been offered the same roles. Boys and not been offered the roles of 'fashion follower' or 'stay at home', while girls were not offered the role of 'leader'. The design of instruments was riddled with such assumptions, leading to sex differences in the results, due to bad methodology, which stereotypes boys and girls.

Not only were the research instruments designed for the study stereotyped - the researchers went on to distort their own findings. All pupils were asked whether they went around in a group of the same sex, a mixed sex group, or just with a particular boy or girl friend. Boys said they spent their leisure with a group of boys. Girls said they spent time in a mixed group. Murdoch and Phelps report the finding that boys go around in single-sex groups - that is they chose to believe the boys' answers, discount the girls', and ignore the really interesting finding. That is, they failed to see that their research had shown a fascinating *difference* in the social construction of reality by teenage boys and girls. This was, again, bad research, not male research.

Murdoch and Phelps (1973) may seem long ago now - but a glance at David Marsland's (1982) review of the research on adolescence shows that all the same problems still characterised the field a decade later. Marsland writes a literature review on youth which never mentions girls. All the research covered is on boys, and no mention is made of females. This is an unscholarly, inaccurate paper - because blatent sexism produces bad research. This must be improved by adopting the blueprint of the ideal researcher outlined by Ian Morris (1981)

> Somewhere there is someone who is totally objective, has no preconceived notions and who collects data unsullied by selective perception.

Ian maintains that the SED:

> seek out this paragon for every project but always finds that she is already employed on another project and will not be free for two years.

17

Note that this paragon is not an exponent of feminist methodology, but good methodology.

Woman's place in education

So what **is** woman's place in education? At the centre of the discourse, receiving equal attention from researchers, earning equal salaries, attaining an equal proportion of all the jobs - salaried and honorary - and doing only half the domestic work in society. This last point is important because one cannot be Dean of the Faculty, President of the BPS, Director of the Research and Intelligence at the SED or Master of Baliol if one has *all* the childcare, *all* the cooking, all the care of aged parents, all the housework, and all the domestic planning on one's shoulders. So woman's proper place in education is one of equality - but that can only be achieved when man's place in the house becomes one of equality too. Woman's place in education will be nearer when Mothercare is renamed Parentcare.

2. Everyday life in today's schools: The female pupils' experiences

Preface

This Paper was prepared for a Festschrift which never got published, and so has not previously been in print in the UK. It has been published in Malta. It was written in the winter of 1991/92.

Introduction

On November 1st 1991 *The Times Educational Supplement* published a letter from a school governor querying the activities of the headmistress of a primary school. Among the problems was:

> Finally, we had put in our behaviour guidelines that no punishment should be embarrassing to the child. Now we've heard that she's made girls wear boys' caps if they're caught fighting.

If this disciplinary strategy has been accurately reported, the gender stereotyping is marked. Not only does the school have uniform, with different headgear for boys and girls, but fighting is seen as a 'male' pastime, and discipline is partially based on shaming one sex by comparing them to the other. Managing boys by comparing them unfavourably with girls, or *vice versa*, were common control strategies in British middle and comprehensive schools in the late 1970s (see Delamont, 1990 p.29 and p.59) and in lessons for slow learners in some Welsh comprehensives in the mid 1980s (Delamont, 1990 p.60) but to hear of them thriving in 1991 is a shock. This paper examines what is known about everyday life in British schools as it is experienced by female pupils, drawing on the research done in the last twenty-five years. There are five sections, on the research background, on teacher-pupil relationships, on same sex pupil relationships, on male-female pupil relationships, on myths and fantasies, and on an agenda for future research.

The research base

Research on everyday life inside schools and classrooms is a relatively new branch of educational research. In Britain and pioneers were Hargreaves (1967), Lacey (1970) and Lambert (1976 and 1982). In the USA, educational anthropologists were first to study classroom processes, both inside the USA Canada (e.g. Wolcott, 1971) and abroad (Spindler, 1974). Gender was not a focus of the early work. In the USA anthropologists were interested in describing minority cultures that came into conflict with dominant values inside schools, while in the UK researchers focused on social class and school achievement (see Atkinson and Delamont, 1980, 1990 for details).

Various methods have been used to study school and classroom processes: questionnaires, interviews, observation by non-participants and participants (working as teachers of role-playing pupils), audio-visual recording, and the collection of documents such as pupils' diaries, essays or life-histories.

The rise of the contemporary feminist movement produced educational researchers who wanted to examine sex differences in school outcomes (such as exam results), to explore how female pupils experienced schooling, and to try and change both the experiences and the outcomes. The work on school experiences has not been extensive but there are British and American studies of girls in nursery (Lloyd, 1989: Paley, 1984), infant (King, 1978; Serbin, 1978), primary (Clarricoates, 1987; Best 1983), secondary (Measor, 1989; Grant and Sleeter, 1986), and further education classes (Cockburn, 1987; Valli, 1986), as well as a much greater sensitivity to gender issues in school process studies generally. However there are still many gaps in our knowledge; many aspects of the schooling of girls we know little or nothing about. Before reviewing what is know in the rest of this paper, these gaps in the research need documenting.

The British research is, first, lacking in coverage of Northern Ireland. There is no monograph on the school experiences of young women in Northern Ireland either in Catholic or Protestant institutions. As Northern Ireland has many single sex schools *and* maintains academic selection at 11, comparisons could be drawn between Northern Ireland and other regions of the UK if research on women were carried out. The lack of data on gender and schooling in Northern Ireland is not the only gap in the regional coverage of our knowledge of the issues. Wales has not yet had much research carried out on gender and education. There is a brief overview of the statistics in Jones (1989) but no process studies have been published. In particular, the lack of research on girls' experiences in the fast growing Welsh-medium sector is unfortunate. There is an evaluation of one innovation aimed at broadening young women's experiences: the Women's Training Roadshow programme (Pilcher et al., 1989), but little else.

Scotland has yet to produce the range of school process studies focused on women that its unique education system deserves. The impact of moving to secondary education at 12 rather than 11 on girls, and the comparative success of Scottish comprehensives at reaching working-class teenage girls and harnessing their educational potential (McPherson and Willms, 1987) both deserve Scottish-based process studies.

Most of the British research on girls' and young women's schooling has actually been done in England, especially urban England. Like most of the British ethnographic research it has concentrated on pupils in state schools. There is shortage of work on girls'; experiences in denominational schools (especially fee-paying ones), and in elite 'public' schools. The young women I studied at 'St.Luke's' are now 36, and mine is still the only published research on the processes of schooling in the high prestige, high cost and explicitly *feminist* independent sector (Delamont, 1989). Because of the sexist biases in the sociology of education in the 1960s and 1970s (see Acker, 1981) there are gaps in the historical records of girls' schooling in Britain. The only data on young women in single sex grammar schools were collected by Lambert (1976, 1982) and Llewellyn (1980) and are mostly unpublished. There are no data on young girls' experiences of the 11+ or 12+ exams, or of streamed primary schooling; none of young women in the few Technical High Schools established after the 1944 Act, and none of life in secondary modern schools before CSE and the raising of the school leaving age to 16. All these experiences are now past and therefore lost, and sociologists failed to collect data on them when they existed. There has also been a pattern of research on male adolescents being published in monographs, while equivalent data on young women has been only available in journal articles or research reports, which have lesser impact (see Delamont, 1989, Appendix 1). Hargreaves (1967), and Lacey (1970) are frequently described as pioneers of school ethnography, while Lambert (1976, 1982), their contemporary, is ignored, because her study of the girls in 'Lumley' and 'Hightown' was never a monograph.

There is also a shortage of research which compares the lives of females in mixed and single sex schools or classes of otherwise similar types, which

21

means we are often unable to determine whether findings are due to the dynamics of schooling *or* the presence of males and females in the same rooms. The arguments advanced by Hammersley (1990) could only be addressed by such comparative research. Race and ethnicity are also topics where the data on gender are still too few in number. There are a few studies of British West Indian and South Asian women in education, but not enough, and some other ethnic groups (e.g. Greek and Turkish) have not yet been the focus of published research. The school experiences of a female pupil of Chinese origin are unlikely to be 'the same' as the British West Indians studied by Furlong (1976), Fuller (1980) and Mac an Ghaill (1988). No one could suggest our data on the latter were adequate, but we do have a few studies of British West Indian women in school, whereas we have nothing on the Chinese.

Bearing these limitations in mind, the paper now considers what is known about the school experiences of girls in contemporary Britain, in the next three sections on teacher-pupil, same-sex pupil, and opposite-sex pupil relationships. Because most of the studies conducted in the last fifteen years have been done in mixed schools, the findings reported here are from mixed schools. The feminist calls for the reintroduction of single-sex schooling (see Deem, 1985) have not yet produced a body of research on interaction *in* girls-only schools.

Teaching-pupil relationships

Female pupils in Britain are likely to be taught by women most of their classtime before the age of 11 or 12, and by women and men thereafter. The head of their school, however, is likely to be a man, and so are senior teachers such as deputy heads. Whether their teachers are men or women, however, the female pupil is likely to be viewed as *naturally* more compliant, more nurturing, more verbal, and more dependent than male pupils. Most teachers hold stereotyped, determinist views of sex differences, believing males and females to be biologically distinct: and the effects of such beliefs are conservative. Teachers who believe boys are "naturally" more gifted at scientific and mathematical reasoning are unlikely to spend time and trouble on developing scientific and mathematical prowess in girl pupils (see Delamont, 1990 pp.25-26 and 75-78). Believing phenomena to be natural has doubly conservative effects: not only are believers unlikely to try to change the phenomena, they also fear that attempts to tamper with the *status quo* will be damaging to individuals and the social fabric.

22

When pupils hold stereotyped views about male and female behaviour, then the school teachers' reinforcement of them makes classrooms uncomfortable places for the pupils who diverge from the stereotype. Wolpe (1977) and Abraham (1989a and 1989b) have both reported teachers' repulsion when faced with boys they see as 'effeminate', (see also Mac an Ghaill, 1991) and Hargreaves, Hestor and Mellor (1975) and Llewellyn (1980) report similar distaste for girls who behaved like boys.

Ironically, some studies have shown teachers reinforcing the behaviours in girls that they dislike. Serbin's (1978) research showed nursery school teachers objecting to girls 'clinging' and keeping close to them. Yet, when observed, it became clear that girls could only get teacher attention and responses when physically close; unlike boys who received teacher attention wherever they were in the nursery, girls beyond touching distance were ignored. Lloyd's (1989) observations in the South East of England in reception classes at two schools show teachers similarly trapped, as do Hilton (1991) data on playgroup workers. These latter two studies found no evidence that Serbin's conclusions had reached teachers of young children.

Other studies of teachers (see Delamont, 1990), and of recruits to the occupation (e.g. Sikes, 1991) reveal an occupational group unaware of feminist perspectives, ideas of gender as socially constructed, and unconscious of the school's role in reinforcing conservative messages about sex roles.

The only British study which runs against the trends is Smithers and Zientek (1991) who surveyed 218 infant teachers and 84% said that they tried to encourage both sexes to try activities traditionally associated with the other sex. The introduction of the National Curriculum was also thought to have potential for lessening gender stereotyping by 63% of the respondents.

There has not been very much research into sex differences in teacher-pupil interaction, and the interest in the topic has not led to large-scale projects such as ORACLE (Galton, Simon and Croll, 1980) or the American Beginning Teacher Study (Denham and Lieberman, 1980). Some of the best known and most frequently cited studies have been based on very small numbers of teachers and tiny amounts of classroom interaction (see Delamont, 1989, pp.270-272). Hammersley (1990) has challenged the conclusions of two previous sets of researchers both philosophically and in terms of the small size of the data bases used to draw conclusions that there are unjustified gender imbalances in talk in primary classrooms. The available data on primary classrooms in Britain has been reviewed by Croll and Moses (1990), who conclude that 'there is a consistent tendency for girls, on average, to receive slightly less individual teacher attention than boys' (p.197). This is largely, but not entirely, because boys are reprimanded more than girls. Croll and Moses are able to come to this conclusion in part because there have been a series of large scale observational studies of primary classroom in Britain. The data on secondary classrooms are sparser and do not allow for such generalizations to be made. Claims have been made that boys take two-thirds of the dialogue in secondary classroom, but these data are not robust.

It is easy to blame teachers for the conservative and conformist sex roles routinely reported from schools. However teachers who wish to challenge conventional male and female behaviour, dress or speech patterns can find themselves pilloried by colleagues, *and* facing resistance from pupils, who can be upset and angered by such challenges. Pupils' adherence to stereotyped sex roles is one striking finding of the research on pupils and sex roles which needs reiteration here. Study after study has shown that there is a triple standard in operation as far as children's and adolescents' sex stereotyping is concerned. Children and teenagers are relatively relaxed about their own gender-related behaviours, relatively stereotyped about their same sex peers, and highly rigid about opposite sex peers. Thus Tom believes it is fine for him to learn ballet, dubious for Philip to want to be a nurse, and outrageous for Mandy to aim for veterinary medicine. Mandy feels confident that she can be a vet, doubts whether Pauline would strip down motorbikes as a hobby, and is *sure* Philip should not be a nurse and Tom should not learn ballet.

Such beliefs were reported by many of the respondents to the Smithers and Zientek (1991) survey. As one teacher reported:

> (Boys) never turn round and say that boys can't do cookery when we have cookery activities but they turn round and says that girls can't play with the Lego with them, or girls can't play with cars (p.12)

The conservative perspective on sex roles held by pre-adolescent pupils shows up in the research on scarey stories told before transfer to secondary school (Measor and Woods, 1984: Delamont 1991), and in pupils' response to teachers who try to be different (see, for example, Beynon, 1987). Guttentag and Bray (1976) discovered that teachers who tried to challenge pupils' stereotypes *could* actually accentuate and reinforce them. A wholehearted and well-conducted intervention could change pupils' ideas, but a half-hearted or badly constructed intervention had the effect of exaggerating pupils' stereotypes. Many of the projects designed to widen pupils' horizons about the labour market, or change their ideas on sex roles, have run up against such ingrained prejudices (see Delamont, 1990, chapter 5 passim).

For the female pupil, relationships with teachers are important, but equally central to school life are peers.

Same sex pupil relationships

Young women at school place a high value on their same sex friends. In *Jackie* for May 15th 1991 the problem page carried eleven problems, four of which concerned relationships with female friends. One girl complains her friend is nice when they are alone but horrid when others are present; one fears her long standing relationship with her best friend is breaking down; a third has one friend who is unpopular with her other 'mates'; the fourth suffers because her friends think she is too well behaved in her school where her father is head of year. The co-ordinators of the problem pages in all the teenage magazines report a similar bias in the letters they receive: relationships with same sex peers matter a great deal to young women. Nilan (1991) has discussed the moral order to two cliques, one in a middle class Sydney school, one in a more working class rural Catholic school in New South Wales. In both contexts, survival in a friendship group depended on 'fairness', 'honesty' and an 'obligation to show caring', and in both settings, the maintenance of the friendships was extremely significant to the young women. For twenty years researchers have been chronicling the peer group structures of schoolgirls in mixed and single sex institutions. Lambert (1976), Meyenn (1980), Llewellyn (1980) and Delamont (1989) all found girls' peer groups in schools during the 1960s and 1970s which functioned as important parts of their of their members' lives and mediated school experience through group attitudes. Meyenn (1980) found that the twelve and thirteen year old girls in an English middle school did have groups of friends rather than one best friend, and their groups were important to them. One girl, Diane, is quoted as saying 'if we had to say somebody was our best friend you wouldn't say one person. It would be all this lot'. Meyenn found that the sixteen girls were in four groups, which he called 'P.E.', 'nice', 'quiet', and 'science lab'. The quiet girls saw themselves as 'dunces' and were in bottom groups for lessons. Yet they were not anti-school, but accepted their low status and co-operated to have fun. The 'nice' girls were apparently concerned to go through school unnoticed, neither excelling nor failing. The two more visible group were the 'P.E.' and 'science lab' girls. Both these groups wore fashionable clothes and make up, but differed in the relationship to the school. The P.E. girls were noisy and aggressive, and helped each other with schoolwork. The science lab girls were regarded by the teachers as mature and had internalized the idea that schoolwork was competitive and individual. Their 'maturity' meant they were allotted the task of caring for the animals in the science lab and recognized the value of their privilege. The science lab and P.E. girls did not get on very well together, for as Diane (a science lab girl) says, 'When we get good marks they all say "teacher's pet" and things like that', while a P.E. girl, Betty, told Meyenn about the science lab group. 'They're always trying to get round the teachers and everything. They're always teachers' pets, them four'. Meyenn's data are very similar to mine on upper middle class fourteen year olds collected in Scotland (Delamont, 1984a, 1989). At St Luke's there were similar distinctions between girls who had adopted fashion and makeup and those who had not, and between those who accepted the school's ideas about intellectual effort against those who saw schoolwork as a task to be completed by fair means or foul (e.g. copying).

The interaction between the girls in any particular friendship group can be important for the academic involvement and achievement of all of the members. Solomon (1991) is the latest in a series of observers to follow a group of 11 and 12 year old girls through their first months of science. One clique, Karen, Sheila, Mary and Anna, begin science with Karen very keen on the subject. Within two months the whole quartet have decided that they cannot 'do' science, their experiments do not work, and they are directing all their effort towards writing beautifully neat accounts of other children's successful experiments rather than trying to do their own practicals. There are not enough studies of how peer group membership can influence school performance yet, but those we do have routinely show girls valuing unanimity and consensus in their group over controversy and innovation. Boys' groups are less concerned to reach consensus and argue more enthusiastically. Because even in mixed schools, co-educational friendship or working groups are rare, pupils get little school experience of cooperating with those of the other sex.

Male-female pupil relationships

In mixed schools, although boys and girls are taught in the same rooms and spend their leisure time in the same playgrounds, the evidence is that males and females avoid each other. Pupils do not sit together or work together, unless a teacher forces them to do so (Delamont, 1990, pp.38-40). The features of pupil culture which produce this avoidance have been most sympathetically described by Raphaela Best (1983). She followed a cohort of pupils through childhood and into adolescence, learning about their culture and simultaneously confronting them with the illogicalities in their sex role stereotypes. Her central argument is that schools teach children three curricula, one overt, two hidden. The academic curriculum and the official school rules are manifest, but behind them, and largely invisible to adults were the rules of appropriate male and female behaviour learnt from peers and enforced by them. Concealed behind that first 'hidden' curriculum was a third, even more secret children's, culture, where sexuality and obscenity were crucial. The third area was the most carefully hidden from adults.

As Bauman explains:

> The free peer group activity of children is by its very nature a privileged realm in which adults are alien intruders, especially so insofar as much of the children's folklore violates what children understand to be adult standards of decorum
>
> (Bauman, 1982 p.178)

Fine (1987, pp.238-40) reports the complex process of getting pre-adolescent boys to trust him with the vulgar-obscene aspects of their culture, as do Canaan (1986), and Measor (1989). This deeply concealed pupil culture is revealed in the scarey stories told about school transfer (Measor and Woods, 1984; Delamont, 1991), and researchers can gradually gain access to it, if, like Best, they reveal themselves to be unshockable and trustworthy. Such things as sexual harassment (Mahoney, 1985; Herbert, 1989), attacks on cissies as 'poofters', and accusations about young women being sexually immoral flourish in this arena.

Research priorities

Despite the research done in the last twenty years there are many areas of female pupils' school experience which are not yet properly investigated. Apart from the lack of studies in Northern Ireland, and in Wales, some research on young women in rural areas of England is needed. The school experiences of females in fee-paying schools, both single sex and co-educational, need studying. The percentage of 16 year old women opting to stay into the sixth form has risen over the last decade without any research on why these 16 year olds are staying on rather than leaving as their predecessors did. Many of the initiatives designed to change women's experiences of education, such as Women Into Science and Engineering buses have not been evaluated by researchers (see Delamont, 1990, pp.114-115).

Most serious, however, is the lack of a large, reliable database on classroom interaction patterns from 4 to 18 in all subjects, which compares females' experiences of classroom interaction in mixed and single sex classes. It is a matter of urgency to discover whether girls are routinely receiving less teacher attention, and/or teacher attention of different kinds from boys, and how their learning experiences are different when only girls are in the room. Only when we have this large body of data can we really claim to know what the female pupils' experiences of schooling are.

3. Adolescent resistance to sex equality messages

Preface

This paper was prepared to be given as a lecture at the Annual Meeting of the British Association for the Advancement of Science held in Swansea in 1990. It has not been published in this form.

Introduction

This paper draws on two sets of data gathered by the author and colleagues in South Wales and the South East of England between 1987-1990. One set of data are drawn from a Welsh Office funded evaluation of the Cardiff Women's Training Roadshow and have been partially published (see Pilcher *et al*, 1989). The other data consist of folklore about school transfer collected by the author from sixth formers in South East England.

This paper is in four sections: the material from the Roadshow evaluation is presented, then the folklore material, then there are suggestions about why sex equality messages are failing to reach those pupils, and finally proposals for planning in next wave of programmes.

The roadshow evaluation

In June 1987 over 2,000 female pupils mostly between 12 and 18, visited the Cardiff Women's Training Roadshow: an exhibition, filmshow, careers convention and workshop designed to widen their horizons about non-traditional jobs (Pilcher *et al*, 1988, 1989a, 1989b). This was the eighth in a series of such events held round Britain run by the Women's National Commission between 1985-87. Roadshows are unusual compared to most of the other programmes designed to challenge sex role stereotyping in education because they were a *national* initiative. Venues included Cardiff and Glasgow. The Cardiff Roadshow was the only one to be evaluated, and the researchers' conclusions are a useful starting point for thinking about initiatives since 1980. The full results are published (Pilcher *et al.* 1989a, 1989c), so the issues raised here are brief and selective. Overall the Roadshow was a great success for sponsors, exhibitors, participants and visitors. However, the benefits were unevenly spread in the locality and among the schoolgirls who visited it.

A Roadshow costs a good deal of money (raised from industry, commerce and government agencies) and involves many people in a vast amount of work. For a school, visiting a Roadshow is a cheap and easy way to do something about sex equality, because the costs fall elsewhere. All the secondary schools with female pupils in three local authorities in South Wales were invited to send parties of pupils and teachers to the Roadshow. Many did not even reply to the invitation, which indicates how little importance most heads attach to female careers advice and equal opportunities. There are, for example, four Welsh-medium secondary schools in the area, but only one accepted the invitation. A few schools were enthusiastic and sent large numbers of girls, but many others were uninterested in the opportunity.

There were also noticeable differences among those schools which did send pupils in the amount of preparation for the visit that had been done, the plans made about what pupils would do there, and hence the benefits for staff and schoolgirls. For example, the adolescents were given an activity booklet to structure their use of the Roadshow, schools had been told about this in the precirculated materials, yet almost all schools allowed young women to come without pens or pencils! Following one pair of young women as they ambled round the exhibition hall (who had drifted past most of the stalls without engaging in conversation with the staff or taking part in activities) this lack of preparation in their school was apparent. When they went to the area containing role models (real live women who were bus drivers, engineers, dentists and carpenters), the girls appeared to be unaware of the purpose of this part of the Roadshow. I intervened, saying "Have you found a role model to talk to?" and steered them to the veterinary nurses. One girl commented "We haven't been told anything about this", and followed up a talk with the veterinary nurses by speaking to the women bus driver and inspector. They had had *no idea* of the active part they were supposed to be playing.

Not all the exhibitors were properly prepared to encourage teenage girls into non-traditional occupations either. The evaluation team found that people staffing the stalls were not necessarily volunteers, and/or interested in promoting sex equality at all. For some, it was just a job. As Guttentag and Bray (1976) showed, halfhearted attempts to challenge sex roles are *not* even half-effective: attempts that are poorly done or done by non-believers tend to reinforce conservatism in pupils.

As a fifteen year old complained:

> some stalls were only there to advertise and not to speak to the girls.

The research on the VISTA (women scientists and technologists visiting schools to explain their jobs) element of the Girls into Science and Technology (GIST) project (Whyte, 1985) makes it very clear that the role models only work if they are properly prepared and briefed and the 'lessons' to be learnt by pupils are made explicit.

Five hundred of the 2,000 schoolgirls who had attended the Roadshow were subsequently visited at their schools and asked about their responses to it. There was a wide range of attitudes according to the young women's ages and the type of school attended. A sixth-former at a private school who had been exposed to WISE (Women into Science and Engineering Year), been on a work-shadowing programme, done three sciences to 'O' level and planned to be a doctor told us almost wearily:

> Being at this school, everyone is told that they can do anything. We have had it all.

In contrast, younger pupils - those of 12, 13 and 14 - were surprised to discovered that women 'were allowed' to be plumbers, bus drivers and solicitors. As one said:

> It was very interesting. I didn't think there were so many jobs available to women

One of the role models, a chemical engineer, reported two younger women asked her three times if she was 'really an engineer'. She enquired why they doubted her, to get the answer "because you've got a handbag". These pupils were still at primary school in 1984 - WISE Year - and held precisely the attitudes that it was designed to change. One lesson from this is that all these initiatives have to be done for *every* generation of women: the first year pupils do not 'know' what the fifth form were taught about sex roles four years earlier.

31

One of the striking findings of this evaluation was the young women's surprise that important national companies - such as BP - thought they were worth putting on an exhibition for. Many of the school girls were flattered that firms thought they justified such effort and expense.

The Women's Training Roadshow aimed to give girls and women information about the opportunities available to them in non-traditional female occupations. The general message of the Roadshow did get over to its audience - perhaps especially so to the younger pupils who enjoyed their involvement in the participatory activities. Each schoolgirl's visit to the Roadshow lasted less than three hours. The follow-up visits to the schools took place some four months after that. The impact the Roadshow made on the girls can be judged by their recall of the event, which was detailed and vivid, and by the level of support for future events. Our analysis of the girls' attitudes towards women and work and issues of child care reveal that they generally hold egalitarian and non-stereotyped views. Yet, however egalitarian and non-sterotyped the views of the girls might be, this does not mean that they are considering attempting non-traditional occupations themselves. The occupational aspirations of the majority of the schoolgirls are safely within the well established realms of 'women's work' and they were not doing physics and CDT after 14.

The girls in our study maintained that their decisions about which subjects to study to examination level were made on the basis of their interest and ability and whether a subject would be useful for a job that they had in mind. However, from comments that were made in the discussion sessions in relation to physics and other non-traditional subjects, it is clear that a 'hidden agenda' is in operation involving their perception of the subject matter and their consequent ability to do well in it. The girls described physics as a subject which was 'boring' and 'hard'. They explained that boys are less likely to view the subject in this way because the subject matter, as the girls perceived it, is more likely to appeal to them. A sixth former, from a private school told us;

> boys are encouraged in these things from an early age with toys.

Many girls also believe that physics teachers, who were invariably male, had a negative attitude towards girls, who were most often a minority in their classes. It was explained to us frequently that physics is a subject which 'leads to male careers' and that this is a further reason why girls choose not to study it. The 'hidden agenda' in relation to physics thus involves the girls' perception of the subject matter and their ideas about its

32

occupational implications. It is the subject matter of physics, or more probably, the way it is presented, that needs to be addressed if the number of girls choosing to study the subject are to increase.

We asked about the girls' own plans and hopes: both expected and desired destinations after leaving school. There is a large literature both international (Kuvlesky and Bealer, 1972) and local (Cowell, Rees and Read 1981) showing that adolescents separate their ideal jobs from their occupational expectations which are more conditioned by local labour market conditions.

Table 3:1 shows what the pupils hoped and expected to do after leaving school. The sample included a wide range of abilities yet a large proportion of the girls (35%) hope to go to university after they leave school. Thirty percent of the schoolgirls hope to get a full-time job whilst just over 20% hope to train in a college. A comparison of their expectations for the future rather than their hopes is revealing.

Table 3:1   Hoped for and expected destinations after leaving school

Destination	Hope		Expected		Differential	
	No:	%	No:	%		%
University or Poly	173	35	144	30		-5
Full-time job	150	30	81	17		-14
Training in a College	107	22	110	23		+1
Studying GCE	58	12	57	12		0
Part-time job	22	4	46	10		+6
Start a family	14	3	16	3		0
YTS	12	2	30	6		+4
Help at home	4	1	9	2		+1
Don't know	8	2	46	10		+8
Other	17	3	14	3		0
% do not add up to 100 due to some respondents naming more than one destination						

Aspirations to attend university and to get a full-time job are greater than expectations. Getting a place on a Youth Training Scheme, getting a part-time job or training in a college, are expected more frequently than desired. An examination of the explanations for the gap between their expectations and their hopes reveals a concern about the young women's ability to gain appropriate qualifications (59%) and unemployment (19%). Other explanations include changing their minds (11%), financial concerns (4%), the responsibilities of marriage and family life (4%) and that achievement of aspirations requires determination (4%). It is clear that the girls view barriers to achievement of aspirations in personal and individual terms, expressed as failure to obtain appropriate levels and types of qualifications, or a lack of determination or conviction on their own part. Societal or structural barriers are mentioned less.

Most of the young women wanted secretarial jobs (10%), or to enter nursery nursing (10%), hairdressing and beauty (10%) or teaching (9%). Six percent of the sample wanted to be 'lawyers' or 'solicitors', and smaller percentages chose medicine, dentistry, three veterinary science, and accountancy. Very few girls aspired to non-traditional manual occupations, such as plumbing. Only 1% of the sample favoured engineering for themselves. Overall, the girls were aiming to enter occupational areas which are safely 'female', with a minority aiming for 'professional' occupations, such as law and medicine.

The main effect of the Roadshow, and any other sex-equality information the young women had received in the past was to make them aware that women *could* do non-traditional jobs, *not* to change their own preferences for traditional female ones or the professions of law and medicine.

The folklore material

The second source of data on the sex role stereotypes still held by adolescent pupils is very different. For several years researchers have been studying how pupils face up to transfer to secondary school, and have found they are frequently full of anxiety about the change. (See Delamont and Galton, 1987).

In Flecker's poem, the *Gates of Damascus*, the four gates of the city are each given a specific character. The West Gate leads to Lebanon and the sea, the North Gate is the route to Aleppo, and the South to Mecca. Travellers are able to pass through these in relative serenity. The East gate, guarding the road to Baghdad, is a different matter. To the east lies the desert, nameless terrors, and probable death. Travellers are urged 'Pass not beneath' and the gate is labelled:

> Postern of Fate, the Desert Gate, Disaster's Cavern, Fort of Fear.

Pupils preparing to transfer from junior schools to secondary ones face their *status passage* with similar apprehension. It is clear from all the studies of pre-transfer anxieties that issues of gender are one important strand within them. Pre-adolescent and adolescent boys believe that they are moving to an institution where their credentials *as males* will be inspected and their masculinity tested. This is clear from two sensitive American books (Best, 1983; Fine, 1987) and from all the UK work on transfer anxiety. The commonly told 'scare stories', urban legends (Brunvand, 1983), myths (Morin, 1971), or rumours (Shibutani, 1966) about what awaits pupils beyond their postern of fate carry some awful warnings about what happens to small, new pupils at secondary school.

An example of the tall stories spread among pupils comes from a ten year old friend who wrote to me in 1991 the summer he was transferring to secondary school.

> Last time you visited us you told me to tell you about the horrible (*sic*) things I had heard about BIG school. Here are the ones that are not too rude to even write.
>
> 1.   THEY make you eat the skin off a bulls eye.
> 2.   THEY throw your school bag over the fence.
> 3.   THEY beat you up.
> 4.   THEY make you drink -
> 5.   THEY set fire to your hair and
> 6.   THEY bully things out of you.
>
> Looks like I'll have to avoid them.

The letter, from a well-balanced boy, big for his age, from a middle class home in a quiet English suburb, going to a secondary school his older siblings have attended happily which his parents believe to be child-centred and friendly, is typical of the material that adults can collect from British children about to transfer to secondary school. The transfer is accompanied by a rich array of scarey stories that circulate year after year, from child to child.

See (Measor and Woods, 1983, 1984; Delamont and Galton, 1986, 1987). The gender implications of these rumours is the focus of the next chapter. As Measor and Woods pointed out, these myths suggest that secondary schools are places where there will be:

> New demands of harshness and toughness... in both formal and informal cultures (p.19)

For Measor and Woods:
> The secondary school represents a new, more impersonal state, where the inner self cannot any longer be safely revealed
>
> (p.20)

Boys have to face up to these new demands, or they will be branded as poofters. Male pupils have to claim that they are looking forward to dissecting the rat, doing that 5-mile run, and so on. They have to be prepared to face up to the bullies in the lavatories and playground and to the most weird and fearsome types of teacher.

The informal culture of pupils circulates these stories, which carry clear messages about what proper male and female secondary pupils do. To the adult outsider, primary schools may look sexist. To pre-adolescents, the approaching secondary school is the place where sex roles will become critical and very traditional sex roles at that.

Since 1980: What have we learnt

The Roadshow has many features in common with other national and local attempts to reduce sex differentiation and stereotyping in education. These features are particularly important if the next decades' efforts are to be consolidated and extended. There are: locational, directional, 'vocational'/'cultural', and psychological issues. The locational issues are that Roadshows and other initiatives are concentrated in:

(a) England rather than Wales, Scotland and Ireland;
(b) urban rather than rural settings.

The directional issues are that Roadshows and other initiatives are:

(a) aimed at girls and women not boys and men;

(b)   directed to secondary and tertiary sector students not nursery, infant and primary school pupils;

(c)   aimed at school pupils rather than parents, trade unions employers and teachers.

The 'vocational'/'cultural' issues are that Roadshows and other such initiatives are:

(a)   focused on science and CDT, not humanities and aesthetic subjects;

(b)   based on an assumption that schools and work places are sites for labour, not primarily places for socialising;

(c)   concentrated on the serious rather than the pleasurable.

The psychological issues are that Roadshows and other initiatives are:

(a)   focused on what adults believe will change pupil's ideas rather than starting from what pupils actually believe (their 'folk model');

(b)   sanitised to avoid all discussion of sexuality, orientation and sexual politics.

The issues that are of relevance to the sex equality programmes of the 1990s and to challenging the types of sex role stereotypes revealed in this paper, are explored further below. A fuller discussion of *all* issues can be found in Delamont (1990).

Lost boys? The directional issue

The Cardiff Women's Training Roadshow, and the others in the WNC series, were for females. Schools were asked to send parties of girls, and the publicity was aimed at women. The stallholders, role models and workshops were designed to challenge women's ideas about the labour market. This is typical of the majority of initiatives designed to change the sexual division of labour in Britain. Few projects have been aimed at discovering why boys avoid foreign languages and home economics, choose 'masculine' jobs and plan to stay in the labour market rather than stay home to rear their children. The research that has been done receives less publicity, and generates less concern than that on girls. Powell (Powell, 1979, 1984 and 1986; Powell and Littlewood, 1982 and 1983) has been voicing concern for a decade about the small numbers of boys gaining a foreign language qualification, but there has not been a single project like GIST aimed at boys. Noticeably, Powell's research is not even cited in the Burchell and Millman (1989) collection, or in Askew and Ross (1988). In 1973 only eight percent of male sixth formers in English LEA schools were taking 'A' level French compare to 24 percent of girls. Yet nowhere in the DES documents produced in the 1970s was this raised as a problem. While the shortage of female scientists and technologists has generated research and action, the shortage of male linguists has been ignored. No one has suggested that all soldiers stationed in Germany should seize the chance to learn German, or those in Cyprus be taught Greek, yet these are wasted opportunities to reach young men.

The focus on female pupils rather than males is not the only directional issue that needs comment. Many employers still do not have any interest in recruiting, training and retaining workers in non-traditional occupations; many trade unions have yet to take sex equality on board at a workplace, everyday level; and many parents, teachers and even careers staff have very stereotyped ideas about male and female behaviour.

Rees, Williamson and Winckler (1989) report that many employers in South Wales, studied in 1986 and 1987, held

> stereotyped beliefs about differences in the technical and social abilities of men and women...(and) such stereotypes were further consolidated by cultural assumptions about the gender-appropriateness of different jobs - and where men or women...entered 'inappropriate' jobs, it was often the employer who guided them away... into other work.

Encouraging young people into non-traditional occupations is pointless if their employers are going to redirect them away from those jobs. Cockburn (1987) has shown vividly how hard it is for an adolescent who chooses an unconventional job to sustain it under pressures from adults and peers.

Projects and initiatives designed to challenge sex stereotyping have to be aimed at males and females, employers and workers, teachers and taught, parents and children, advisors and advised. If they are not, the initiative suffers the Lake Wobegon effect. Lake Wobegon, Mist County, Minnesota, does not appear on any map of the USA. As Garrison Keillor

(1986: 90-92) explains, four teams of surveyors began from the four corners of Minnesota, working towards the centre.

> The southwest and northwest contingents moved fast over level ground, while the eastern teams got bogged down in the woods, so that when they met a little west of Lake Wobegon, the four quadrants didn't fit within the boundaries legislated by Congress in 1851... The legislature simply re-proportioned the state by eliminating the overlap in the middle, and that little quadrangle is Mist County.

Ever since 1866, therefore, Lake Wobegon has not been on any map. Education reforms tend to vanish in the same way.

The same Wobegon effect occurs in the area of reducing sex stereotyping. Teachers blame parents, pupils and the labour market; parents blame schools, pupils and employers; employers blame schools, parents and young people; young people complain about adults. No group admits that they can change the *status quo*: and the educational equivalent of Mist County (sex equality) stays missing from the centre of the map.

Science or sculpture? The vocational/cultural issues

The musical *Salad Days* featured a magic piano which made everyone who heard it start dancing: even a killjoy cabinet minister. The initiative designed to reduce sex segregation and differentiation desperately need such an instrument. The programmes and innovations have been serious, prosaic and leaden-footed: Apollonian not Dionysian: there has been very little joy, gaiety and dancing. The thrust of the initiatives has been towards science and technology, towards vocational subjects and towards the intrinsic rewards of work. Very little has been done about sex equality in the humanities and the aesthetic curriculum, in leisure activities, as a way of having a more pleasurable life, and to the social and emotional aspects of working. There are no programmes designed to enthuse girls with the ambition to be poets or sculptors, to get boys enjoying ballet or *petit point*, or to encourage the sexes to practice working together and sharing hobbies and recreational chatter. Tickle's (1987) collection on the arts in education does not include a single report (in eleven chapters) of any initiative to challenge sexism in these areas. There is a desperate need for projects that focus on all areas of the curriculum, and those which stress that liberation from rigid sex roles makes life fun for both sexes. The school children studied by Raphaela Best (1983) were quite clear at 15 that:

> they could do and say what they wanted, they were indeed egalitarian, they were indeed non-sexist, they could indeed relate to one another on the basis of common interests - as friends - without resorting to macho aggression or female wiles.
>
> (178)

Elaine told an interviewer:

> we had a fun time

in Best's anti-sexism programme. Such fun is too often missing.

The lack of gaiety in the programmes to reduce sex differentiation in education is closely related to a second characteristic they share. Initiatives are heavily biased towards the view that life in schools, further education colleges and workplaces is centred on the work that goes on there, which should be intrinsically satisfying. This is contrary to the experience of most pupils in their schools and at their part-time jobs, and to research on workers; it therefore makes the emphasis of the programmes seem irrelevant and rarefied.

This is ample evidence that many pupils value school as much or more for the social life - seeing friends and catching up on news - as they do for the lesson or eventual qualifications. As a Scottish school-leaver put it:

> Once I left school I thought it was great, then you miss all of your pals, you miss all of the laughs.
>
> (Walford, 1989: 260)

In the labour market, the same criteria apply. Carol Buswell's (1988) study of 55 adolescents in YTS placements in clerical and retail workplaces, reveals how important for the trainees the social relations were. The intrinsic nature of the work was dull and repetitive, but a good placement resulted from friendly, supportive, colleagues. Buswell (1988: 170) quotes a girl on a clerical placement whose workmates "invited me to the dinner-dance and paid for me and everything", while one in a shop said hers were "very helpful and nice" and treated her "like an equal". Most of the research on the types of work that the majority of the population does show it to be undemanding, uninteresting and repetitive. (See, for example, Blackburn and Mann, 1979; and Pollert, 1981).

Blackburn and Mann pointed out that most of the men they studied used more skill when driving *to work* than they needed to perform their tasks at work. It is the social relationships that differentiate good and bad jobs, and the lack of them is one reason why unemployment is so depressing (see Coffield *et al*, 1986; Walford, 1989). Few people are privileged to have jobs that are intrinsically absorbing or satisfying. A major problem for young people who try to enter non-traditional jobs is the lack of supportive, enjoyable friendships in the workplace. (See Cockburn 1987, for example, where this lack affects both boys and girls on YTS). Too much of the effort put into reducing sex differentiation is based on a model of working life where intrinsic satisfaction is enough ignoring the realities of the jobs young people actually face. It is no use persuading a girl to get an apprenticeship in a garage if none of the men is able to be workmates with a female.

Advice about choosing non-traditional occupations will be 'written off' if it is offered in careers lessons riddled with misapprehensions about the world of work adolescents already know. In 1985 I watched a careers lesson for remedial and ESN(M) pupils in a Welsh comprehensive school, Heol-y-Crynwyr, taken by the Deputy Head, Mr. Despenser.

> The lesson is centred round the book about starting work. Frank starts his first job, and does everything wrong: he is late, he hasn't brought his NI card etc., he is cheeky and does not radiate keenness etc.

> His boss is angry with him. The pupils read the story aloud and then discuss it. They all side with Frank, and regard the boss as quite unreasonable for shouting at him.

> Mr. Despenser tries to refocus them onto their responsibilities, such as punctuality and politeness. He asks for their ideas on what happens when a young person starts work, and then disputes all their ideas. Frederick said the worst thing about starting work was that it would "be a new place, wouldn't know nobody there".

> Mr.Despenser said that was irrelevant and asked what time a shopworker has to start work in the morning.

Claudette said "7.00" and Mr. Despenser told her that was too early, shops did not open that early in the morning. She tried to tell him about shops that do, but he ignored her.

The shop at the end of the road outside the school, a newsagent and general store, announced on its door that it was open from 7.00 a.m. to 7.00p.m. Too many of the initiatives fail to use the knowledge pupils have and face the realities they face.

Whose heads are we in? The 'psychological' dimension

At first glance school physics, smoking in pregnancy, a proper roast dinner and Basque cheesemaking have nothing in common with each other, and no place in a book on sex roles and the school. In fact all those topics have been the focus of research on how ordinary people think about the world around them and the everyday things in it. Experts frequently despair because people do not follow good advice or behave in self-damaging ways or fail to learn what they are taught. Doctors, nurses and midwives, for example, are distressed when mothers smoke, drink and take tranquillisers even in pregnancy.

In a range of areas, researchers have decided to start at the other end of the problem: to find out how ordinary lay people understand their everyday worlds, and then compare their 'lay' or 'folk' models with those held by experts. Frequently, it transpires that the people in the street have a clear logically consistent folk model which is quite, quite different from 'scientific' or 'expert' models. When a folk model conflicts with expert argument, the former usually wins out: because it was developed over a person's lifetime, in their home, school, job and family setting *and works there*, it is more powerful than the abstract 'theories' of outsiders.

A concrete example from the area of food and eating will illustrate this. Anne Murcott (1983, 1988) studied the folk models of food and nutrition held by women in South Wales. Although her respondents had learnt about vitamins, minerals and protein in school, and could describe food in those terms, it was not the model they used when planning menus, shopping and cooking. When actually getting food on to the table, the model used was one of 'meals and platefuls'. For example, everyone had an idea of a 'a cooked dinner' or a 'a proper dinner', consisting of roast meat, roast and boiled potatoes, a green vegetable and another vegetable, plus gravy. This was contrasted with snacks, salad meals, chip-based meals, curries, Chinese take-aways and so on. When organizing their family's food, the lay model of types of meal, plus the likes and dislikes of family members, plus the constraints of time, money, availability and, importantly, the views of the husband, governed what was cooked and eaten. The dietitian's model, though known, was not relevant compared to the folk model of what a good wife put on the table in front of her family.

Exactly the same findings came from science education. Even people who have done 'A' level sciences still have 'folk models' or 'misapprehensions' about how scientific phenomena (such as gravity) work. If you ask fifteen year olds a science question framed like a school science task, they use their school science to answer it. If they are asked a question needing the same scientific information to answer it, but phrased like an everyday enquiry, commonsense lay models are invoked. So, for example, the same pupils who can answer a science question about expansion of heated metals correctly, fail to explain why sausages burst their skins when cooked. The scientific information does not displace the folk model, it merely sits in a compartment alongside it. The research on this topic (e.g. Driver, 1983 and Gilbert and Watts, 1983) is mostly read within science education, but there are implications beyond that Aggleton, Homans and Warwick (1988) have shown how adolescents' understanding of AIDS is based in folk biology which often conflicts with official health education information. Some of the folk models about biological phenomena are undiluted descendants from the ideas of Aristotle: the Basque shepherds studied by Ott (1986) for example still have Aristotle's theory of conception.

Many people reject, or compartmentalise, scientific theory, because it conflicts with their deeply embedded folk models. People also balance information from each model they have, which explains why people 'damage' their own health. Mothers knew smoking was bad for them, but also knew if they did not smoke their families suffered because they were tense and stressed. Relaxing by smoking led to benefits for the health and welfare of the rest of the household.

The consequences of accepting that pupils have their own folk models of how the world works are potentially far-reaching. In school science, the proponents of the misapprehensions approach want teachers to discover what pupils' folk models of, for example, weight, mass and density are; and then design a series of experiments to demonstrate that the folk model is not sufficiently robust or universal to explain all phenomena relating to weight, mass and density. Pupils would recapitulate parts of the history of science as they moved from their models to scientific truth which *would* displace the folk originals. Measor (1989) has argued the same point in relation to sex education, although she does not refer to the science education authors at all.

The lessons for initiatives designed to change sex roles in schools are clear. First, it is important that such programmes start from the target group's current lay beliefs about science, or CDT, or sex roles, or engineering, or childrearing. Most of the initiatives that have been tried in Britain have ignored the ideas that teachers and/or pupils may have in their heads already. If teachers believe that sex roles are genetically determined (women are naturally more patient with small children), or pupils, that any adolescent girl who takes an apprenticeship in a garage is 'boy mad' and any boy interested in fashion design is gay, programmes to change their ideas and practices have to start from those premises.

4. The "hit list" and other horror stories: Sex roles and school transfer

Introduction

The paper analyses the messages about sex roles transmitted in the scarey stories told among school children when they are facing transfers from primary to secondary school. The data are 217 stories written for the author in 1988/89. The majority of the stories were written by 16-21 year olds, and refer to transfer which took place in the 1980s. None of these stories has been published previously. There are four sections making up the paper: on data collection, on the main themes in the stories, on a theoretical framework for understanding the messages carried by such stories, and on the sex role norms that are emphasised in those messages.

The data and their collection

The data analysed in this paper are stories about transfer from primary and secondary school recalled by young adults, and written down at the author's request. Three groups of young people provided the 217 stories which are analysed in the paper. These were produced anonymously, in a standard format.

The first group of young people were sixth formers from schools in Ledshire (an English county) attending day conferences at the county university. There are 90 to 100 students at each conference, and they wrote their stories before the author's lecture. Seventy-eight stories were handed in from this group in 1988, and 103 in 1989.

The second group of young people were aged 18-21 and were attending an occupational training school. There were 20 students in the group and 16 of them handed in 22 anonymous stories, again at the beginning of a lecture by the author. The third group were training for a 'caring' occupation, ranged in age from 21 to 50, and 42 students handed in 14 school related stories (plus a set about their professional training not analysed here). They too wrote their stories at the beginning of a lecture, and handed them in anonymously.

In all three settings the author asked the students to 'write down any scarey stories' they could remember from their own transfer between junior and secondary school (or if a parent, any their children had heard). The respondents were offered a standard format:

> Before I went to........school, I was told by ....that
> ....

To stimulate the groups, and indicate that fantastic stories no adult would believe were acceptable, an example, *not* based on any story gathered by previous researchers was offered.

> Before I went to Tenby Boys Grammar School I was told by
> my brother who was already there that the Biology teacher
> kept adders in the lab and wrapped them round your neck if
> you were naughty.

The 217 stories are the largest bodies of material collected about school transfer. Other research on pupils; anxieties and anticipations about school transfer (e.g. Bryan, 1980; Measor and Woods, 1984; Delamont and Galton, 1986 and 1987; ILEA, 1988a and 1988b) has focused on rational fears and hopes as well as myths or rumours, and has studied the eleven and twelve year olds at the time of transfer. These studies have the advantage of gathering their data 'fresh' while the pupils are actively involved in the status passage. However children of that age are inhibited from mentioning some of the common myths to adults because they are vulgar, sexual, or both. As Bauman (1982), Canaan (1986), Grugeon (1988), and Fine (1981, 1987, 1988) have shown, children learn early in life to keep quiet about aspects of their culture that adults will be repulsed or shocked by. The sixth formers and students felt free to recall stories with 'unmentionables' in them, and used their sophistication at 18 or older to distance themselves from the myths they had been told at 11.

The material can be regarded as myths (Leach, 1969), as rumours (Shibutani, 1966) or as urban folklore (Brunvand, 1983, 1984, 1985; Dale, 1978). Sociologists of education have concentrated more on gathering the 'rational' accounts of young people about schooling than on their jokes, tall stories, atrocity stories or folklore about it. The status passages, or transfers, from each sector of schooling to the next are, however, known to be times of anxiety, and folklore often conveys that more vividly than factual accounts. (See for example Blatchford *et al.*, 1982; Cleave *et al.*, 1982 and Delamont and Galton, 1987).

All the stories handed in were coded, by each main theme found, and also to record the source of the story (e.g. 'brother'). The themes found are presented in the next station, and then a theoretical framework for examining their sex role messages is presented.

The main themes

Before presenting the thematic analysis, it is worth quoting one story in full to get a flavour of the genre. It is longer than average, but has all the vividness of the stories collected.

> When I started at Laverlaw Boys' Grammar School I was told by older boys who lived in the same street as I did, and with whom I played, that the Physics teacher and the laboratory assistant were having an affair, and that failure to pass the weekly Physics test in the first year resulted in boys being caned by the teacher in the backroom of the Physics laboratory, on their bare bottoms in from of the laboratory assistant. This behaviour apparently 'turned her on'.
>
> (Male undergraduate, 1989)

The student states that the rumour was not true: he failed the test several times and was given lines. Although this is the only example of a story about a sado-masochistic lab assistant, the general issues: violence from a teacher. humiliation for a pupil, sexuality, science labs, and harder academic work: turn up in most of the tales. The main theme of the 217 stories which from the database for this paper were:

1)   The 'bogwash' theme
2)   The violent gang theme
3)   The fierce/weird/sexually harassing teacher theme
4)   The humiliating experience theme
5)   The supernatural theme

Each of these is illustrated with one example, and then its variations explored. The lavatory story is the most common (99 of the 217 stories collected) and is regularly recalled by audiences after the stories have been collected during the discussion of the exercise.

A typical example of the 'bogwash' story, from a Welsh occupational trainee is:

> Before I went to secondary school I was told by other children (my own age usually) that older boys at the school would stick our heads down the loos and flush them (the loos that is).

Earlier researchers (e.g Measor and Woods, 1983, 1984: Delamont and Galton, 1987; Delamont, 1989; Fine, 1987) have also found this to be the commonest story that circulates about secondary schools. Apart from the polluting nature of the 'bogwash', it is also a story about hazards new children face from their fellows pupils. The theme of violent gangs of children roaming the secondary school is also common. A typical example is:

> Before I went to Westhaven High School. My brother told me they used to put little kids on the roof of a hut and not let them down until the teacher arrived when the older kids would run off and leave them up there. (Ledshire sixth former).

Fifty-five of the 217 stories were about such bullies pushing children into holly bushes, down banks, into dustbins and/or extorting their money.

While the bogwash and the gang are pupil-centred dangers, the third theme is that of teachers: especially those who are fierce, weired and eccentric, or sexually harassing to pupils. Examples of a fierce and of a sexually exploiting teacher from the Ledshire pupils are:

> Before I went to Westhaven High School I was told by my sister that there was a history master who hung people from the light fittings by their toenails if they didn't do their homework.

and

> I was told by an older friend already there that the hockey teacher was a lesbian nymphomaniac (*sic*)?

There were 39 stories about extraordinary teachers among the 217 collected. A smaller number of stories (eleven) concerns humiliating ritual/ceremonies/ordeals which secondary schools were believed to operate. One of the occupational trainees remembered.

Before I went to Grammar School I was told by a friend that
we had to wear 2 pairs of knickers; a white pair underneath a
navy blue pair and regular inspections were carried out.

The humiliation here comes from the inspection rather than the rule
about uniform. The ordinary minority theme consisted of (five) stories
about the supernatural, such as this one from Ledshire.

Before I went to Slepham Halt School I was told by some of
my older friends that my school was haunted by a ghost. A
ghost of a pupil who was locked in a room and wasn't found
for a long time... *dead*

The remainder of the 217 stories concerned a range of ideas: three about
science teaching, two about sex, one about school dinners and so on.
Before exploring the themes. Table :4:1 shows the frequency of the
different *motifs* among the 217 stories.

Table 4:1   **Frequency of themes in 217 stories**

Theme	No. of stories
'Bogwash'	91
Gang and bullies	55
Teachers	30
Humiliations	11
Supernatural	5
Miscellaneous	25
Total	217

Within these broad categories there are some differences between the
stories told to boys and to girls, and the expectations male and female
pupils have about secondary schools. While exploring the five themes in
more detail, the gender differences involved will be the main focus. The
themes will be examined in reverse order of frequency.

The supernatural stories are a small minority of the total, and are similar
to several collected by other researchers in Britain and the USA. Stories
about ghosts and witches are the exciting centre-pieces of:

the neighbourhood story which gives a certain glamour - literary resonance - to the otherwise unremarkable places where children grow up... (Knapp and Knapp, 1976 248-9)

The Knapps collected two such stories from American children:

One boy from Kanas City told us that at his school the little kids believed that the former principal was buried under the mound at the base of the flagpole, which came right out of her grave.

Other children told us of a teacher who looked like a witch; if she touched you, you would get warts.
(Knapp and Knapp, 1976: 248-9)

The Ledshire stories were all about school ghosts, except for one concerning a dangerous house on the route to school:

Before I went to secondary school I was told by a friend that the house we were walking past at the time was lived in by a witch.

The ghost stories were

Before I went to school at Birleton School I was told that there was a ghost in the bell tower that rings the bell after 12.

Before I went to the senior school at the Ledchester Convent I was told by older pupils that the corridors by the chapel were haunted by the 'white lady'. Once some boarders had ventured down one night and had seen this apparition. The nun had lunged at one of the girls, missed, and hit the wall where the imprints of her fingernails can still be seen.

The girls' toilets were haunted by the 'hairy hand' which grabs your legs when on the loo.

Before I went to Ledlington School I was told by older friends that there was a ghost under the stage. (Ledshire sixth formers, 1988).

These are strikingly similar to a tale collected in 1986 from a graduate student about her girls' grammar school:

> Throughout my junior school years I was told that the comprehensive school I would be attending (which was then a grammar school housed in an old building) was haunted by the ghost of a 'blue nun'. The ghost was described in graphic detail and was said to appear mainly in the girls' toilets. I remember being frightened of being alone in the toilet block and still am - though I now rationalise this as being frightened of attackers etc.

These appear to be typical haunted house stories, transposed to schools.

The stories about humiliations share with the ghost stories their source: young women. Most of the ghost stories were told about girls' schools, and the humiliation stories mostly came from women too.

Typical humiliation stories are:

> Before I went to Westhaven High School I was told by some friends that if you forgot your PE kit you would have to do it in your underwear
>
> (Ledshire, 1988)

> Before I went to secondary school I was told by current pupils of that school that every new girl had to have an 'identity bath' in front of the school doctor (to measure body volume or something!) basically just getting into a bath in front of him.
>
> (Welsh Occupational Trainee, 1988)

> Before I went to Radhurst School for Girls (secondary school) I was told by a girl already attending the school that one of the PE teachers made you have a shower after PE, and those people who forget their towel were given one paper towel to dry themselves with and if they were not dry they had to run naked round the gym to dry off.
>
> (Welsh Occupational Trainee, 1988)

The only man to recall a humiliation story had been threatened with debagging by older boys, which belongs more to the bullying stories than

51

these, where it is the school rules and staff which humiliate girl pupils. The girls' humiliation stories lead towards the tales of teachers who are eccentric, fierce or sexually harassing.

Both sexes told stories of sexual harassment from gay teachers and one young women had heard of a heterosexual rape. Previous research on 11 and 12 year olds had revealed a few stories about gay men in teaching (Measor and Woods,1983 and 1984) but not about lesbians. Measor and Woods found that the myth of the gay teacher was so secret that it was only revealed to a researcher who was really trusted, and it is possible that the lesbian teacher story existed among the children studied by Measor but was even more shameful than the gay man and could not be revealed to any adult.

The Ledshire sixth formers felt free to write the following stories about lesbians:

> Before I went to Westhaven High School I was told by my sister that the PE teacher was gay and watched you changing for PE and made you have a shower and watched you while you had it.

> Before I went to Merefields School I was told by older pupils that the games teacher was a lesbian and that she watched everyone whilst they changed and that she was the reason we didn't have showers.

and about gay men:

> At Rowberry Common School... the PE teacher molested you!

> That the art teacher was gay and put favourite boys in his dark room.

> The drama teacher locks boys in his cupboard and is very scarey.

The latter is only 'about' homosexuality by implication - it may have been another fierce/eccentric teacher story.

The tale of the rape is the only of its kind the author has ever been told, and no other researcher has reported anything similar.

> Before I went to Prior's End School I was told by a friend
> that was already there a teacher Mr.Paradine had raped one
> pupil (girl) and hadn't been asked to leave because he owned
> the helicopter that the boys took apart and put together
> again. They also said Mr.Paradine got girls into the book
> cupboard and touched them up.

Note that in this story the pupil feels it necessary to report that the rape
victim was female. The only other story which is as bizarre as the rapist
helicopter owner is that of the Physics teacher and the lab assistant already
quoted.

That story - which continued with the assistant leaving her job to run a
donkey sanctuary because she was pregnant by the physics teacher - centred
on discipline. Teachers' strategies for keeping classes controlled, or for
terrorising them, are commoner. In the stories, staff are strict beyond the
bounds of proper teacher behaviour (see Beynon, 1985, for a discussion of
this). The Ledshire sixth formers recalled:

> Before I went to Prior's End I was told by some friends of
> mine that the headmaster was a madman who was always
> telling people off and suspending them for no reason.

> Before I went to the Embank School I was told by my sister
> that one of the chemistry teachers was a mad, vindictive
> scientist who would give detentions for coughing in class
> without asking permission to do so.

The occupational trainees had heard of several strict teachers including
the headmaster who 'canned (*sic*) everyone with a variety of sticks!', the
woodwork master who 'beat up kids with lumps of wood with nails on the
end!', and the man who 'kept his belt in vinegar over the holidays for the
new first years'.

Those violent teachers overlap with the eccentric and peculiar ones.
The occupational trainees produced:

> The Latin master was an ex-Japanese POW who had had his
> cheekbones   removed   rendering   his   declensions
> unintelligible.

and

Scripture teacher getting class to kneel and pray for any 'sinners' in class e.g. if found to be talking or eating in class for example.

The second world war still haunts, the schools of Britain. The Ledshire sixth formers had been told about:

A teacher told all his pupils that he shot Hitler through a key hole

and they too had an equivalent to the Latin master

Before I went to Ledlington School I was told by my sister that the science teacher only had one nostril.

Sometimes a teacher's name adds colour to a story. Delamont and Galton (1986) report a girl scared by mishearing her new teacher's name as 'Slaughter' (it was Salter) and deciding he must be very fierce. One of the occupational trainees had heard that:

Mr.Oddy was actually Odd and did lots of mad things.

The stories about gangs and bullies are of five main kinds. New first years are thrown about (into bushes, down banks), marooned on top of things, have food or money extorted from them, are beaten up, or are humiliated. The majority of these were told by boys. Typical examples of stories about gangs and bullying from the Ledshire pupils include the marooning on the roof already quoted and

Before I went to Westhaven High School I was told by a pupil at the school that people threw newcomers (cheeky) into the huge dustbins in front of the school.

Before I went to Poynings School I was told by friends that there was an older boy who had been in trouble with the police for GBH (Grievous Bodily Harm) using a chain with spikes on and the rest of the fifth years were to be scared of.

Similarly the occupational trainees had been told about:

Before I went to grammar school I was told by older pupils that I would be thrown in the thorn bushes as part of my initiation and had to come out bleeding!

On your birthday you might get thrown into the 'galley pit' (a stairway fenced off leading underground) and then everyone in the yard would stand on the railings and spit 'greenies' on you.... until rescued by the teacher. (It did happen on occasions.)

All these stories reflect similar tales recorded by Bryan (1980).

I have horrible thoughts of my new school which is Seacombe High. I think there is no discipline (*sic*) from what my friends have told me. They told me that groups of lads go around battering people up, they are supposed to be from the dreaded B.E.B.B. which stands for the Brightsea Estate Boot Boys.

These fearsome Boot Boys are clearly a close associate in the myths of a gang at Old Town reported to Measor and Woods (1984:27)

There's these boys, and if you have a fight, they wear punch gloves with spikes, and they hit you and leave punch holes in your face.

The Ledshire corpus is unusual in that some of the stories were told by young women, concerning violent gangs of girls. In most cases, the gang stories are told about dangers for boys, but in Ledshire there were stories of female hit lists:

Before I went to girls' school I was told by a friend that certain people were put on a 'death' list and if you were on it you would be beaten up on your first day (Ledshire, 1988)

The lavatory stories are a variation of the bullying and gang tales, of a particularly polluting and unpleasant kind. Most researchers (e.g. Measor and Woods 1983, 1984; Fine, 1987) have recorded that while both male and female pupils have heard the rumours, only boys expect it to happen to them. Sometimes females wrote that they were glad to be girls so it would not apply to them. In the Ledshire sample, however, there were reports of the 'bogwash' happening in girls' schools too. One version from a boy and one from a girl about different schools will suffice.

Before I went to Poynings Community College I was told by pupils there already that disliked pupils received the 'bogwash' where their head was put down the toilet and the chain was flushed. This was done by the oldest, toughest children there.

Before I went to Merefields school I was told by a 'friend' that the prefects took girls into the toilets and gave them a 'bogwash'

In some versions the bogwash happens on the victim's birthday, as in this example from the occupational trainees:

Before I went to a Secondary school I was told by my next door neighbour that I would get my head put down the toilet on my birthday.

Because this threat is so common (see Measor and Woods, 1984; Hanna, 1982; Fine, 1987; Delamont and Galton, 1987; Phillips, 1986) it is worth examining the details of it that are sometimes provided. The story regularly turns up with details of aggressors, victims, timing and a rationale for the attack. Table 4:2 shows the details provided in the 44 'bogwash' stories.

Table 4:2   The bogwash aggressor

Type	Number of mentions
Older pupils	12
Fifth year	6
People	2
Bigger pupils	2
Prefects	2
Bullies	.2
Fourth and Fifth years	.1
Middle school girls	1
Oldest/toughest Pupils	1
Older bullies	1
Fourth years	1
'Wrong People'	1
'Some girls'	1
No detail provided	58
Total	91

While the specific group mentioned varies, their overall characteristic - being older, larger, and fiercer - is clear. It is not your own age group who attack you in the lavatories, but pupils already established in the school. The likely victims of bogwashes are less frequently specified, as Table 4:3 shows.

Table 4:3   Who suffers the bogwash?

Category	Number of mentions
All new pupils	8
All Form 1/first years	8
Younger pupils	1
Second years	1
1st and 2nd years	1
No victim specified	72
Total responses	91

When a reason is offered - rather than the bogwash being seen as inevitable/routine - it is one of 3 kinds: pupils' behaviour, pupils' stature, or a calendar date. Table 4:4 shows the reasons given:

Table 4:4   Reasons for the bogwash

Reason	Number of mentions
Victim's birthday	11
Aggressor dislikes victim	7
Victim is cheeky	1
Victim is caught in the toilet	1
Initiation ceremony	1
First day at school	1
Victim is small and weedy	1
Victim is 'too clever'	1
Victim is 'unlucky'	1
No rationale mentioned	66
Total stories	91

These then are the main themes which occurred in the 217 stories collected during 1988/89. Before examining the messages about sex roles in secondary school which these stories are transmitting, there is a brief theoretical discussion.

A theoretical framework

The theoretical framework which is best suited to analysing *rites de passage* and rituals of reversal is structuralist anthropology as developed by Levi-Strauss (1966, 1967), Leach (1969) and Douglas (1975a, 1975b). A thorough-going structuralist analysis of this corpus of material is beyond the scope of this paper. Levi-Strauss's (1967) analysis of the myth of Asdiwal (a trickster figure in the mythology of the Tsimshian Indians of British Columbia) takes 47 pages. Leach's (1969) exegesis of *Genesis as Myth* fills a small book, while Douglas (1975a, 1985b) spends 35 pages on Lele mythology about the pangolin. However the outline of a structuralist approach can be presented.

The school transfer is a process of leaving the familiar for the strange, and moving from the top of one hierarchy to the bottom of another. A common finding of structuralists is that people draw a distinction between US (the normal, proper, human group) and THEM (people elsewhere who are not normal, and may even behave in nonhuman ways). Thus, among the Lugbara of Uganda witches (who are men in Lugbara cosmology) are described in terms which emphasise their oppositeness to proper humans.

> Some, the most common 'walk at night'... Certain qualities
> are always ascribed to witches: they are said to be incestuous
> and cannibalistic, to be grey or even white in skin colour, to
> have red eyes, and even to walk about upside down.
> (Middleton, 1965: 81)

Proper Lugbara, in contrast, stay home after dark, do not commit incest, are not cannibals, are black, have whites to their eyes, and walk about the 'right' way up.

Such an oppositional reversal can be seen as the common theme in the fears expressed abut destination schools Figure 4:1 sets out the characteristics of the primary and the secondary school as typified by pupils. (See Measor and Woods, 1984; and Delamont and Galton, 1986 for details of children's descriptions of secondary schools.) Transferring pupils are about to make a major status reversal, from the top of the hierarchy to the bottom of the next:

Current School	Destination School
Small building	Big building
Small pupil population	Large pupil population
Environment familiar	Environment unfamiliar
Pupils do not get lost	Pupils may get lost
Full of friends	Full of strangers
Safe place	Dangerous place
Few staff	Many staff
Staff all or nearly all female	Many male teachers
Curriculum simple	Curriculum complex
Subjects familiar	Subjects new and strange
Skills needed have been mastered	New skills needed
Teachers know individual child	Teachers do not know individual children
Personal	Impersonal
Pupils are oldest in school	Pupils are youngest in school
Pupils are biggest in school	Pupils are smallest in school
Pupils are top of school	Pupils are bottom of school
Pupils lack sexuality	Pupils are sexual actors
Teachers lack sexuality	Teachers are sexual actors/predators

Figure 4:1   Characteristics of current and destination schools as seen by pupil

Their world is about to be turned upside down: given that reversal in their status, the lavatory myth becomes explicable.   If the lavatory immersion is the worst kind of degradation and besmirching a child can imagine, it fits with the lowly status they will have in their new schools. The new children are like rubbish in the new hierarchy.

If the new school is a strange and unfamiliar world, it is possible to fit the most common myths into the same framework as Lugbara witchcraft beliefs. In the topsy-turvey world that is coming, there may well be ghosts, gangs and humiliations; staff may well be ogres, and the lavatories unsafe. Figure 4:2 shows the contrasts children draw between their known world and the one they are moving to. In the current school children are small, and teachers known, friendly women who know pupils. In the destination school, children, are big and fierce: teachers are strange, harsh men who do not know pupils.

Primary School		Destination school
Known world	versus	Unknown world
Pupils are smaller than me and lack sexuality therefore safe	versus	Pupils are larger than me and are sexually knowledgeable therefore dangerous
Teachers are women well known and sexual: safe	versus	Teachers are men and women, strangers and potentially sexual: dangerous
Sex roles are known, clearly defined, unproblematic	versus	Sex roles demanded by new curricular/personnel are unknown, not yet defined, highly problematic

Figure 4:2   Oppositional perceptions of pupils

Elsewhere (Measor and Woods, 1983: Delamont, 1989) there are analyses of the commoner myths using this approach Here the focus is the sex role messages carried by these atrocity stories, so one of these is analysed before the more general discussion of gender issues raised by the tales. The story to be analysed is that which provided the title of the paper: 'THE HIT LIST'.

> Before I went to Marbury Church in England High School for Girls I was told by my older fiends that I was on the 'HIT LIST', a selected group of disliked girls, and I was going to be beaten up and have my hands tied (*sic*) together and have my hair shaved off. (Ledshire sixth former, 1988)

To produce a structuralist account of this myth we must start by searching for binary discriminations. As Leach (1969:11) puts it:

In every myth system we will find a persistent sequence of binary discriminations as between human/superhuman, mortal/immortal, male/female, legitimate/illegitimate, good/-bad... followed by a 'mediation' of the paired categories thus distinguished.

A range of binary discriminations can be seen even in these short 'myths'. Among the oppositions that are stated or implied are: before/after, newcomer/old hand, younger/older, weak/strong, free/bound, liked/disliked, safety/danger, aggressor/victim, shaven head/hair.

The last opposition listed above - between having a full head of hair and having a shaven head - suggests a particular message being carried in that folktale above and beyond the general ones about dangerous older pupils. The symbolic meanings of long hair, short hair and the shaven head were explored by Leach (1958) in his Curl Bequest Prize winning essay 'Magical Hair'. Leach argued that:

> marked changes in hairdressing very commonly accompany the changes in sexual status that occur at puberty and marriage. (Leach, 1958:89)

Although different cultures signal the changes in different ways. In some cultures adulthood involves *longer* hair than childhood, in others the reverse. However across many cultures the symbolism of hair length, Leach argues, is as follows:

1)   long hair equals unrestrained sexuality
2)   short hair or tightly bound hair equals restricted/restrained sexuality
3)   closely shaven heads signal celibacy.

The act of shaving the head is frequently part of rituals that separate an initiate or novice from their old life and incorporate them into a new one (becoming a nun, a convict, a soldier, a Krishna devotee). In contemporary Europe there is a particular meaning attached to a women who has her head shaved by others which is a version of the message of celibacy. A women who had her head shaved in Belgium or France after the 1939-45 war, or had it done in Northern Ireland in the 1970s, was bearing the public label of a women punished for having sexual relations with the enemy. By shaving her head, a period of celibacy was being forcibly enjoined, in that no man would wish to have sex with a collaborator.

The pupils who tell the story of the HIT LIST may not be consciously aware of the liberation of Paris. However there is enough research on the rigidity of adolescent girls' beliefs and practices about 'slags' and 'sluts' to support the interpretation that new female pupils need to be wary about how they dress, walk, and relate to boys if they wish to avoid being ostracised or abused by other girls. The research of Smith (1978), Wilson (1978), Lees (1986), and Measor (with Woods, 1984, alone, 1989) is clear about the ways in which female adolescents 'police' the sexuality of their age mates. Measor particularly records older sisters warning new girls not to dress in ways that will produce ridicule and labelling by more experienced pupils. The HIT LIST story is a fantasy version of the same warnings. The sheer nastiness of the story is not unreasonable, given the negative consequences of the 'slut' label once it has been bestowed, and the powerlessness of women to repudiate it. In this frame of analysis, the tying of the hands is also a double symbol, of submission and of powerlessness.

Leach (1969) argues that individual myths should be analysed in the context of the totality of myths that occur and recur around a point of social tension. Once a corpus of myths is fully explicated the message they carry becomes clear. Leach argues that

> even though the ordinary listener is not fully conscious of what has been communicated the 'message' is there in a quite objective sense. (1969:22)

Following Leach, the final section of the paper addresses the sex role messages that are carried in these urban legends, centred on the particularly scarey passage to secondary school.

The sex role messages

Apart from the general messages conveyed by transfer stories, there are clearly specific warnings and prescriptions for male and female pupils that are different. Measor and Woods (1983,1984) have suggested that the stories they found carried the message that secondary school would be a tough area for boys to prove their masculinity. Their set of stories included some about endurance trials in PE. and about Science dissections, which coupled with the lavatory and gang tales made up a set of expectations about appropriate *macho* behaviours. None of the 217 stories examined here focused on endurance feats in PE, and only two mentioned science lessons (both from the occupational trainees):

> I was told by my sister that the school kept live toads in one
> of the biology labs. Also told by friends that school kept
> live mice in biology class, we would have to kill them
> ourselves to be able to dissect them.

The former is hardly a scarey story at all, unless the pupil concerned
was phobic about toads.

Focusing on the types of story that the 16-21 year olds had remembered
the sex role messages will be examined using the structuralist perspective
already outlined. Messages for boys are considered first.

Everything in the batch of 217 stories confirms the findings and
conclusions of Measor and Woods (1983, 1984). Boys facing transfer were
told stories about the need to be tough in secondary school. Boys have to
cut up rats, run 8 minutes miles, slog round cross country courses, while
facing both gangs of bullies in the yards and lavatories and savage
woodwork masters. Only the miniature John Wayne, Bruce Lee or Rambo
will be a hero in the new world. In the recollections of older adolescents
and young adults, the stories about PE and rats have been forgotten,
although the bogwash, the gangs and the harsh teachers are remembered as
motifs. Looming larger in the retrospective data are the stories about
sexuality: stories that can be retold by 17-25 year olds more freely. In the
confused world of the pre-adolescent and young adolescent boy (Fine,
1987; Best, 1983; Beynon, 1985; Delamont and Galton, 1986) the male
who cannot fight and run the 8 minute mile and cut up the rat is a 'poofter'.
Stories of art, drama and photography masters who lock pretty boys in dark
places are not only - indeed perhaps *not at all* - about adult homosexuality,
but about the gender labelling of subjects, and about vulnerability. Clearly
Rambo did not enjoy drama at his comprehensive, he cuts up rat and ran 8
minute miles and fought off gangs. The 'gay master' stories are warnings
that male sexuality is a potential problem *and* a warning about measuring
up as a male oneself.

The young women's stories are equally clear about dangers ahead, but
dangers of psychological harassment rather than physical violence. Shame
is the recurrent *motif* rather than actual bodily harm. The appropriate
subjects for girls are clear: the lesbian teacher is always a PE mistress, the
sweaty, trouser wearing, unfeminine woman.

The world of the secondary school, as portrayed in these stories, is one
where men are men, women are women, all the standards are double, and
all the behavioural norms caricatured extremes. Recalled in young
adulthood some of the topics are different from those gathered from 11 and
12 year olds but the underlying themes: of self presentation, subject choice,

and developing dangerous and/or unmanageable sexuality, are both enduring and depressingly conformist.

Conclusions

Status passages are frequently times of anxiety and of rumour, folklore or mythology. British school pupils not only generate scarey stories of urban legends at the time of their transfer to secondary school, they can also recall them vividly when asked six years or more later. An analysis of the themes implicit and explicit in such stories is illuminating about various aspects of secondary schooling, especially about sex roles and sexuality in the early adolescent years.

Notes

1.   I am grateful to all the sixth formers and occupational trainees who have written stories for me since 1987. Mrs. Pat Harris has word processed this paper several times with skill and speed, and I owe her a great debt.
2.   The county in England, all L.E.A.s, all schools, all training institutions, all teachers, and all pupils/students have been given pseudonyms.

5. Lessons from St.Luke's: Reflections on a study of Scottish classroom life

Preface

This paper was prepared for a Festschrift for J.G. (Ian) Morris, a central figure in Scottish Educational Research in the 1960s and 1970s. It was published in 1983 in W.B. Dockrell (ed) An Attitude of Mind (Edinburgh: SCRE). Since its publication there have been several publications (e.g. Bamford, 1988; Paterson and Fewell, 1990; Brown and Riddell, 1992) which begin to fill the gaps in our knowledge of Scottish women's schooling that were so glaring when I wrote this paper.

> The movement to provide a more solid form of education for girls than that hitherto considered sufficient to satisfy the claims of gentility, and of the female intellect, began in England towards the middle of the nineteenth century..... In 1873 the Girls Public Day School Company was formed and started to found schools all over England, and the example of these spread to Scotland. St.Leonard's School, St.Andrew's was opened in 1877, and in December, two years later, a public meeting was held in Glasgow....... to establish a school for girls.
>
> (Anon, 1930)

This paper describes research conducted in the 1970s on a school, called St.Luke's which was founded in the late nineteenth century in a Scottish city to provide a sound academic education for the daughters of the upper middle class.

As the history of the Park School, Glasgow (Anon,1930), captures it St.Luke's:

seemed to appeal direct to the business and professional men, the professors of the University, and, quite clearly, to the active-minded minister. (p.27)

These parents were unhappy with the standards of education then available to girls, either at home, or in schools which were neither academically sound, nor healthy. The campaigns to establish serious education has been discussed elsewhere (Delamont, 1978a and 1978b) and is not analysed here. However, it is noticeable that there is no scholarly work on the development of such schools in Scotland, as opposed to England, although Scotland is neglected in the standard texts (e.g. Kamm, 1965; Turner, 1974; Burstyn, 1980 and Dyhouse 1981)

The research, consisting of participant observation in third year classes, has been described elsewhere (Delamont, 1973, 1976a, 1976b, 1976c, 1983, 1984) and is not recapitulated in this paper. Rather, this paper discusses the four aspects of the study which can be seen to have accompanied and foreshadowed important developments in subsequent Scottish educational research. The four themes highlighted are: systematic classroom observation; school ethnography; cultural reproduction in Scotland; and the socialization of women.

The research at St.Luke's used two kinds of observation, interviews, questionnaires, and some historical investigation, to produce an evocation of the school lives of fourteen and fifteen year old girls at a public school. The school and the main concerns of the research are summarised, and then the four themes are considered in greater detail.

St.Luke's school

St.Luke's is a public school for girls situated in a Scottish city. It takes day girls from kindergarten to sixth year, and some boarders from the age of 9. It was founded in 1888 by a group of feminist educational pioneers (Delamont, 1978a and 1978b). The establishment of St.Luke's was part of a wider campaign to improve women's education in Scotland. Since the 1880s it has been both academically and socially exclusive, while today the school prospectus announces that the school's aims are 'providing a liberal education and maintaining the pioneering spirit of its founders'. The links with the nineteenth century feminists were still visible in 1973, when the school magazine carried the obituary of one of the first pupils to enrol at St.Luke's in 1888. She had just died at the age of 95, after graduating in medicine at the turn of the century and spending a lifetime practising *zenana* medicine in India (Scharlieb, 1924).

The socially exclusive nature of St.Luke's is exemplified by my particular study population: the 43 girls who made up the third year in 1970. All had fathers with occupations in Social Class 1. The school is popular with senior staff at the local university, with professional families, and with business men. The social exclusiveness is related to the costs of St.Luke's. In 1971, it cost £95 a term for a day girl in the secondary school and £52 in the kindergarten. Boarding fees were an additional £100 per term. These fees included the loan of textbooks, and not stationery or 'extras'. Needlework is available, cookery is not. Unlike many girls' public schools (Dyhouse, 1977) St.Luke's has never given into pressure to train "good wives and little mothers". The high academic standards are maintained by admitting only girls who pass a difficult entrance exam. All but one of my group had IQ's of over 110. The public examination results (discussed in Delamont, 1984) show the standards obtained by St.Luke's. All the girls were given strong encouragement for taking Sciences and Latin at least to 'O' grade, and the majority stay on to 17 and take Highers. In the sixth year 'A' levels are taken, not the Scottish Certificate of Sixth Year Studies (see McPherson and Neave, 1976).

The school buildings represent various architectural styles from 1914 onwards, and are set on a bleak hilltop in a suburb which contains several other fee-paying schools. There is a House system and the five Houses are called after famous Scottish castles: Traquair, Craigievar, Bothwell, Tantalon and Dunvegan. The school plays lacrosse and hockey in the winter, tennis in the summer, and offers fencing, squash and badminton. St.Luke's girls are a source of recruitment for the Scottish girls' fencing team, one of my sample captaining it in her sixth year.

The research methods

The research at St.Luke's used two distinct types of observation. Part of the time was spent using two pre-specified coding schedules (Flanders, 1970; Delamont, 1973), and the rest doing 'anthropological' or 'ethnographic' observation (Hammersley and Atkinson, 1983). A detailed account of the whole study is given in Delamont (1973), and a brief summary only is presented here.

During the first two weeks of the research I used Flanders Interaction Analysis Categories (Flanders, 1970) in all lessons, before I knew any of the participants. This was my main source of data on teaching behaviour at

St.Luke's. Then I watched the lessons concentrating on the pupils, coding their contributions with a schedule of my own devising (see Delamont, 1983 and 1984, for this schedule), and made *verbatim* 'fieldnotes' of 'interesting' pieces of dialogue.

It was not possible to do anything but sit silently in lessons, because that is what the girls did. The lessons at St.Luke's were silent, or had one person talking at a time. Pupil conversations were rare, because the girls worked nearly all the time, or switched-off. In lessons where talk was allowed, I mixed with the pupils: for example Physics, Chemistry and Biology group work, and P.E. However, I tried to be passive - I did not play hockey or lacrosse as Mandy Llewellyn (1980) did - but did tie the girls' team numbers on for them if they asked. At break and lunch I went to the staff-room and chatted to the teachers. I interviewed the boarders one evening in the boarding house, and the day girls in a city centre flat during the holidays. They came in groups (if they wished) and sat reading magazines while I interviewed them one at a time in a separate room. The groups they formed to come for interview gave me an unobtrusive measure of their sociometric structure, which I also researched in the interviews and by drawing seating plans for lessons.

The research strategy employed was highly unusual, combining Flanders' Interaction Analysis Categories (a pre-specified coding scheme) with ethnographic work, in a manner which had not previously been attempted. In retrospect it is clear that, embodied in the study, were the four themes mentioned above which came to be important in Scottish educational research in the 1970s and 1980s. These are now discussed in turn. The growth of classroom studies in general is considered first, both in general and in its two main methodological variants, before turning to the themes of cultural reproduction and the education of girls.

The growth of classroom studies

Direct observations of teachers and pupils in classrooms over the last twenty years has been carried out by researchers from a range of different disciplines. In addition to psychologists (McIntyre and MacLeod, 1978); there have been anthropologists (Wilcox, 1982), linguists (Edwards, 1980; Green and Wallat, 1981), and sociologists (Hammersley, 1980 and 1982). All these approaches were evident in Scotland in the late 1960s, and Scottish researchers were central to the growth of classroom research in Britain.

Among the various disciplines, while there are theoretical differences, there are two different approaches to the direct observation of classrooms in terms of method and philosophy. One school of researchers has concentrated ˙ on developing coding systems for recording their observations, so that the observer classifies what is seen and heard into pre-specified categories. Thus, for example, in coding system devised by Flanders (1970) if a teacher is heard to say Can anyone tell me what we call these blue crystals?", the observer codes this in a category of 'Teacher Questions' and records that coding ('4' in the case of the Flanders system). The behaviour of teachers and pupils is classified, according to a set of rules, into particular categories and these are recorded.

Many famous studies done in recent years, such as Neville Bennett's (1976) *Teaching Styles and Pupil Progress* and the Michael Rutter *et al.* (1979) study *Fifteen Thousand Hours*, have used the coding system approach. It was predominantly popularised by researchers with backgrounds in psychology, has clear links with psychological theories of learning and teaching, and will be one central focus of this paper.

There is, however, a contrasting approach to the direct observation of classrooms, which is currently enjoying a vogue in the USA, and has always had vocal adherents in Britain. This is usually called the 'anthropological' or 'ethnographic' approach, because of its origins in social anthropology. The most obvious differences between ethnographic observation and the coding system are that the former does not pre-specify what will be recorded, and tries to record in the natural language (direct speech) of the teacher and pupils, rather than classifying it. Ethnographers are usually interested in the participants' subjective perspectives on, and accounts of, interaction, rather than being concerned to classify it objectively.

Underlying the methodological differences are deeper philosophical and theoretical theories about the nature of social science, in particular whether social science should be 'normative' or 'interpretive'. Cohen and Manion (1981) have produced a lucid and coherent discussion of these contrasting research approaches to the study of schools and classrooms, and it is not elaborated here.

Both methodological approaches, and all the theoretical angles, were being employed in Scotland at the time of the St Luke's study. The use of Flanders Interaction Analysis Categories (FIAC) in the St.Luke's work was closely paralleled by Arnold Morrrison's (1973) evaluation of the impact of modern studies in Scottish secondary schools. In Glasgow Sue Kleinberg (1975) was working with similar techniques in teacher training. As Wragg (1975) and Brown (1975) show, much of the work advancing the use of

FIAC in Britain was going forward in Scotland. While there have been many criticisms of this research approach (see Hamilton and Delamont, 1984) the spread of FIAC in Britain led to a redirection of scholarly attention to teacher-pupil interaction after decades of neglect.

The St.Luke's study also employed a schedule for coding pupil talk, which was an independent creation. This compilation of a novel schedule was a regular part of Scottish educational research. Duthie's (1970) pioneering study of Scottish primary schools used one of the first pre-schedule coding schemes to be developed in Britain. Also active in schedule development was Ray McAleese who is represented in Maurice Galton's (1978) compilation of 41 systems by no less than seven different schedules. Scottish researchers provided 14 of the systems anthologised, which show a diverse range of educational problems under scrutiny.

The St.Luke's study was unusual in that it focused on differences between pupil's classroom participation patterns. The analysis showed that one group of girls, who shared a self-conscious identity as 'intellectuals', had a measurably different pattern of contributions to the classroom discourse from their classmates. These girls were the only ones who regularly and habitually challenged the teachers' definitions of school knowledge. The rest of the girls very rarely queried the staff' pronouncements, being, as one girl put it, 'quite content to take facts' (see Delamont, 1976, and 1984 for further details). In using both FIAC and a uniquely developed schedule, the St.Luke's research was typical of the Scottish classroom studies of the 1970s.

Alongside the schedule-based observation, Scotland was also one major British source of the ethnographic tradition in educational research.

The group of research students gathered to Edinburgh by Liam Hudson (1977) were instrumental in developing school and classroom ethnography in the UK. Alongside the St.Luke's ethnography is the work of Nash (1973), Hamilton (1976), Stubbs (1975), Atkinson (1981), Torode (1976), Reid (1982). The Hudson department also produced two critiques of the prevailing paradigms in classroom research (Hamilton and Delamont, 1976 and 1984) and curriculum evaluation (Partlett and Hamilton, 1972) which advocated ethnography. Accounts of the Edinburgh Department in this period of paradigm change and personal turmoil can be found in Hudson (1977), Bell (1983), Delamont (1983) and Wragg (1982). Although Bell has claimed that the Hudson students 'could just as easily have carried out their work in England, Ontario or Wisconsin' (p.170), the product of the studies is an important body of information on Scottish educational practices of the period 1968-74. Indeed the contribution made to the study of Scottish cultural reproduction is made apparent in the next section.

Cultural reproduction in Scotland

The publication of *Scottish Culture and Scottish Education* (Humes and Paterson 1983) has brought the relationship between education and cultural reproduction in Scotland to the centre of educational research. Yet Humes and Paterson (1983) Smith and Hamilton (1980), and Gray *et al* (1983) all neglect to consider the role of the girls' fee-paying schools (private or grant-aided) in reproducing Scottish culture. The girls at St.Luke's came from two distinct sectors of the upper middle class : the intelligentsia and the bourgeoisie. The girls who challenged the teachers' definitions of knowledge came from intellectual homes where *both* parents were graduates and the mothers had careers. The rest of the pupils lacked graduate, working mothers, came from bourgeois homes, and had an unchallenging attitude to the school's knowledge. The 'intellectual' girls left school with better qualifications than their peers, as Table 5:1 shows, but the rest of the pupils achieved a high standard of exam passes. Table 5:1 shows the exam results obtained by the girls studied in 1970 when they took 'O' grades, 'H' grades and 'A' levels. The average number of passes obtained by each of the three large friendship groups, and by the rest of the sample, who remained at school till 18 are shown.

Table 5:1   Public examination results by clique

	(1971) 'O' Grades	(1972) Highers	(1973) 'A' levels
Group 5 ('intellectuals')	9.3	5.4	2.6
Group 1 (boarders)	8.6	5.2	1.6
Group 2 (adolescents and sports women)	8.4	5.1	1
Rest of the year	8.4	5.0	1

The 'intellectuals' had been noticeable at 14 for abhoring school sport, and being uninvolved in adolescent subcultures. They hated team games and were not keen on pop music, discos and coffeebars. The other two groups shown in Table 5:1, the boarders, and the 'adolescents and

71

sportswomen', both enjoyed school sport and spent their leisure with boys, dancing and listening to pop music. At 14 the 'intellectuals' were labelled 'swots and weeds'. At 18, the school offices (e.g. Head Girl, House Captain) were equally spread across all the girls, but the intellectuals dominated the scholarly offices. (e.g. president of the debating society) and the other two groups provided the school sports captains.

Captured within one year at St.Luke's are two sectors of the Scottish upper middle class reproducing themselves. The pejoratively - labelled 'swots and weeds' are the bearers of cultural capital (Bourdieu and Passeron, 1977) and the representatives of the 'new' middle class described by Bernstein (1974). (See Delamont 1976a, 1984 and 1989) for the elaborated version of this argument.) The concern with the reproduction of Scottish culture is shared with other educational researchers, notably Andrew McPherson (1973, 1983). Yet none of the papers in Smith and Hamilton (1980) or Humes and Paterson (1983) addresses the socialization of the middle or upper middle classes, and the major research effort (Gray *et al*, 1983) pays little attention to the issue. It is noticeable that Gray, McPherson and Raffe do not bother to discuss John Scott's (1979, 1980) research on Scottish capitalists and land owners, nor do they refer to the material on elites in Parsler (1980). This is a serious lack in the recent Scottish educational research, paralleled only by the lack of data on the school experience of girls, which is the subject of the final section.

Women's education in Scotland

When the St.Luke's study was conducted, research on the schooling of women was unfashionable, marginal and discounted. Since 1970 'women's studies' and educational research on women has boomed (Acker, 1982; and Walker and Barton, 1983). However research interest in the education of Scottish Women has been slow to develop, and an examination of bibliographies on British women's education reveals little on the distinctive Scottish system. There are no published classroom studies or school ethnographies of girls in state schools, and the St.Luke's material remains the only account of the processes of women's education in Scotland. Sutherland (1981) is the only general text on the education of women which includes Scottish material, and her evidence is largely statistical in nature unbalanced by interactionist work. In England there is a detailed study of sex differentiation in infant schools (King, 1978), in primary schools (Clarricoates, 1980), in middle schools (Meyenn, 1980, Delamont, 1980), in secondary schools (Fuller, 1980) and in further education (Stanworth,

1981). All these sectors of the education system are different in Scotland, but the processes of sexual differentiation in them have yet to be researched. Scotland has the study of female undergraduates' and trainee teachers' attitudes to sex roles (Galloway, 1973) which tells us more about the staff role in sex role socialization than any other British research. Otherwise this important topic is badly neglected in Scotland. It is sad that the St.Luke's study was not merely the first of many such investigations.

Conclusions

The group of students gathered by Liam Hudson have become notorious for developing qualitative methods in educational research. In this paper I have argued that the ethnography of the St.Luke's is actually part of several movements in Scottish educational research. The Edinburgh department under Hudson, despite his views, was actually contributing to our knowledge of Scots education.

Note

1. St.Luke's is a pseudonym, as are all the names given to teachers and pupils in this paper. The research at St.Luke's was financed by an SSRC studentship, and the material was written up while I had a research assistantship funded by SCRE. I am deeply grateful to both funding bodies.

6. The old girl network: Recollections of the fieldwork at St. Luke's

> In England we possess, in the great boys' schools, what is (in spite of all defects) probably the finest system for the training of men in manly qualities that the world knows; it is all the more pity that we have so signally failed to evolve a corresponding organization for the rearing of womanly women.

Meyrick Booth wrote that condemnation of the education provided in the girls; public schools in 1927. In 1971 Mallory Wober described the *English Girls' Boarding Schools* and came to an effectively similar conclusion when he criticised them for failing to teach cookery and childcare. In 1969 and 1970 I was engaged in research in several of the fee-paying, elite girls' schools in Edinburgh, imbuded with the opposite conviction. I had, as I still have, a belief that such schools were an embodiment of the best kind of education for girls. Single-sex, academic, achievement-oriented institutions dedicated to producing scholars rather than womanly women seemed to be highly desirable. This paper is an autobiographical account of my Ph.D. fieldwork at St.Luke's: the pseudonym I gave the expensive girls' public school where I did observation in 1970

The full ethnography is written up in Delamont (1973) and remains substantially unpublished.

There are 4 main sections to this paper. The first is essentially a *caveat*, because I have certain reservations about discussing the material so long after the events. The central core is made up of extracts from the relevant chapters of the Ph.D thesis with an intercalated commentary written in the 1980s. This is followed by a discussion of some further issues on data collection and analysis which have relevance to the current state of educational research and to this volume. The fourth section is a postscript, in which some 'if only' comments are made.

Caveats

At the outset I would like to stress how long ago this work was done. I graduated in 1968, spent 1968-69 working on paper and pencil tests about study habits, and did the observational work in 1969-70. At that time the 'new' sociology of education was not public'. I had completed my data collection by the 1970 BSA conference at which the paradigm change was announced (Brown, 1973). Also work on females was very unfashionable, and 'women's studies' had barely begun even in the USA. This means that there are at least two major research topics - gender and the content of the curriculum - which would have been treated as problematic if I had done the fieldwork in the mid-1970s. However, they were not seen then as central or even significant topics for research, and I cannot say much about them. I believe that bad ethnographic writing comes from taking data collected with one frame of reference and writing it up using a different one, because the researcher has usually focused on issues and personnel relevant to the first perspective, and lacks insight on different questions. The work of Sharp and Green (1975) seems to me a particularly vivid warning for other ethnographers in this regard. It does not appear either possible or desirable to write about the St.Luke's work as if I had read classification and framing (Bernstein, 1971) or Millman and Kantor (1974) while I was doing the research. The study is, therefore, notable for failing to make either the curriculum, or the issues of gender, problematic.

A second caveat concerns the status of the research, and its historical context. Since the St.Luke's fieldwork I have never had the luxury of spending longer than a month engaged in research full-time, so in some ways the three years full-time study (and two years of part-time work) spent on the project should make it a model ethnography. However, it was a higher degree project, and therefore a learning exercise; an apprenticeship. I would not want any other researcher, novice or experienced, to do exactly what I did, and I would not now tackle the project in precisely the same way myself.

The whole context of classroom research has changed so markedly since 1969 that many aspects of the St.Luke's study seem quaint; sepia-tinted; "long ago and far away". As the extracts from the thesis, used in the next section, show the combination of a novel research topic and method with being a candidate for a higher degree gives the thesis a defensive tone. My recollections of writing up the thesis are that, as well as being extremely hard work, the process was frightening. The criteria for success were largely indeterminate, my supervisor had no experience in submitting ethnographic work for higher degree examination, and the Professor (who controlled the selection of an external and an internal examiner) capricious. I now know from a survey of higher degree students (Eggleston and Delamont, 1983) that most feel worried by the indeterminacy of thesis examination, and that inexperienced supervisors are common. Today I warn graduates that research is a lonely, unsettling experience, and doing a thesis is rather like an initiation ceremony where young warriors have to live all alone in the wilderness for long period before rejoining the tribe as adults. At the time, the intellectual isolation and responsibility I felt scared me.

It can be argued that such isolation is necessary, as well as common among postgraduates (Eggleston and Delamont, 1983). I can see that, as one of a group of research students Liam Hudson had gathered in Edinburgh, I was lucky to share my stumbling discovery of school and classroom ethnography with a group of others. Hudson (1977) has written an article about the student ethnographers he fostered in Edinburgh, in which he describes us as an intellectual and social clique with considerable hostility to other schools of methodology. His detailed analysis of the internal structure of the student group is highly inaccurate, but his general characterisation of us as mutually supportive both intellectually and personally is reasonable. The central links formed then can still be seen in the publications of the core members of the clique.([1]) The Edinburgh group was not only mutually supportive in developing ethnographic methods in education, it has also become seen as a pioneering centre for developing educational ethnography. Professor E.C.Wragg's (1982) evidence to the Rothschild Enquiry, for example, cites us as a shining example of the role of SSRC studentships in fostering scholarly work of major national importance. Certainly if I had not had the friendship of Paul Atkinson, David Hamilton, Michael Stubbs, Margaret Reid, Brian Torode and Margo Galloway I would never have written the thesis and submitted it. As it was, I planned carefully to submit while Liam Hudson was on sabbatical, and was awarded the degree by Don Swift and Boris Semeonoff.

The final caveat is that, because the bulk of the research is unpublished, much of what follows may be obscure. The data on St.Luke's lie, relatively unknown, in the Edinburgh University Library. This is not because I was ashamed of my work, but the result of a series of accidents. I submitted the thesis in August 1973, and started work at Leicester in September. I had asked Routledge, who had published Roy Nash's Ph.D (1973), if they wanted to see mine, and despatched it as I left for Leicester. Some 6-9 months later, having heard nothing, I wrote to ask for my manuscript back. Routledge replied that they had lost it, would pay for a Xerox, and wished to have a photocopy so that they could consider it for publication. The second submission reached an academic referee (Brian Davies) who recommended that a revised manuscript be published. Routledge rejected this advice, pleading the economic climate, and so I was back at Square One. However, by this time John Eggleston had asked me to write *Interaction in the Classroom* (1976a), so the thesis was put aside. Thus apart from four papers (Delamont, 1976b, 1976c, 1984; Atkinson and Delamont, 1977) the research described below is only known from *Interaction in the Classroom*. The material which follows therefore describes the collection, analysis and presentation of a Ph.D thesis, not a book or a research report to a sponsor.

The next section presents material from the PhD thesis, *Academic Conformity Observed: Studies in the Classrooms*, set in italics, with a commentary written in 1982/83.

Doing the research at St.Luke's

The introduction to the thesis describes the central features of my research at St.Luke's, in the context of 1972/73.

The scope of the methods

> *This thesis discusses the intellectual perspectives and work-habits of adolescents at a variety of Scottish schools; with particular emphasis on one sample of girls who are analysed in the context of the teaching they experienced and their institutional and social setting. Three traditionally separate methods of data collection have been used, together with aspects of their related theories.*
>
> *The first of these three normally distinct methodologies uses inventories, questionnaires, or mental tests; and has traditionally formed the cornerstone of most educational psychology and educational sociology. Both the other two methods are based on observation, but used in rather different ways. In one tradition, which I have called **systematic** observation the observer uses a schedule of some description, which has been devised in advance, and allows the observer to code behaviour as he observes it, usually so that it can later be quantified, (Medley and Mitzel, 1963). The other tradition of observation I have called **unstructured**, because the observer is concerned to **discover***

77

the interrelationship of variables in the social situation by observing social action.

These three particular methods of data collection have not, to my knowledge, been used in conjunction before. As a result there is no obvious precedent in the literature either for combining the results gathered in the separate traditions or for presenting it in a coherent monograph with the related theory. This lack of precedent has affected the form which this thesis takes and the style in which it is written. The authors who have conducted research in the three traditions relevant to this thesis have done so largely in mutual isolation. In consequence I have dispensed with the standard 'review of the literature' chapter, in favour of discussing the relevant literature at the appropriate point in the thesis. Stylistically, the lack of precedent has led me to expose the 'bare bones' of the research design rather more than usual - to explain and justify my use of the various data collection techniques at each stage of the discussion.

The comments today on this extract are firstly: it is odd that I use 'he' for 'the researcher', and secondly, I am surprised by the defensiveness. The thesis had 10 chapters in 3 sections - one on the pupils and the teachers based on questionnaires, interviews, and documents; the next on the systematic observation; and then one on the unstructured observation which built to a theorised crescendo. After the description of what was in the 10 chapters, I reviewed some basic literature on the 'Three Traditions', in the following ways:

THE THREE TRADITIONS: Paper and Pencil Measures, Systematic and Unstructured Observation

My work on teacher and pupil's styles has only a tangential connection with the mainstream of work in either the mental testing field or that of questionnaire and survey based educational psychology. However, it does have close ties with some of the less orthodox work which has developed from that tradition, in particular that of Hudson (1966, 1968a, 1968b) on differences in intellectual styles, which grew out of intelligence testing, and Parlett (1967 and 1970) on individual work-styles. The study described below used a variety of questionnaires and inventories, in particular a version of the syllabus-bound inventory developed by Parlett for use among students at MIT (Parlett, 1967) and also Hudson on English schoolboys, (Hudson, 1968a). The questionnaire and inventories, used in this study have provided much of the quantifiable data, and the means of comparing samples of pupils at different schools. The main emphasis of this study was, however, placed on observation within schools rather than an inventories, questionnaires or tests.

Here I rehearsed the growth of systematic observation in the USA via Medley and Mitzel (1963) and Rosenshine (1971). I said that:

Some of these systems are mentioned briefly later in this chapter. A more thorough review of the relevant literature occurs in Chapter 6. At this point it is enough to say that this part of the research is well documented and has clear precedents.

This was to draw a contrast with:

Unstructed observation techniques [which] have remained largely neglected. Handbooks of research methods in the social sciences, particularly anthropology, discuss unstructured observation, but handbooks on educational research do not. There have, however, been a few studies done in recent years using unstructured techniques, in particular the work of Becker and his associates in higher education and professional socialisation (Becker et al. 1961, 1968)..... Four studies of schools using unstructured techniques have been useful during my research; two studies of English secondary schools (Hargreaves, 1967l; Lacey, 1970), and two of American elementary classes (Smith and Geoffrey, 1968; Jackson, 1968).

Writing today, it is very striking how little observational work was published on schools in 1970-1973, and how unknown some of the available studies from the USA were in Britain. None of the ethnographies I traced was about girls, and the few books on girls' schools (e.g.Wober, 1971) were not recognisable to me as research. I corresponded with Audrey Lambert about her Manchester study, but at that time she had not written up her Master's thesis and so had nothing to send me. To date her work is less well-known than the classics (Hargreaves, 1967 and Lacey, 1970) by her colleagues , and only one article Lambert (1977) has been published. Since 1973 there have been a few papers on the schooling of girls published (Fuller, 1980); Llewellyn, 1980) but a contemporary research student studying St.Luke's would not find a full-length published ethnography of girls to use as a model. I based the structure of my thesis on *Making the Grade* Becker *et al*, 1968), and it would have been easier to have a British ethnography of a school to use as a blueprint. At the time, I did not labour those points, but emphasised to the reader of the thesis that I had used Flanders Interaction Analysis Categories (1970) *with* a loosely symbolic interactionist-observational approach. I explain this at the time as follows:

> *The decision to integrate data gathered from different traditions into one coherent monograph was initially the project of disappointment. During 1968-9 I conducted a study of syllabus-bound and syllabus-free pupils in some secondary schools based solely on questionnaires and inventories. This research raised more questions than it resolved. I found that differences between samples from the various schools visited were great, even when the pupils were of the same age, sex and social class. Nothing in the questionnaire data explained the wide range of scores, and the answers appeared to lie in the internal structures of the schools. A research project which was based on observation within one or more schools, designed to illuminate the subtle variations which had eluded the questionnaire-based study, was indicated.*
>
> *When I came to the literature on observation in schools I was intrigued by the existence of two disparate traditions of observation - the systematic and the unstructured apparently in mutual isolation. I felt that the two types of observation had been used for tackling different research problems, and so were not necessarily incompatible. The project at St.Luke's was therefore planned to involve both methods, each in the area where it was most appropriate. While in the field I found that the two techniques were indeed compatible, and the problems which were raised by the combination of methods were relatively slight. However, the difficulties of producing a coherent report of the study*

utilising all the data are considerable. This is due, at least in part to the lack of any previous work attempting the same combination of techniques, and the resulting lack of any established conventions for presenting such data.

Writing in 1983 this is still true, in that no published work has attempted to do what I did! However the ORACLE book on transfer to middle and secondary schools (Galton and Willcocks, 1983) does draw on data collection with Deanne Boydell's two observational schedules and ethnographic fieldnotes (see Galton and Delamont, 1985). At the time I stressed the uneasy relationship(s) between quantitative and qualitative data.

The relationship between the unstructured methods of observation and either the data produced by 'paper and pencil' measures or that from systematic observation is an uneasy one. It is, of course, merely a part of the wider problem which faces anyone using unstructured techniques: how to handle and present the data and whether or not to attempt to quantify them. A comparison of those authors whose work with unstructured observation has influenced this research shows vividly that there is no consensus about the extent to which other types of data should be incorporated.

At one extreme the two books produced by the Manchester 'anthropologists' Hargreaves (1967) and Lacey (1970) contain far more data derived from written questionnaires than actual accounts of the observation. Lacey includes a long historical section derived from published records, and quotes at length from diaries kept by the boys, apparently at his request. Hargreaves uses questionnaire responses extensively in his book, although his subjects would probably have been more articulate in interviews than on paper. Both men relied very heavily an sociometric data to establish social relations among the boys, and apparently paid little attention to recording actual patterns of interaction among the boys while they were in the schools. This reliance on written material means that their books tell us more about social relations expressed in writing than they do about what the fieldworker actually saw. Neither book contains detailed accounts of the lessons

observed: nether their intellectual content, nor the teachers'
actions, nor the pupils' reactions and classroom behaviour.

This passage shows how dominant Hargreaves (1967) and Lacey (1970) were at the time, and how I saw my work as an attempt to do better. I wanted to see how far Hargreaves and Lacey were producing findings about boys which would not be applicable in girls' schools; *or* about streamed schools which would not turn up in institutions with subject sets and mixed ability groups; *or* about schools with an intake from different social classes or home circumstances. That is, if one looked at girls, and at a non-streamed school, and at a 'one class' school, would one find polarised peer groups? So I wanted expensive, single-sex schools where there were subject sets but not fixed streams, where I could study peer-group formation. When I came to write up the thesis I dignified the choice of school type as 'theoretical sampling' (Glaser and Strauss, 1967) *but only when writing up.* In 1969 I just thought Lacey and Hargreaves had 3 variables confused, and it was necessary to separate them.

The thesis chapter goes on to compare the role of the observer doing FIAC with that of the ethnographer. I contrasted the non-involved FIAC-user with Becker talking to medical students as they sat around in Kansas, emphasising that 'full' participation is not possible in the type of school studied. The thesis chapter continues:

In my study I attempted to play both types of observational role within the school, depending on the situations which arose. Within the ordinary, largely silent classroom I acted as an entirely non-participant, 'fly-on-the-wall' observer, and concentrated on using two systematic schedules, augmented by notes of other events. In those lessons where the girls were sometimes free to move around and to talk amongst themselves (such as Needlework, Art, the three sciences, and games), I circulated among the pupils during the appropriate periods, talking to them and to the teacher. In the episodes where attention was focused on the teacher I reverted to the non-participant role, and used my systematic techniques if they were applicable. Throughout the rest of the school day I concentrated on participating in the life of the staff-room and the playground, engaging in conversations with teachers and pupils, during breaks, lunch-hours, free lessons, the intervals between lessons and the extra-curricular activities.

With this combination of techniques I tried to make the best possible use of my time in the school, to provide coherent accounts of both the highly regulated, and the relatively free, episodes in the school day of my sample. It appeared to be perfectly possible to play both roles while observing in the same school, because each role is used in the context where it is closest to the behaviour of the people being observed. Within a secondary school, at least, the two methods of observing are not incompatible.

As part of the contrast, I did stress that Jackson (1968), Smith and Geoffrey (1968) and Blanche Geer (1964) had tried to make the familiar strange, and that was what I, too, had tried to achieve. There is more detail about the FIAC observation in a later chapter, but no more discussion about the ethnography. For this paper I have written something on access, data collection and recording, analysis, and ethics, none of which is discussed in the thesis. In retrospect it appears that I took 'participant observation' as a relatively unproblematic, taken-for-granted, activity, which did not need further discussion.

Some previously unconsidered trifles

In this part of the paper I comment upon several aspects of the research which were not discussed in Delamont (1973) and are previously unpublished. Access, Data Collection and Recording, Analysis, Writing Up, and Ethics are recollected in this section.

Gaining access

The general strategy for gaining access to a school to observe, interview or give out questionnaires, was a polite, but vague letter asking to see the Head. Once inside her room, I would specify what I hoped to be allowed to do. All the schools studied in Edinburgh were independent, fee-paying girls' schools, so the local authority and the SED did not have to be approached. As far as I know all the heads made their own decision, and did not consult the Governors. When I saw heads I always wore a conservative outfit and real leather gloves. I had a special grey dress and coat for days when I expected to see the head and some pupils. The coat was knee-length and very conservative-looking, while the dress was mini-length to show the pupils I knew what the fashion was. I would keep the coat on in the head's office, and take if off before I first met pupils. When observing I tried to dress like the student teachers who were common in all the schools: no trousers, unladdered tights, and no make up.

No head ever asked me to explain my project to her staff, bur rather did any explaining herself. I do not think any head let me into her school without warning her teachers, an experience reported by Atkinson (1984) and Llewellyn (1980). I never approached teachers myself, and the pupils were never asked, by anyone, if they minded completing questionnaires or being observed.

None of the 'posh' girls' schools in Edinburgh refused access. I visited six elite girls' schools (including the one used for the Jean Brodie story) for questionnaire-sessions, or observation, or both. Paper and pencil 'test' were done in several girls' schools during 1968-69, and I had negotiated observation of a few lessons. When I decided to concentrate on observation of methods I did a short period (2-3 weeks) in December 1969 on one school 'The Laurels' as a 'pilot' for a half-term at St.Luke's. Some observation was done in four different schools, but the thesis was concentrated on the half-term at St.Luke's. Accordingly I have focused on that work in this paper. However I can honestly say I did not have any access problems, and all the heads - gatekeepers - were very cooperative. I used to be nervous before I saw them, but no-one every objected to the research taking place.

The phrase 'old-girl network' is used as the title because I think the fact that the headmistress of St.Luke's was an old Girtonian and warmed to me when told I had been at Girton, led to allowing me to stay in the school for half-a-term and leaving me unharassed. She asked the staff if they would let me into their classes, but in my absence. Only one teacher refused to have me in her lessons, her public reason being that she had just had a student teacher for eight weeks and wanted some privacy. The girls told me that she frequently lost her temper and 'explained' her refusal in that way. This refusal meant I only saw one French teacher in action, although I was able to see German and Spanish taught. Mrs. Michaels, the head also wrote to parents asking them to allow me to interview her pupils. Only one set of parents among the forty-four girls in the year I was studying refused me permission to interview their daughter, Deborah. With the inevitability of sod's law, Deborah was the isolate of the year, chosen as a friend by no one, and was a highly significant, negative reference point for all the other girls. They thought her parents were over-protective and that she was babyish and yielded too much to her family! I regret to this day that I did not get to talk with her, because her classroom behaviour was unusual: she volunteered a lot in class, but the teachers ignored her raised hand to a noticeable degree. (Her school career was reasonably successful however, in that she eventually left with 9 SCE '0' grades and 6 'Highers'). (2) The other girls either gained their parent's permission for the interview, or were given the freedom to make their own decision. (They were fourteen and fifteen during the study). All in all Mrs.Michaels was extremely supportive towards the research, as were the staff of St.Luke's, who largely treated me with benign neglect.

Sampling

I worked with a whole year group, of fourteen/fifteen year olds who were third year in Scottish terms (fourth year in English terms) - that is one year away from SEC '0' grades. There were 44 girls in the year in two parallel forms, taught as ability sets for some subjects and in option groups for others. I had a sampling problem over which lesson to watch when three or four were sometimes happening at once. For example, Physics, Biology, Greek, and Dress and Design were timetabled simultaneously, so that I could not observe the girls taking Greek *and* those doing needlework. I chose to concentrate on large classes (i.e. Physics with 20 girls rather than Greek with 3) and avoided the languages I did not speak myself (German and Spanish). However I made sure that every teacher had me at least once, so they all shared the burden, except the 'refuser'. I kept a careful record of where I had been, and watched an equal number of lessons taught by the 'majority' teachers: that is I systematically went to one English teacher and then the other to make sure I had an equal sample of 'A' and 'B' English lessons. The whole year group was my 'sample' or rather population, and all the teachers who taught them, except the visiting music teachers of violin, trumpet etc. (Among these peripatetic staff were the only males in the building apart from the caretaker).

Data collection and recording

Overall I do not think what I did can usefully be called *participant* observation, because I did not participate in any meaningful way. Instead I 'lurked' and watched. I think I fell into the category in the school occupied by student teachers, who also lurked about the school, often without any clear function.

There were four kinds of data: questionnaires completed by the girls; tape-recorded interviews with pupils; the FIAC data and my fieldnotes. Specimens of all the questionnaires, and the interview schedule, are reproduced in an Appendix to the thesis, and are not discussed further here. I taped pupil interviews, *and* took notes on them, in case of the recorder failing, which it did on one occasion. The interview covered peer group membership, perceptions of teachers elicited with their names on cards presented in threes following Kelly's procedure (Bannister and Fransella, 1971), career ambitions, leisure activities and general views of St.Luke's. The interviews also went into some detail about subject choice, and the role of parents and teachers in the process. I also asked what sort of pupil teachers liked and disliked, eliciting a description of a 'Good Pupil' Ideal Type. These data have subsequently confused several commentators, notably Rosemary Deem (1978: 40-41). Drawing only on *Interaction in the Classroom* rather than the thesis or published articles, she says that the girls of St.Luke's:

> seem to have almost an obsessive concern with being quiet, good at school work, and getting teachers to like them.... Boys seldom perceive their role in this way and there can be few boy pupils of whom it could be said, as it was of one girl in Delamont's study... that 'she only answers when she's sure she's right'.

While I fail to understand how anyone could misread the relevant section of *Interaction in the Classroom* (pp.68-71) so thoroughly, I have amended the section in the second edition (Delamont, 1983). I asked the girls "If you had a sister coming to St.Luke's who wanted to be popular with teachers, and asked you how, what would you tell her to do?". The characteristics of the ideal pupil elicited in this way were in no sense a description of behaviours any of my sample wished to engage in. Every girl said that only 'goody-goodies', 'wets', 'swots' and 'babies' wanted to be popular with teachers and no sister of theirs would be so feeble. However, they did produce descriptions of a 'teacher's pet' for me, which is revealing about *their* views of what *teachers* like. But, in justice to Alexandra, Zoe, Wendy and the rest, I must record that they did not *want* to be swots and weeds.

There is, to my knowledge, no evidence that boys' perceptions of what teachers like are different. Boys also think teachers like well behaved, quiet, clever, hardworking pupils, and there are plenty of quiet, conscientious boys who only answer when they are sure they have the

86

correct reply in the classrooms of Britain. Beynon and Atkinson (1984) show a thoroughly rebellious boy describing 'teachers' pets' in language almost identical to that used by the St.Luke's girls, twelve years later and in a South Wales comprehensive.

The two kinds of observational data were recorded in different ways. Coding classroom talk with FIAC involves writing a number every 3 seconds (800 in a 40 minute lesson) with the sequence preserved. I sat at a desk with a stopwatch, and wrote the coding numbers on A-4 lined paper turned sideways to give me columns; each minute of interaction took one column. (I prepared pages with horizontal lines at 15, 30, and 45 seconds to keep the coding neatly arranged and to enable me to check that I was recording at 3 second intervals). My other observational records were kept in spiral bound shorthand pads. The 'notes' in the shorthand books included: a seating plan for each lesson and the mixture of notes and my pupil talk schedule. Things that happened in the staffroom, at hockey or on the bus home got noted down in the same books. I did not keep a separate field diary, nor did I rewrite my notes afterwards in any proper way. Looking back I realise how badly I did the recording: *but* I do have an excellent memory. I take better, fuller and more kinds of notes today because I know better, from reading books on ethnographic methods, and other people's 'methods' appendices: I would not let any graduate student I supervise escape with so little in writing, or such undigested records.

Data analysis

Other students at Edinburgh, notably Brian Torode, constructed elaborate indexes of their material. I did not do any indexing of fieldnotes, because I usually remembered which lessons included examples of whatever behaviour or person I was interested in, and was able to turn to it. If I wanted any incident I knew where to find it, by running the fieldwork through my head and picturing the relevant pages in my notebooks. I still do this - running the 'film' of a lesson in my head, and then running over the 'film' of my notes till I can 'see' where the incident is.

Analysing the FIAC data took a long time. I followed the instruction manual, now superceded by Flanders (1970), transferring each code number onto a 10 x 10 matrix and then totalling the codings. I worked out all the ratio - 1/D, TTR etc. by hand. As this was done according to an explicit, published manual I will only say here that it was a chore - if I ever do that again I'll use a computer!

All the paper and pencil tests and questionnaires were coded or scored, and the numbers were punched (by me) and handled with SPSS, mainly to do cross-tabs. Liam Hudson was very hostile to factor analysis, and we were none of us urged to use multivariate analysis. Charles Jones taught me how to prepare punch cards, and get simple SPSS runs done by the Edinburgh Regional Computer Centre, and sorted out my botched jobs. In return I spent time collating, stapling and distributing the questionnaire on which his Ph.D was based. Brian Torode had invented a cluster analysis program, for his seating plans, and he used it on mine, too, though I did not report any detail of it in the thesis. The results did not seem to make sense, and neither Brian nor I could see why a programme that produced beautiful sociometric clusters in his school, did not on the St.Luke's data. The idea was to put the seating plans drawn in every lesson into the cluster analysis, and see which pupils habitually sat together, weighting the tie between a pair who sat side by side more heavily than the links between those sitting one behind the other, or separated by gangways. In his school this produced magnificent sociograms, at St.Luke's it seemed to reflect only the setting arrangements: girls who said they were not friends, but were in the same set for maths, English or French, came out as highly associated. I went to a series of seminars on cluster analysis and multi-dimensional scaling run by Peter Buneman and Tony Coxon, heard several experts in maths and computing science show cluster analysis to be very problematic, and quietly abandoned the data from the Torode programme.

The 'fieldnotes' were not analysed. I read through them over and over again, and picked out bits to illustrate the argument I was developing.

When I wrote up I was still analysing data, and I tried to say things for which I had evidence of two different kind (e.g. a questionnaire and a classroom extract). I was unselfconscious and non-reflexive at the time and it is hard now to reconstruct what I did. I can describe how I arrived at the sociometric structure of the year group I presented in the thesis and elsewhere (Delamont, 1976c). I had two sources of data, apart from the seating charts. In each girl's interview I asked who she went around with in school, who her friends were. When the girls arranged the appointments for their interviews I suggested that they could come in groups, and so I was able to see a pattern of voluntary, holiday time, association which gave me an unobstrusive measure. Thus, when Tessa told me her closest friend was Zoe, and when she arrived for her interview with Zoe (and Zoe's sister) I felt I had tapped something solid. Some girls said they did not see school friends outside, and they all came alone, or with a friend who was not from St.Luke's. The confidence I had in this as an unobtrusive measure was strengthened when the clique who prided themselves on being 'mature' and 'grown-up', because they had boyfriends, wore make-up, drank coffee, smoked, dressed fashionably, and went out dancing, arrived with a group of boys having been thrown out of a coffee bar for noisy behaviour. The party sat in the flat playing strip poker (though none of the girls took off anything more than shoes, hair-ribbons, watches and jackets) while I interviewed members of my sample.

It was important that, as we wrote our theses, we all read bits of each other's work, and commented on the analyses. David Hamilton, for example, read my chapter on FIAC very thoroughly, while I read Margo Galloway's work, and so on. This gave us, I imagine, some similarity of style, and of literature cited, and meant that we tried out our arguments for plausibility in a sympathetic atmosphere.

Finally in this section, the issue of ethics in the St.Luke's research has to be mentioned.

Ethics

Too many researchers, especially the illuminative evaluators, discuss 'ethics' instead of focusing on methodological reflexivity or theorising. This argument is made elsewhere (Atkinson and Delamont, 1984) and I do not wish to elaborate it here. There were some problems which arose during the fieldwork, because every enthnographer in a school learns things about pupils which could cause them trouble with staff, and possesses 'guilty knowledge' about teachers pupils would relish. The St.Luke's girls were not engaged in criminal acts, but because it was a school used by University families (a Dean of Social Sciences had a child in the school), I knew the parents of two of my sample. The two girls concerned took the double relationship in their stride, but it could have caused problems. The main ethical issue on which I felt, and feel, strongly, is the importance of protective pseudonyms. Until this paper I have always used the coy phrase 'a Scottish city' instead of Edinburgh. In talks great stress was laid on the research being conducted in *all* the fee-paying girls' schools in Edinburgh, to confuse those who knew the city. When challenged by anyone who had guessed the real identity of St.Luke's, I have always refused to make any comment, and pointed out that it could have been X, Y, Z or W school instead. The official history of the school was mentioned in the thesis, but no reference is given in the bibliography. All the teachers and pupils have pseudonyms which have been used so often it is hard to remember their 'real' equivalents. I am a believer in pseudonyms rather than real names because the individuals should be protected whether they like it or not.

Any school prepared to have a researcher in deserves that protection, because researchers know what harm can be done to teachers and pupils better than schools can. The determination and care exercised in protecting the participants at St.Luke's was rewarded for me when a colleague announced that his/her research assistant was one of my sample. The young woman had been given *Interaction in the Classroom* to read, and returned having recognised her schooldays in the examples. Finding that one of the sample is now an active educational researcher seems a good enough reason to maintain all the pseudonyms twelves years on.

Maintaining pseudonyms is aided by spending considerable time inventing them with a logical relationship to the real names, attaching them early on, and always writing and talking abut the research from the earliest drafts and most informal chats with the pseudonyms. It soon becomes easier to remember that Tessa and Zoe are friends than that A and B are. Indeed it is harder today to recall the real names of my sample than their pseudonyms.

Retrospect and prospect

In retrospect, greater attention to the content of the curriculum, especially the reasons for the large number of girls doing science; and to the importance of the school as an all-female institution, should have been paid. The school had a feminist tradition, founded in the nineteenth century as part of the pioneering educational campaigns, and the large numbers doing Physics in 1970 symbolised the high academic standards. Gender was, therefore, important but not a matter thought about at the time. I was glad that the school was of that kind and not the 'finishing-school' type, but I only thought through the implications of the gender issue much later when writing 'The Girls Most Likely to' (Delamont, 1976c) which tried to look at St.Luke's as a school reproducing Scottish elite strata. The historical tradition is recounted in the thesis, and the concept of 'double conformity' (Delamont, 1978) was evolved (in discussion with Paul Atkinson) for the thesis. It would have been nice, I now realise, to enquire systematically about the impact of that pioneer tradition on the school in 1970.

The lack of a published monograph on the material is a cause for regret. In addition to a 500 page thesis, there is enough unused draft to produce a further 250 pages. Data lying unpublished sadden me. It is probably *hubris* to imagine that a full-length monograph would have had the impact of Lacey (1970) or Willis (1977), because sociologists of education are uninterested in research on elite groups. It would be nice if the data from

St.Luke's were to make a dent in the inverted snobbery of sociologists, which makes it OK to research the bad and the poor, but not to study elite groups. However the St.Luke's work is always rejected as 'irrelevant' because of the class, ability, and elite status of the school (e.g. Deem, 1978) (3) as if the way the upper class is educated were unimportant. For five or six years this study was also 'written off' because its focus was girls, and that at least has changed. I still believe there is a desperate need for ethnographies in prep, public and other elite schools, so we know how the top people are educated. We are also very short of published work on girls in all social classes.

There is one further paper on these girls awaiting publication (Delamont, 1984c) including data on their '0' grade, 'H' grade and 'A' level results and school careers until the upper sixth. These data allowed me to 'follow-up' the pupils, and even test my hunches about who would 'succeed' in the school. The characterisation of St.Luke's as a highly academic school can be seen in the exam results obtained in 1973 (when my sample left the sixth). In the fourth year 47 girls took 381 '0' grades and only 10 results were graded below 'C'. Girls in their fifth and sixth years added 28 further '0' grades in 16 subjects to their fourth year totals. 'Highers', taken in fifth and sixth years, produced 234 passes in 17 subjects among 80 pupils. Thirteen different 'A' level subjects were available, and 8 pupils took 3 subjects, 8 took 2, and 7 took 1. There were 40 passes, and three of my sample (Jill, Penny and Evelyn) got 3 'A' levels at Grade A. In 1970 there were three large cliques, two small ones and a few marginal girls. The three large cliques were the boarders, the 'debs and dollies', and the 'intellectuals'. One small group consisted of the keen horsewomen, and the other of the weakest pupils academically who spent their leisure time with their parents. At 14 the boarders and the 'intellectuals' were the most academically successful, and the keenest sportswomen came from the boarding house and a subset within the 'teenage' group. These patterns of abilities and interests at 14 were sustained until the girls left at the end of their school careers.

The group who described themselves as 'academic' were the most successful in obtaining exam passes, university places, school offices in the intellectual activities and provided the Head Girl (Jill). Three members (Jill, Penny and Evelyn) got 3 'A' levels at Grade A. Michelle went to Oxford, Henrietta to medical school, Evelyn won a bursary to St.Andrews, and Charmian a prize as an outstanding scientist. None of this group were involved in sport, but they were the presidents of the school societies (Historical, musical and literary).

The boarders had been the most enthusiastic sportsmen at 14, and in the sixth form they were the dominate presence in the school teams. Mary was captain of hockey, squash and badminton as well as playing tennis and lacrosse for the school. Alexandra was captain of tennis, and in the first team of hockey and lacrosse. The boarders also provided the mainstay of the choir, and most got enough 'H' grades and 'A' levels to enter higher education. The sporting members of the 'deb and dollies' clique had survived into the sixth, also getting entry qualifications for university. Tessa became captain of lacrosse and vice-captain of hockey, and Monica not only captained the school fencing team but represented Scotland. The prefects, house captains and winners of merit badges came from all three groups.

This pattern came as a relief, because the thesis argued that the involvement in youth culture shown by the 'debs and dollies' was *not* a signal that they were to be school dropouts or academic failures. However data on their occupations and marriage patterns in 1990 will be needed to test the hypotheses about elite reproduction made in Delamont (1975c)

Conclusion

The study, as conducted, has many flaws of omission and commission. However the basic topics, the choice of school, and the structure of the thesis still appear to me to be soundly chosen.

Notes and acknowledgements

During the fieldwork I was supported by a 3 years SSRC award. The thesis was written in the evenings while I worked for Dr.J.A.M.Howe supported by a grant from the Scottish Council for Research in Education. I am grateful to both these funding bodies. Paul Atkinson and Bob Burgess have given me substantial criticisms of this paper, and I am very grateful to them. Mrs.Myrtle Robins typed this manuscript into an acceptable form, and I am deeply indebted to her.

1.   Most obviously in the contributions to Chanan and Delamont (1975), the volume edited by Stubbs and Delamont (1976) *Exploration in Classroom Observation*; papers in Delamont (1984b); Atkinson, Reid and Sheldrake (1977); Dingwall, Heath, Reid and Stacey (1977), and Adelman (1981).

2. Readers unfamiliar with Scottish education may need to know that the Scottish Certificate of Education (SCE) exam system has '0' grades at 16, Higher 'H' grades at 17 and then a certificate of sixth form studies for 18 years olds. Fee-paying schools like St.Luke often put pupils heading for university in the English 'A' levels at 18, so they take major public exams 3 summers running. At St.Luke's the brightest girls did this, so Charmian got 10 '0' grades, 6 'H' grades and 3 'A' levels.

3. Deem (1978:40) dismisses the whole ethnography (without having read the thesis) by saying that 'in any case the girls studied are a quite atypical group in class terms', as if that made them unworthy of research attention.

7. The lost enchantment? Re-focusing the history of science education for girls

Introduction

This paper raises three issues for discussion about science education for girls and women. It deals with the loss of enchantment with science among women educational writers, the failure of the science education literature to address or explain that loss, and then suggests a way to recapture the early delight and harness it to change the science education experiences of the majority of girls and women.

The overarching theme of the piece is that too much of the scholarly and polemical writing on women and science education in the last thirty years has been pessimistic, negative *and* lacked an understanding of historical features.

The paper is in four sections. It summarises the contemporary debates on girls, women and science education, and then outlines two bodies of literature which tell a different story. The fourth part then outlines how these two sets of materials can be used to refocus current deabtes. The connecting theme of the paper is the enchantment with science expressed by women involved in it. As a biochemist interviewed by Gornick (1984:136) put it

> Biology was like having a whole lot of beautifully wrapped
> and beribboned boxes suddenly sprawling all over the bed,
> and you know, you just *know*, whichever box you open
> there's going to be a lovely surprise in it. No bad surprises.
> Only beautiful ones.

This paper is an attempt at providing more women with 'beautiful boxes'.

The title of the paper comes from the autobiography of the poet Kathleen Raine (1975:11) who went up to Girton in 1926 to read Botany. In her autobiography she recalls the lure of doing science in a women's college in the 1920s, spending:

> long enchanted hours in the little botany laboratory, learning to cut and stain specimens for the microscope.

This sense of enchantment is expressed by many of the contemporary women scientists interviewed by Vivian Gornick (1984:46-47). Sharlene George, another of Gornick's respondents, tells how she had 'a eureka moment' in the shower one Friday night. She goes on.

> Five years work and it had come out so beautifully! It was one of those times you think, Jesus, I've put a tiny piece of creation in place. I was *flying*.

These two women, separated by sixty years and the Atlantic Ocean, both recount being enthralled by science. That enchantment and involvement has not been captured in the science education literature. This paper focuses on that lost enchantment. Once the existence of the continuous trickle of women who have loved science is established, the paper then argues that research on the enchanted will be more likely to help us design attractive science education for the 1990s, and offers a programme for addressing popular stereotyping.

The current debate on girls and science

Both scholarly and popular writing about girls' education in the last thirty years has assumed that the majority of females are not interested in, or good at, mathematics and science, especially physical sciences.[1] Manthorpe (1982) and Watts and Gilbert (1989) have both discussed the material on women and science and there have been several books published about the topic (e.g. Kelly, 1981; Kelly, 1987; Harding, 1986)

Reading this literature on 'girls and science' the dominant refrain is that young women, especially in adolescence, are repelled by, or bored by, mathematics, science and technology as currently presented in schools. (See for example, Watts and Gilbert, 1989 pp89-89 for a summary of this).

The 1980's saw several action research programmes in Britain designed to encourage adolescent girls to persevere with physics and chemistry after

95

fourteen (when most UK schools allowed pupils to become relatively specialised). Thus there was the Girls into Science and Technology (GIST) project in Greater Manchester, the Girls and Technical Education project (GATE) in London, the Women's Training Roadshows, Women into Science and Engineering year, and various leaflets produced by the Equal Opportunities Commission. (See Delamont, 1990 for details). All these projects were designed to open the eyes of young women to the attractions of science and technology and to their vocational relevance.

Various 'explanations' are offered for the perceived lack of interest and involvement by girls. These include biological explanations, cultural explanations, and those which place the blame on school processes. Thus Moir and Jessel (1989) and Gray (1981) have argued that women's brains are less suited to mathematical and scientific thought, and many school teachers and parents believe that boys are 'naturally' more scientific. (Spear, 1987). Cultural explanations have been advanced both by those who want more females to do science (e.g. Kelly, 1985) and by those who are content to leave science and technology as masculine preserves (eg Overfield, 1981; Elliott and Powell, 1987). Kelly (1985) outlines four ways in which science in Britain is masculine, and the aggressive culture of experimental research has been discussed by Keller (1983) and Traweek (1984). Authors in this tradition argue that British society socializes young women into a set of behaviours which unfit them to be successful scientists, and that British science (like American) has been made by men in their image. The cultural explanations do not contradict the argument that school processes put girls off science, but complement them.

The authors who see school processes as crucial include Lynda Measor (1984). She describes a class of twelve year old girls 'resisting' their comprehensive's attempts to teach them any science: it makes them feel sick, it marks them with dyes, it involves dangerous equipment, and so on. The pupils she observed in a mixed comprehensive were extremely ingenious and determined in their avoidance of science, but responded well to cookery and needlework. Some authors have suggested that in mixed classes boys dominate girls, muscling in on the equipment and grabbing the attention of the teacher (Crossman, 1987).

Those who see women as 'naturally' less suited for science and technology do not, of course, support schemes to encourage females into those areas. The scholars who locate the problem in the culture or the schools want either more energetic and well-designed schemes, or wish to change the culture of science itself. All three groups tend to write as if an opposition to or rejection of science and technology was almost universal among females, and of long standing. This paper argues that the discussion of females and science education needs refocusing, to emphasise the attraction of some women to science, explore it, and trace its (long) existence. In the attraction science holds for some women lies an alternative route for research into making it appealing to more of those who currently disdain it.

Those authors who have suggested that women are not naturally suitable for science, such as Ronald Butt (1990) in *The Times*, think they are expressing a universal truth, and write as if all females throughout human existence have rejected science and technology. This is clearly wrong. The journalists who wrote the conservative articles a century ago believed that a completely opposite position was the universal one. When British and American education were dominated by classics, conservatives argued that women were *more* suited to science than to classical subjects. Thus in March 1899 *The Spectator* informed its readers that women

> have a distinct proclivity towards science and mathematics, finding them less exhausting than either history or classics ... (women) will produce a Laplace or a Lord Kelvin before they produce a Paul of Tarsus or a Shakespeare.
> (Quoted in Sharp, 1926: 137)

The recent books by Schiebinger (1989), Rossiter (1982) and Phillips (1990) all show that in that historical period science was not as important for gentlemen as classics and therefore not so firmly classified as 'masculine' *and* therefore not constantly described as unappealing to women. The current orthodoxy came when classics lost its centrality in elite men's education.

None of the scholars addressing the scientific ladies of the nineteenth century has explained satisfactorily *why* the perception of science shifted during the twentieth century. English Literature which was equally derided as a subject for elite men in the nineteenth century, has risen in esteem throughout the twentieth, yet it has not been reclassified as an area for males only. Why have we developed this idea that science and technology are unappealing to women; this notion that women are bad at science; this concept that school sciences are *boring* for adolescent females? As long as our focus is on women who apparently dislike science, our hopes of producing more female scientists will rely on either changing women's minds and/or making school science more girl-friendly or human-centred.

The authors like Phillips (1990) and Schiebinger (1989) not only fail to explain *why* or *how* the nineteenth century female enthusiasm for science faltered, they also neglect one of our major sources of data on keen women scientists: histories of schools and colleges. It is to this neglected source of inspiration that the paper now turns.

The evidence on enchantment

There are two places where women's enchantment with science can be found: the reminiscences of schoolgirls and students collected in institutional histories; and the autobiographies, oral histories and biographies of women scientists, collected and prepared by contemporary feminists. These two bodies of research describe women's positive feelings towards their science. The evidence from the histories of schools and colleges is considered first.

Institutional histories

When the campaigns to establish academic secondary schools and higher education institutions for women began in the mid-nineteenth century in the UK, the USA and in Australia and New Zealand, science was not the highest priority of the feminist pioneers. Mathematics was a priority, but sciences were much less important than classics, and technology almost unheard of.

The pioneering girls' schools in the UK, the USA, Australia and New Zealand were concerned to offer girls the high status 'masculine' knowledge available to elite boys' schools. (See Delamont, 1989 for details of this campaign). The same curricula issues were also crucial in developing women's colleges, espoused by a group I have called elsewhere 'the uncompromising' feminists. As David Riesman (1976:*xxiv*) has pointed out, the uncompromising feminists needed to create 'a platform of seriousness' in their schools and colleges, and:

> women could no more afford spontaneity in curriculum than
> in contraception, for they had not yet become equal...

This seriousness meant curricula dominated by classics and a wide range of responses to the developing science education debates of the era.

Layton (1984) argues that because the number of academic girls' schools grew rapidly from the 1870s onwards, and because:

> nothing comparable to the dominance of classics in boys'
> schools constrained innovation (34).

women's educational institutions 'yielded a rich diversity of curricula'. His evidence shows that some girls' schools gave science 'an established and prominent place', some gave it only a subsidiary place in the curriculum, while many taught no science at all as late as 1928. Even in the schools which valued science there was no consensus about which branches of it should be taught. As Layton (1984:34-35) puts it:

> The competing educational claims of nature study, botany, physiology, chemistry, physics and domestic science were familiar topics at conferences of women Science Teachers and headmistresses.

Manthorpe (1985) has done detailed research on this topic in the UK, and it is a striking gap in the feminist scholarship in the USA and in Australia and New Zealand that there are not yet equivalent histories of how the pioneering schools came to teach science. Delamont (1989) uses material from the histories of schools in all four countries, to trace the difficulties facing them, such as the costs of laboratories, the shortage of teachers, and public prejudice.

The previous work on girls schools (Delamont, 1989) used material from eighteen British schools histories, two Australian, three American and one New Zealand to illustrate the discussion on science training. Here the focus is the positive side of scientific education: the evidence on the women who felt the same enchantment as Kathleen Raine. It is clear that the more seriously a school took academic matters overall, the more likely it was to put sciences other than biology into the curriculum. Those schools which were predominantly charitable, or religious, or simply socially exclusive, started science later in their histories, and spent less money on it, than the highly academic ones such as those started by the GPDST.

Many school histories say very little about science teaching, and do not include many memories of it by 'old girls'. Nor do the books include many pictures of laboratories. In an examination of twenty volumes of girls' school histories (Delamont, 1992), a content analysis of their illustrations revealed that sports teams were much more commonly shown than academic matters. Table 7:1 shows what appears in the illustrations in twenty school histories.

Table 7:1   Frequency of subjects in illustrations

Topic	Number of Illustrations
Exterior views of school buildings	88
Headmistresses	84
Sporting activities	61
Visiting dignitaries including Royalty	36
Staff groups	36
Groups of staff and pupils	32
Drama, Art and Music	31
Pupil groups	29
School governors	26
Guides	26
Interior views of schools	18
Science teaching	8

Table 7:1 shows that the most common subjects for illustrations are the exteriors of buildings and the headmistresses of the schools, followed by a variety of sporting teams and activities. Hockey alone provides 21 pictures in these 20 books, while science teaching is only shown eight times. Hockey is the most commonly shown sport, followed by drill and gym (eleven pictures). Within the aesthetic area, drama (shown 22 times) is more commonly shown than art or music.

The casual reader of a few volumes of school histories would not be impressed with the importance of science in the nineteenth century girls' school. However, a careful study of the reminiscences of pupils at the most academically ambitious girls' schools reveals that some young women loved science in the nineteenth century when it was well taught to them. The autobiographical accounts of pupils' lives in them between the 1870s and 1918 contain many accounts of the *pleasures* of learning science. Two old girls of the Oxford Girls' High School in the 1902-1932 period catch the flavour of the best girls' science education at the time.

> My enthusiasm for Science, faintly awakened at the school I had been at for one year before coming to Oxford, was stimulated and increased by Miss Macdonald. She was a delightful person, humorous and friendly. She always made us start our experiments with an open mind, instilled in us love of discovery and eschewed any kind of text book,

which certainly nurtured a true scientific spirit but made the rate of progress somewhat slow. There was an acute lack of apparatus, particularly physical apparatus, and when I took my scholarship examination at Cambridge, I had never used most of the pieces of apparatus with which I was faced, though I knew their pictures and the theory of their use. This shortage of apparatus cut both ways, for we became ingenious in constructing home-made things and got a great thrill when they worked, and we certainly understood the fundamental principles underlying their construction far better than many pupils of today who have only to plug in a terminal or touch a switch to get what they want.

Marguerite Cam quoted in Stack (1963:79).

Cam's contemporary, Muriel Palmer, expressed similar enthusiasm:

Our one teacher of natural science was Evelyn Macdonald, half Irish, full of energy and enthusiasm. She was one of the Girtonians, and therefore had the Cambridge training in three fundamental science subjects, so that O H S was more fortunate than most schools that had only one science specialist. The botany lessons were informal and seemed impromptu - we had no dull textbook to kill our interest, nor were we plagued by dictation of notes. During our progress through the Upper School we were taught the fundamental facts of elementary physics and chemistry, and my own later experience of teaching showed that the apparently informal methods were in fact the result of long practice by a teacher of genius.

On reaching Form V, I was flattered to receive an invitation to do some extra science with "Smac", as we always called Miss Macdonald. Four close-packed years followed, full of intense interest and wide teaching, such as was then available in very few girls' schools. The one mistress had to cope with the whole of the teaching of science in the schools, and manage the laboratory and keep apparatus in order with no help, giving instruction regularly in the three usual subjects, physics, chemistry and botany, and at times in geology (which with chemistry had been E M's subjects for Part 11 of the Tripos). Therefore, apart from extra afternoon work in the laboratory the coaching for a scholarship candidate was crammed into short period probably filched from E M's extremely limited free time. This meant that one was given books to read, plenty of them, with advice on the portions to be covered in any given week, and sharp questioning on the knowledge acquired, but we were given no pre-digested work with ready-made notes and summaries. I owe far more to her memory than can ever be expressed.

Muriel Palmer (nee King) quoted in
Stack, 1963:72-73).

Similar engrossing interest in science is implied in the history of the Park School, Glasgow, founded in 1880, which had science teaching from early on.

In 1884, upon the suggestion of Professor Young, chemistry was introduced into the curriculum, and a laboratory was fitted up - surely one of the first laboratories to be introduced into a girls' school (Park School, 1930:11). This laboratory was upstairs in the school and when the enthusiastic chemists were absorbed in their investigations they were apt to leave taps running with disastrous results to the classrooms below (p.42).

This does not sound like reluctant female pupils, but committed and absorbed ones. So, too, does the account provided from the Newport High School for Girls founded in 1896 which had problems in getting a laboratory. The official history records that as the first headmistress put it:

From the first we were much curtailed in our Science work by the lack of a Laboratory which fifty years ago, was not considered essential for a Girls' School. As our building was practically complete before I came to Newport I had no chance then of pleading for one. So for the first few years we had to borrow a Laboratory in the Boys' School, only available after 5p.m.: a very difficult time.

(Jubilee, 1946:13-14).

Five years later the school had grown so much an extension was necessary and it had a lab in it. An old girl, Maude Lyre (1899-1904) remembered

the excitement of .... going to our own Lab instead of the
"conducted" tour to the Boys (27).

Again, the female pupils are recalling pleasure in their science. By
modern standards, girls who did *not* want to go over to the boys' school for
a lesson would be seen as almost unnaturally keen on science.

Most institutional histories say little about the content of syllabuses or
the methods of teaching. Those authors who do comment on the content
and form of the science teaching tend to stress the practical heuristic,
experimental nature of the pupils' work. Thus Grylls (1948:91) argues that
the man who visited Queen's College in Harley Street to teach chemistry
'aroused interest in the subject' by

> The freedom - and the courage - with which he allowed
> practical experiments to be made ....

Gadesden, the head of Blackheath Girls' High School, writing at the end
of the nineteenth century was optimistic about the state of science teaching,
and claimed that:

> Science rooms which allow of free movement, and are
> provided with firm benches, and gas and water supplies, are
> being universally fitted up ... The heuristic method is
> adopted in most schools where a course in elementary
> physics and chemistry follows the nature study of the lower
> forms.
>
> (Gadesden, 1901:10)

Armstrong, generally credited with the pioneering of heuristic school
science teaching, sent his daughters to Blackheath High School. Malim and
Escreet (1927:46) describe the teaching of sciences there between 1886-
1920.

> The method employed in the laboratory was based on the so-
> called Heuristic Method ... the learning of real "scientific
> method" is a training in self-reliance and honesty of thought.
> (p53).

Among the Old Girls, H.M. Foster (1884-1898) talks of 'the excitement'
of starting chemistry. Rachel Hamlyn (1896-1908) then describes

it was with a feeling of intense interest that as a member of
the Lower IV, I was, for the first time, allowed to take part
in the practical work ... (p55)

The UK schools which started science enthusiastically were those
which produced the majority of women teaching science in British
Universities in 1971-72. Burrage (1983) gathered data on 154 women
scientists teaching in English and Welsh universities. One third had been to
fee paying schools, and most of the rest to Grammar Schools,
overwhelmingly single sex. Only 23 of the 154 had been to mixed schools.
It is no surprise that Rosalind Franklin came from St.Paul's Girls School -
not an elite finishing school, nor a mixed school, but an *academic* single-
sex institution.

The histories of female college education also include examples of
women enjoying science, and making it their own. For example the early
students at Berkeley, California had hygiene classes from Dr. Mary
Bennett, the first woman lecturer at the University. Then in 1894 women
began to form subject-based clubs and societies. As well as the ZYZ club
for women interested in maths, there were the Chemistry Friends. They
pioneered 'girl-friendly laboratories':

> to make themselves feel more comfortable in the chemistry
> building, an all-male preserve, women practised traditional
> female activities: they held evening parties there, making
> fudge and coffee over the bunsen burners.
>
> (Gordon, 1979).

The institutional histories of girls' schools and women's colleges
frequently contain accounts of enthusiastic scientific practices. Yet there is
no secondary source which brings out this enchantment and excitement. If
there were an accessable book for GSCE or A level history students on how
nineteenth century women fought for the right to study science and enjoyed
doing it; if all the women's studies courses had access to a book on the
same theme; if teachers in training were shown a good video on those early
schools, then there would be three groups of people who knew of that lost
enchantment.

More seriously, there is a gap in the research on the history of women's
education. None of the scholars who write on the topic has discussed what
happened to that committment to science after 1920. There is evidence in
the school histories that women took to science with alacrity - why was that
initial committment 'lost'?

104

There are several possible explanations. Perhaps the enthusiastic scientists were always a minority, and as mass secondary education for females came in, they became more and more submerged and deviant. Perhaps the content of school science changed and became less exciting for girls. Perhaps the teachers in the early days were more gifted than their successors, as other careers opened up for women scientists and teaching ceased to be their only possible vocation. Until serious research is done on science teaching in girls' schools after 1920, and through into the 1950s and 1960s, these will have to remain unanswerable questions.

At present the only data available are drawn from the biographies, autobiographies and oral histories of women who became professional scientists, to which the paper now turns.

The personal stories

Contemporary feminism has produced a body of research on women and science which has yet to be incorporated into the science education literature in a pro-active way, perhaps because the authors have failed to report on their respondents' schooling and undergraduate careers

Yet in the autobiographies of women scientists, in the feminist biographies and in the oral histories and sociological literature, a passion and committment to enquiry and to science can be found, which has educational potential.

Since the rise of contemporary feminist scholarship there have been published papers and book-length autobiographies from women scientists. Niven (1988) and Briscoe (1987) are examples of autobiographical papers. Among the book length autobiographies is the work of Rita Levi-Montalcini (1988). In the oral history and feminist scholarship category Abir-Am and Outram (1987) contains six biographical essays on women scientists; Kass-Simon and Farnes (1990) contains ten chapters on women in different American scientific fields. while Gornick (1984) is a study of women currently working as scientists in the USA aged between 25 and 80. The most famous biography of a woman scientist is Keller (1983) on Barbara McClintock, following Sayre (1975) on Rosalind Franklin. In an earlier period Sharp (1926) on Hertha Ayrton pioneered this approach. Rossiter (1982), Schiebinger (1989) and Phillips (1990) have all produced historical accounts of women's involvement in science, to which volumes such as Abir-Am and Outram's are successors.

The work done by these feminist scholars predominantly consists of recounting the scientific careers of women who have been neglected in the history of science. The Abir-Am and Outram collection thus includes papers on Cecilia Payne-Gaposchkin (Kidwell, 1987) and Dorothy Wrinch (Abir-Am, 1987), and the Kass-Simon and Farnes (1990) volume profiles Isabella Karle (Julian, 1990) and Icie Macy Hoobler (Miller, 1990). The emphasis of these profiles is usually on the graduate school and afterwards. Little or nothing is said about schooling. The same is true of the interviews with living scientists in Gornick (1984). Feminist scholars keen to discover, or re-discover, women who loved science and were successful at it, have apparently failed to research what the science teaching in their heroines' schools was like. We cannot retrieve the names of the science teachers, anything about the syllabuses, text books, labs or exams, or data on how those women first discovered their gift for, and love of, maths or science. A major opportunity to discover something about successful school science teaching for women has been lost.

The re-discovery of women in the history of science has neglected schooling. Historians of women's education have neglected science teaching and learning. Neither group has begun to explain when the enchantment became lost. Here we have a research project, and a puzzle in the history of education which need scholarly attention.

Implications for today's schools

Much of the writing about girls and science education tries to explain the relative lack of women in science in UK schools either by focusing on girls' brains and socialization, or on the nature of the science taught. Both start from essentially *negative* stances. The time has come to approach the issue from the other end. Let us have studies of females past and present who *like* science, especially those who find it enchanting, and discover what went right for them.

To move forward with this re-focusing, four things are needed. First, historial research on *why* (or perhaps if) the enthusiasm for science recorded by Schiebinger (1989) and Phillips (1990) faded after the 1920s. Second, a published account of the development of science teaching in girls' schools and women's colleges which captures the pupils' and students' pleasure, draws out the implications for current practice, and contrasts past and present teaching in girls' schools and higher education. Third, a recognition of the relevance of work such as Gornick (1984) on adult women in science to school science education is needed. Fourth, researchers on practising women scientists need to find out more about their experiences of school science, to discover why and how they perservered

106

with the subjects when contempories did not. If researchers on science education carried out these four tasks, the insights generated would allow us to produce hypotheses about how the minority's enchantment can be retained for the majority for whom it is presently lost.

Notes and acknowledgements

1. I am grateful to Ms. Elizabeth Renton for wordprocessing this paper.

2. The previous work on girls' school histories (Delamont, 1989) used material from eighteen British school histories, two Australian, three American and one New Zealand to illustrate the discussion on science teaching.

3. The twenty volumes used in Delamont (1992) are as follows:

School and Place	Date Published	Author(s)
Albyn School, Aberdeen	1967	Duthie and Duncan
Bedford High School	1932	Westaway
Bedford High School	1957	Westaway
Bedford High School	1982	Godber and Hutchins
Cardiff High School	1955	Carr
Cardiff High School	1986	Leech
Cheltenham Ladies College	1904	Beale
Cheltenham Ladies College	1953	Clarke
Cheltenham Ladies College	1979	Clarke
Edgehill College, Bideford	1934	Pyke
Edgehill College, Bideford	1957	Pyke
Edgehill College, Bideford	1984	Shaw
Francis Holland School, London	1931	Dunning (Graham Street)
Francis Holland School, London	1957	Bell (Baker Street)
Francis Holland School, London	1978	Hicklin (Baker Street)
Park School, Glasgow	1930	Anon
Park School, Glasgow	1980	Lightwood
Richmond Lodge, Belfast	1968	Robb
Rugby High School	1969	Randall
Shrewsbury High School	1962	Bates and Wells

The content analysis of these twenty volumes included an analysis of what was shown in the illustrations

4.   The author owns 143 volumes of histories of girls' schools in Great Britain and Eire, plus 2 Australian, 1 New Zealand, and 2 American histories.

8. Universities are for women: But you'd never notice it from the Winfield report!

Preface

*This chapter is based on two papers, amalgamated for the volume. One paper was written in 1988 and was published in the new journal, **Gender and Education**, in 1989. It predated the ESRC Training Board's research initiative on the social science Ph.D, which did included funding to focus on gender as a variable (See Burgess, 1994). The paper was a lecture to the Welsh Secondary Heads Association, who have a twice-yearly conference, when they met in Cardiff in 1982. It appeared in their journal - **The Welsh Secondary-Schools Review** in December 1982.*

Universities are, in theory, places of equal opportunity today. A century ago this was not the case, and anyone who argued for a University education for women students, or a career in University teaching for females, was regarded as eccentric. The medical profession was largely convinced that secondary and higher education for women would lead to brain fever, sterility, and even death. (See for example, Duffin, 1978 and Burstyn, 1980). Public opinion was on the side of the doctors, not the feminists who wanted University education. McWilliams-Tulberg (1975) has shown how, although Girton College was founded in 1869, women were not given degrees until 1948, and their position in the University was insecure throughout that 80 year long period. At any time the women were likely to be thrown out of the University. My current employer, the University of Wales College of Cardiff took women from its opening in 1883, but only in a restricted way, to read certain subjects. Indeed, the nineteenth century University student, if female, led an extremely restricted life. As Tylecote (1933) records of Manchester University in the 1880's women students could not use the library:

It would have been the height of impropriety to enter the library and demand a book in the hardened manner, now usual. No, we had to 'fill up a voucher' and a dear little maid of all work aged about 13 went to the library with it. (p.13)

Today, especially since the Sex Discrimination Act of 1970, the explicit barriers to women have gone, and so too have the public expressions of gross prejudice. However, there are barriers to equality for women in universities, at student level and in staffing; and the prejudices against women are still there, even if they are voiced less often. The following examples of sex discrimination in higher education are by no means an exhaustive list.

1. The closure of the colleges of education has removed the opportunity for higher education from many women, and the removal of this route to degrees has not been compensated for by any other opportunities being provided. (See Turner, 1974 and *THES* 19.8.77)

2. Women are still only 35-40% of undergraduates, and the UGC cuts have been aimed predominantly at Arts and Social Science faculties where women students are in the majority. The proportion of female undergraduates will therefore fall unless women opt for different subject areas.

3. The UGC has refused (*THES* 1.10.1982) to support 'conversion courses' to allow women without science 'A' levels to convert to science and technology courses at University.

   Points 2 and 3 taken together mean there is currently an assault on the position of women in the student body.

4. Universities are not equal employers. There are very few women in real jobs - that is permanent, tenured teaching positions - and those who are in careers are not promoted to the higher scales. Nationally, women are only 2% of the Professors, 6% of the Readers/Senior Lecturers, and 14% of the Lecturers. Yet they are 32% of the 'temporary' workers in untenured, soft-money jobs. Overall they are 12% of the University teachers, in the UK (*THES* 1.10.1982.)

110

5.   Cardiff is no exception. There are no women Professors, 1 Reader, 4 Senior Lectures, and 1 Head of Department. So there are six women in promoted posts, in a college that has 450-plus non-professorial staff. 40% of whom are Readers/Senior Lecturers. (University College, Cardiff) *Prospectus* 1980/82.

There are several possible reasons for this inbalance, which are spelt out by Acker (1981). Women lecturers seem to prefer teaching to publishing or committees or administration, and if that is how they direct their energies it would go a long way to explaining a lower promotion rate for women. Perhaps if women were promoted more assiduously, teaching would have a higher status than it currently does in Universities.

It is my firm conviction (and it is shared by the AUT) that Universities need to engage in a affirmative action programme at staff and student levels. Until every department of every University has at least 33% women on its staff, and 40% of women staff are in promoted posts, and 50% of students are female, we have not left the nineteenth century with its prejudices and myths far enough behind.

A detalied critique of one document - the Winfield Report - shows how far from sex equality British higher education still was in 1987. During 1982 two reports on British higher education (Swinnerton-Dyer, 1982; Rothschild, 1982) began a debate about aspects of the social science Ph.D. Concern was expressed about 'poor' completion rates, and about 'falling numbers' of research students. Swinnerton-Dyer (1982) also argued that the scope of the social science Ph.D should be narrowed to improve completion rates, because, he felt, typical projects were too ambitious to be completed in three to four years. Most full-time British social science Ph.D students are funded by the Economic and Social Research Council (ESRC), and by 1985 the ESRC was under pressure from several sources to improve completion rates. They decided to introduce institutional sanctions in universities or polytechnics with poor completion rates. Institutions were no longer allowed to hold ESRC studentships if their completion rate was below 10% in 1985, 25% in 1986, 35% in 1987 and 40% in 1988. The completion rate was taken over a rolling four-year period, and although students only got grants for three years' study they were allowed four years in which to submit their theses before being classified as 'failures' by ESRC. It appeared that only about 25% of ESRC funded students in the early 1980s had submitted a thesis within five years of embarking on a Ph.D.

In addition to the institutional sanctions policy, the ESRC set up an enquiry into the social science Ph.D in 1985 chaired by Dr.Graham

Winfield an industrialist member of its council. The report (Winfield, 1987) was published by ESRC, who issued a policy statement (ESRC, 1987) outlining the future of the ESRC-funded Ph.D based on their acceptance of some parts of the Winfield recommendations. The Winfield Report (1987) drew on data collected by a market research company (Rubashow, 1986), an investigation by a team of social scientists (Young *et al* 1987) and comments by distinguished figures in each discipline. The Winfield Report was controversial and its contents and implementation by the ESRC have been debated widely in Britain and abroad (ALSISS, 1987; Colombo & Morrison, 1987; Holmwood, 1987). One particular aspect of the Winfield report has not been discussed in print, however, and forms the subject of this research note. Gender is absent from the Winfield report and the database underlying it.

Any inadequacies in the Winfield Report and its database or policy recommendations have implications beyond ESRC-funded Ph.D research. State-funded studentships in arts and science are also being scrutinised, and policy changes similar to those recommended by Winfield may well follow in these fields. If, for example, postgraduate awards are concentrated in some institutions, students who cannot be geographically mobile will not be able to take up grants for doctoral study. The postgraduate education of women may be radically changed by Winfield.

This research note demonstrates the absence of gender from the Winfield Report and its accompanying data and debates, and then examines the implications of that deficit. If the whole Winfield debate is examined with a focus on gender it becomes clear that an all-male committee consulted male experts to produce a report focused on male graduate students.

The Winfield Committee had seven members, all men. Only two of the members had doctorates themselves, so having a Ph.D was not a qualification for membership. There seems to be no reason for an all-male committee, and its composition is not explained.

The Expert Witnesses are the eight authors of essays 'by leading academics' printed in the second volume of Winfield (1987). These were commissioned by the committee to represent the main social science disciplines, and all the experts are men. The spread of social science areas is broad, but only one of the authors explicitly recognised that there are women in his subject (Broadbent, 1987, p.120)

These two points - the all-male committee using male witnesses-may seem trivial. Yet they are symptomatic of the invisibility of gender as a dimension in the debate, and the lack of attention paid to research on women in the investigations carried out for the enquiry. Both the Winfield

Report (1987) and the Policy Studies Institute research (Young *et al* 1987) are based on inadequate reviews of the literature. The research studies which are marshalled are an incomplete subset of the published literature, which excludes all the material on women postgraduates.

Among the studies ignored by Young *et al* (1987) and Winfield (1987) is an ESRC-funded research project on postgraduate students in sociology and social administration (see Wakeford, 1985). The omission of this investigation from both the PSI study and Winfield is inexplicable. There are many publications from the Lancaster team who conducted this ESRC study (.e.g Scott and Porter, 1980, 1983, 1984; Porter, 1984; Scott, 1984, 1985; Wakeford, 1985) which are widely available. The only feature of the Lancaster research which could be thought to disqualify it from inclusion in the Winfield literature review is that it focused on part-time students while Winfield was concerned with graduates holding ESRC awards for full-time study. However, other research on part-timers was reviewed by Winfield (e.g. Eggleston and Delamont, 1983) so the committee apparently did not restrict their focus to data on full-time students. The data from Lancaster include material on women, and the failure of the PSI team and the Winfield Report to cite them is inexplicable and undermines their credibility. The Lancaster study is not the only missing work on British women postgraduates. Taylorson's (1984) research is also conspicuous by its absence, yet is easily traced. Again it appears that studies on women were not sought, examined and treated as part of the data base.

Both the PSI team and the Winfield committee have ignored published British research relevant to their enquiries which provided information on women. They also failed to use or cite most of the relevant material from the USA. It is possible that both teams felt that American doctoral students are so different from British ones that the research was irrelevant to a British enquiry. If so, that point should have been made explicitly. Without such a statement, it appears that the authors were ignorant of the American literature. Again the 'missing' American work includes studies of women, so both a comparative perspective and the issue of gender are absent from Winfield's deliberations. Feldman's (1974) work is not cited despite the high quality of the research. Also absent from the PSI and Winifield reports is the work of Acker (1978) on male and female graduate students in the USA, and the collection edited by Vartuli (1982) containing women doctoral candidates' perspectives on their experience.

This catalogue of missing literature (sufficient in itself to raise doubts about the quality of the research conducted by the PSI team and gathered for the Winfield Committee) is indicative of the absence of gender in two reports. If there are gender differences in the attitudes, performance, problems or successes of doctoral students in the UK then neither the PSI team nor the Winfield Report addresses them. Gender is not seen as an important enough topic to merit any discussion. The PSI report does not use gender as a variable in any of its comparisons of the six universities chosen for intensive study. The Winfield Report notes (p.54) that the proportion of women in the population of ESRC-funded students had been rising (to 31% of the total) up to 1982 and provides one table (Vol.2, p.5) on sex differences in completion rates. Otherwise gender is not used as a variable in the committee's deliberations.

There are some published data on gender divisions in postgraduate education, although scholars would welcome publication of much more detailed statistics. The university student statistics are published by the University Grants Commission (UGC), and the Council for National Academic Awards (CNAA) publish figures on postgraduates in polytechnics and institutes of higher education. Table 8:1 shows the number of full-time postgraduates in the UK broken down by domicile (home versus overseas students) and gender in 1980 (UGC,1981). The published figures do not break down the overseas students by sex, and the 'education' figure combines PGCE and research students. In 1980 there were 6419 British women doing postgraduate study of

Table 8:1   Full-time university postgraduates 1980

| | Home students | | Overseas | |
	Male	Female	Students	Total
Administrative business and Social Studies	3840	2574	3886	10,300
Education (including PGCE)	3548	3845	1301	8,694

Source: UGC (1981, table 19, pp.22,23)

Table 8:2   Full-time university postgraduates 1986

| | Home students | | Overseas | |
	Male	Female	Students	Total
Social Sciences	2122	2053	3660	7616
Academic educational studies	952	898	749	2278

Source: UGC (1987, table 6, p.26)

some kind in education plus the business and social sciences. During the 1980s the bases for cataloguing postgraduate numbers were changed, with PGCE students separated from those doing 'academic studies' in education and business studies separated from social sciences. Table 8:2 therefore shows the numbers of research students in education and social science in 1986 (UGC, 1987), again separating home and overseas students. The UGC still do not provide a gender breakdown of the overseas students, but the table shows that there were 2951 British and EEC women doing full-time postgraduate work.

Table 8:3   New entrants to postgraduate study 1976 and 1986

	1976	1986
Arts	19,593	22,099
Science	12,081	14,735
Male	13,779	13,914
Female	7,781	9,713
New candidates for research degrees	9,791	10,758

Source: UGC (1987, table 10, pp.36,37)

There are also figures available on how many people start postgraduate degrees and courses each year. Table 8:3 compares 1976 and 1986 comparing 'arts' and 'science'. (Social science is not shown disaggregated from 'arts'.) Breakdown of gender is given for the whole graduate entry, but not for the students starting on research degrees. Table 8:3 makes it clear that the percentage of females in the total of postgraduate 'starters' has risen from 36% in 1976 to 41% in 1986.

Part-time higher degree students are also reported in the UGC statistical record, and the 1986 data are shown in Table 8:4. This shows that out of 3802 part-time postgraduates in social science there were 646 women doing research degrees, and in education 1827 women doing research degrees out of 4456 postgraduates of all kinds and both sexes. Across all disciplines there were 11,148 women doing part-time postgraduate work, 28% of whom were in education and 13.4% in social science: the two biggest areas of concentration.

Table 8:4   Part-time postgraduates in 1986

	Social Science	Education
Total part-time postgraduates	3802	4456
Part-time females	1497	3138
Women doing research degrees	646	1827

Source: UGC (1987, table 13, pp.40,41)

Not all higher degree students were in universities, but the public statistics on CNAA candidates are not broken down by sex. The CNAA 1986/87 Annual Report shows that there were 347 M.Phil and Ph.D candidates registered (p.50), and that in the previous year 21 Ph.D's and 19 M.Phil degrees were awarded in social sciences and education. A published gender breakdown of these figures would be desirable.

Implications

There are several implications of this complete neglect of gender in the two reports. The first is that an opportunity to improve the database on research students was missed. Dr.Winfield himself (ESRC, 1987, p.10) states that his committee was severely hampered by the lack of useful and consistent data about Ph.D students not only in the social sciences but in all subjects.

The lack of information could have been partially remedied by systematic data collection on gender differences among postgraduates and the reporting of these differences. As Holmwood (1987, p.3) points out, the larger percentage of women (and of mature) candidates for higher degrees in social sciences as opposed to science and enginneering may be related to the lower completion rates in social science. Family commitments are known to be a major cause of delayed completions, and it is at least plausible that women in general, and mature women in particular, will have such commitments. Ignoring gender means that an opportunity to explore the relations between the nature of the students, the disciplines and completion rates was missed.

A second consequence of the failure to focus on gender in the Winfield Report is that the implicit model of the Ph.D student is reinforced. Throughout the whole of the Winfield Report there is an unexamined, taken-for-granted assumption that the actual and potential doctoral student is a 21 year old, white male able to be geographically mobile. Because gender (and age) are missing as variables there is little recognition that doctoral students in social sciences may not fit that demographic pattern, even if it is normal in the laboratory sciences. There is no evidence that the best social science doctorates have been, are being or will be done by full-time men of 21. A policy of concentrating studentships in a few institutions discriminates against the potential student who is not mobile so this unexamined assumption has policy implications. If the candidates most likely to complete were mature women, then the post-Winfield policy would *lower* completion rates! The ESRC's Research Training Board needs to re-examine the interrelations of age, gender and geographical mobility in social science doctoral research.

Thirdly , the complete omission of gender as a dimension of the discussion in the Winfield Report reveals that feminism and its scholarly research has failed to impinge on the committee or its six expert witnesses. This is symptomatic of approaching social science research with the laboratory science model. In laboratory science it is arguable that innovation arises in large centres where big research groups are working. There is no evidence that this is so in the social sciences. Research inspired by feminism has grown and developed without the benefit of powerful patrons, big grants or large teams, and so did other innovatory developments in British social science. There is no ESRC Research Unit on gender, or women or women's studies, for example, whereas such units exist to study race, legal issues, health economics, industrial relations and survey methods. Yet British research and theorising on feminist issues is flourishing. Failure to recognise gender as a significant issue reveals that the Winfield team are not *au fait* with current British research strengths.

In summary then, the failure of the Winfield Committee to recognise the importance of gender divisions among postgraduates in Britain gives cause for concern about the implicit, unexamined model of social science doctorates underlying the whole report. When policy changes, which affect the chances of women becoming doctoral candidates in future follow such a report, this short-coming of Winfield deserves public debate.

This example shows how radically the culture of higher education has to change before universities will really be 'for' women, and how much campaigning has yet to be done.

The role of the schools

There is a role for the schools in this. Schools can legitimately complain that their female pupils are not being given a fair chance of a University education, and protest about the removal of their chances of higher education with college closures. Additionally, schools can stop girls falling into a trap - giving up science and 'switching off' in maths. The call for a common core curriculum in secondary schools (e.g. Lawton, 1975, White, 1973) is usually made in the name of equality and justice. A compulsory science course for all girls is justified in the interests of sex equality.

My own view is that schools can do more than this, and I am very enthusiastic about the work of the GIST (Girls into Science and Technology) Project running in Manchester. This project is being run by teachers in Manchester schools (Smail *et al* 1982) and is designed to encourage girls into wood and metal work, science and maths in school, and into scientific and technological careers. Perhaps the most controversial experiment is single-sex maths classes in mixed schools, to encourage girls to take risks and participate in maths in ways they seem unwilling to do in mixed classes. No one knows if this will produce more numerate women - but it is worth looking at the results of the GIST project to see what schools and teachers can, and are doing. Certainly those Manchester schools put the Universities to shame.

Acknowledgements

The issues raised in the note have been discussed with a range of colleagues in the last three years who helped me clarify my thinking. I have not named them, however, because any blame for mistakes in this piece should rest unequivocably on my shoulders.

9. The great Bangor scandal of 1892

Preface

This chapter is a (much expanded) version of my review article on Evans (1990), published in **The Welsh Journal of Education**. *The new material is about three quarters of the total wordage.*

Introduction

In 1990 W.Gareth Evans published *Education and Female Emancipation: the Welsh Experience*. Many features of this book were admirable and exemplary, and these are outlined before I advance a critique of his lack of theoretical/analytic "bite", and illustrate this by reworking his coverage of "The Great Bangor Scandal of 1892". My analysis is *not* based on a reading of the actual primary sources in Bangor: a feminist historian could easily write a whole book using these archival sources.

The publication of this book is a matter of congratulation. The publishers are to be credited for producing exactly the kind of scholarly work on Wales for which they exist. Dr. Evans deserves the gratitude of future scholars and students for this pioneering work, which is bound to be a basic source on women's education in nineteenth century Wales for generations. Anyone wishing to do further research on Welsh women, or Welsh education between 1840-1914 will wish to begin with this book.

W.Gareth Evans has performed a major service for everyone interested in women's education, in Welsh education and in social movements. He has also filled several serious *lacunae* in the existing literature. There was no published account of the schooling of Welsh girls, or teacher training for Welsh women, or of higher education for females in Wales before this book. Now all the basic issues in Welsh women's education are clearly explained, and the similarities and contrasts with Scotland and England can be seen.

Evans has been diligent in his search for sources. The fifteen pages of bibliography are an invaluable resource in themselves. Dozens of future scholars will be grateful for the details of archives, theses and reports which can be mined for more detailed work. Evans has searched out M.Ed theses, inspectors' reports, and papers from the Charity Commissioners, and set the agenda for the next generation of researchers.

Evans deals with the position of Welsh women in the education system between 1840-1880, and then shows how, after that, women are admitted to the University of Wales, how teacher training developed, and how mass female secondary education came with the Intermediate Education Act in 1889. He has produced the first modern account of the work of the Association for Promoting the Education of Girls in Wales, which campaigned between 1887-1901, and published a series of fifteen pamphlets. The work of several feminist pioneers in Wales, and the Welsh connections of several well-known pioneers of women's education in England has also been explored by Evans. Among the new Welsh figures are Dr.Frances Hoggan, Dilys Davies and the sisters, Ethel and Kate Hurlbatt: heroines for films on S4C (the Welsh Channel 4) and many future student projects.

Evans has demonstrated how the Welsh campaigners, especially the Association, were skilled in their use of Welsh arenas - such as Cymmordorion Society and the National Eisteddfod - to advance and to promote the cause of female education. This was a public platform on which the men (for there were also many male campaigners for improving female schooling) and women could raise the whole issue of Welsh women's rights. The use of the Eisteddfod is particularly interesting, because it shows how a burgeoning nationalist feeling could be harnessed to a feminist cause.

In addition to discovering the Welsh women who advanced the cause of education in the Principality, Evans also documents the efforts of some women already known in English educational history of advance Welsh female education. The Association for Promoting the Education of Girls in Wales included pamphlets in their series by Sophie Bryant (headmistress of the North London Collegiate after Miss Frances Buss, and the first British women to hold a Ph.D), and Elizabeth Hughes (of Hughes Hall, Cambridge who pioneered ladies' teacher training). The involvements of women of Welsh ancestry and/or loyalty in the Welsh movement are made clear in this book, and this serves to 'round out' their compaigning careers. Perhaps surprisingly Frances Power Cobbe, although a Welsh resident, does not seem to have been active in promoting women's education in Wales.

Issues of class and religion are central in this book. Women's education in Wales was not only an issue of gender, it was also a matter of appropriate schooling for different social classes and schooling girls opened up the tensions between liberal Non-conformists and conservative Anglicans. The two Howell's schools for girls, opened in 1860, were surrounded by controversy because they were for upper middle class girls, and controlled by Anglicans, even though the original endowment had been for poor girls, most of whom were, in 1860, Non-conformists. The use made of the endowments of the Howell Foundation - Anglican-dominated schools in a non-conformist country - was a symbol for Welsh liberals of the religious discrimination they suffered. Falconer's attack on the two Howell's girls schools, in 1860, was centred on their 'unWelsh' elitism and Anglicanism. Evans gives ample coverage to the attack on the Anglican control of the Howell's schools, but does not mention any controversy following the Woodard corporation, who were explicitly Anglican, establishing St.Winifred's in Bangor in 1887. Nor does he discuss what negotiations, if any, surrounded the opening of Penrhos College by Wesleyan Methodists in 1880 in Colwyn Bay. Perhaps the religious issues had become less pressing by the 1880s, but if there was a lack of controversy, mentioning that peace explicitly would have been a good idea.

Evans has by no means exhausted the topic of women's education history in Wales. There is still a need for research on a range of topics such as women's adult education (Mechanics' Institutes and so forth), on governesses in Wales, on the lives of the female teachers in both state and private schools, the careers of training college staff, and the women dons in the University Colleges. Also his work ends in 1914, and there is plenty of scope for a sequel, bringing the story up to the recent past: including the admission of women to St.David's, Lampeter. The new history of that institution (Price, 1990) makes very little of the admission of women to the college, which did not happen till 1965. The first woman to be appointed to the permanent staff, Mrs. Renowden, joined in 1956, and Price also skims past that feminist landmark. There are many interesting studies yet to be done and published.

It is to be hoped that the University of Wales will follow up this book with more texts on Welsh women's education. Reprinting the 15 pamphlets produced by The Associate of Promoting the Education of Girls in Wales would be a good start. An account for GCSE pupils of the Hughes sisters, Frances Hoggan, Dilys Davies, and Hurlbatts and the other Welsh women uncovered by Evans would also be a great help to history teachers. Some of the unpublished theses used by Evans could usefully lead to chapters in a collection of essays of original research on Welsh women's education. The publishers could, and should, follow up this pioneering volume.

Although Evan's work is to be welcomed wholeheartedly there is one problem with this book. It has obviously been a long time in the writing, so that Bryant (1979), Fletcher (1980), Burstyn (1980), Dyhouse (1976, 1977, 1981) and Purvis (1981) are described as 'recent' (p.4) and are the latest works on women's education by those authors cited. It is a pity that the author could not have updated his citations of feminist historical scholarship in his final revisions before publication. A reader interested in Wales who wants to turn to current writing on women will not be able to trace it from this book.

Writing personally, if Evans had used my concept of double conformity (Delamont, 1978, 1989) it would have enriched his discussion of several topics, and especially about the 1892/93 scandal at Bangor. This scandal centred on three women, Miss Rhys, an undergraduate of only eighteen whose father was the Master of Jesus College Oxford; Violet Osborn an older, mature undergraduate living in lodgings in the town; and Frances Hughes. Miss Frances Hughes, sister of the Elizabeth Hughes who pioneered teacher training for ladies in Cambridge, was the 'Lady Principal' of the privately owned and run women's hall at the University College of North Wales, Bangor.

The rules of the hall at Bangor were strict, like those of similar residences in women's higher education in the 1890s. Students living in the hall were not allowed to mix with other women students: that is those who lived at home or in lodgings: unless the Lady Principal of the Hall approved of the friendship. Miss Frances Hughes was expected to protect the reputations of the young ladies entrusted in her by 'policing' their social contacts exactly as their mothers would do when they were at home.

In 1892 this routine scrutiny of social intercourse led to a major scandal. Miss Frances Hughes prohibited an ex-resident of the hall, Violet Osborn, from visiting a current student, Miss Rhys, stating that Osborn would corrupt Rhys. The action was reported to Miss Rhys's mother, in Oxford, in a letter from Frances Hughes in which Violet Osborn was described as an unsuitable friend because she was worldly, untruthful, had an impure mind, and was too familiar with Professor Keri Evans, a male instructor. Miss Osborn heard of the accusations; that she was 'untruthful', had a 'corrupt and impure mind' and was 'indecorous' in her behaviour with men: and complained to the Senate.

The subsequent controversy hit the Welsh and the London papers, and eventually there was a libel action, and discussion in both the House of

Lords and in the Commons. The higher education of women in Wales was damaged by the row. Issues of religion (Miss Hughes was an Anglican, most of Bangor's Senate were non-conformists) and of control over the Hall became compounded with the central question chaperoning female students and safeguarding their reputations.

Evans does not set the Bangor scandal into its context, which was the era of 'double conformity' in women's education. Briefly, the feminist pioneers had to ensure that while students and staff did all the academic work that men were doing, they also behaved like *ladies*: sticking with exaggerated care to all the social conventions about hats, gloves, chaperones, avoiding scandalous women, eschewing 'fast' activities like cycling and acting, and staying clear of campaigns like suffrage. In the light of the conventions of the day, the actions of both Miss Hughes and Miss Osborn, and indeed of all the actors in the Bangor scandal make perfect sense. Without the contextualising of the 'double conformity' material, the whole affair seems merely bizarre.

The dangers and safeguards

The feminist pioneers who opened higher education to young ladies in the second half of the nineteenth century did so against a body of medical opinion, religious orthodoxy and widespread belief among their potential clientele (that is middle and upper middle class parents) that such institutions were dangerous. A student, or a member of staff, at an academic college was held to be in physical danger (her health would suffer, she might become subfertile or die of brain fever); in moral danger (away from the control of her mother she might meet *anybody*) and liable to forfeit her marriage prospects. (No man wanted a wife who knew algebra.)

To deal with these dangers, colleges took action to safeguard pupils and staff. The dangers to physical health countered by medical inspection and physical education. However, the new activities of gym, hockey and cricket were in turn attacked by opponents of education. The safeguards installed by feminist pioneers against moral danger, and those intended to provide a safe background for the PE and the academic curriculum were essentially pollution control measures in the terms outlined by Mary Douglas (1966).

As Delamont has argued, the young lady was able to attend a college, play hockey, learn Greek, and even ride a bicycle, *if* her teachers set up very strong barriers between her and the possible pollutants, such as men, women of other classes and denominations, women of doubtful morals, suffragists, and the public gaze. Activities likely to damage the reputations of students and/or staff were forbidden, or confined to the privacy of the college, or governed by strict rules about their performance. Thus acting had to be done in private and male parts must not be played in male clothes; gym slips were only worn indoors or behind high hedges; girls were forbidden to talk to male students and were chaperoned everywhere. These strategies are explored at some length, with illustrations from both schools and colleges, in the UK, New Zealand, Australia and the USA. (Delamont, 1989).

A century later it is hard to reconstruct either the parental fears, or the rationale and efficacy of the strategies. It is equally difficult for the contemporary reader to imagine generations of girls who were forbidden to talk to fellow students, or walk with them except by parental permission, or were forced to act in skirts even when playing male roles, or had to be chaperoned to receive a piano lesson.

The struggle for girls to be allowed to play tennis or netball, to learn Greek and Algebra, to wear a gymslip, and to be a Girl Guide seems quaint today. So too, does loyalty and nostalgia for pioneer schools. As Hicklin (1978:9) points out:

> Sentiments uttered at the turn of the century, and even between the wars, on the subject of the Dear Old School and its denizens might come in for mockery today. The notion that any civilized young woman could have actually wanted to wear an old school tie or hatband.... or to have considered turning up at Harrods clutching a signed authorization from the Headmistress and demanding to purchase the old school blazer.... will seem scarcely credible....

To recapture the controversial nature of education for girls it is necessary to read autobiographies by pioneering teachers and students, who lived through the early days, such as Sara Burstall (1933) an early Girtonian who became headmistress of the Manchester High School for Girls; or study the virulent attacks on the girls' schools by critics such as Meyrick Booth or Arabella Kenealy. The writings of Kenealy and Booth, at a period when the academic schooling of girls was already fifty years old make the bravery of the pioneers starkly apparent. Schools introduced Greek and lacrosse in the teeth of accusations that educating women was the cause of their sterility, promiscuity and masculinity, and that British society and the British family were being ruined. When the pioneers' enemies held views such as these higher education for women proceeded with caution and precautions.

Careful scrutiny of many college and school histories, plus autobiographies and memoirs, and examination of archives, revels the plethora of rules and regulations in their original social context.

The pioneers had to be particularly careful about dress and deportment, sport, class and religion, men, curricula, and feminism. A few examples from pioneering schools, all of which are paralled in higher education, will illustrate the point.

We know from other sources that Cheltenham only accepted the daughters of gentlemen, and demanded references to prove claims to gentility but the three histories of Cheltenham do not mention this. Cheltenham also had territorial rules which kept the pupils away from areas of the town where they might encounter men or boys. In the pre-1914 era girls were forbidden to go to the polo ground, the race course or the Cheltenham boys' school playing fields. These rules are not mentioned in the three histories either. In contrast Godber and Hutchins (1982) are careful to *explain* the rules on chaperonage. The girls' school in Bedford had different hours from the boys' so the pupils would not meet in the street and on keeping the *social* contacts between girls to a minimum.

Similarly we know that religious mixing was considered so dangerous that the school for army officers daughters at Bath nearly failed to get established because admitting catholics was proposed. A discussion of the dangers of admitting pupils from different denominations almost certainly took place whenever a girls' school was opened in the nineteenth century, and many schools were started for *one* particular group (Unitarians, Anglicans, Methodists, or Presbyterians for example). Yet the three histories of Edgehill do not mention any discussions of whether non-Methodists were to be admitted leaving the reader in ignorance of the care taken at boarding schools particularly not to mix denominations. In fact Anglicans *were* accepted, but the books do not analyse the debates, if any, over religious 'mixing'.

An example of a chaperonage entry where the restrictions of an earlier periods are covered, but not set into any explanatory framework is:

> In the 1930s, apart from the prefects who had the coveted privilege of visiting a specially reserved room in Ambler's Cafe for supper on Saturdays, no girl was every allowed outside the school grounds unescorted... Fortunately this state of affairs was regarded as quite normal, for even in the holidays girls did not have the freedoms they have now....
>
> (Hovey, 1931).

Finally, an example of 'mixing' where the reading is told enough about the issue to understand the problems facing the pioneers:

> Religious denominationalism was a burning educational issue in the nineteenth century, and the thorniness of this topic is reflected in the early history of the School.
>
> In November 1875, at the third committee meeting, it was resolved that 'Religious Instruction limited to lessons from the Bible be given as part of the regular school course. Any pupil may be exempted from these lessons on the application of a parent or guardian. Further Religious Instruction according to the scheme of the Oxford and Cambridge Local Examinations shall be provided for every pupil whose parents or guardians desire she should receive it.
>
> From this, to modern eyes, innocuous, resolution there was one abstention, and on account of it, one member of the committee resigned
>
> (Jewel, 1976)

This history goes on to explain that twenty years later, the admission of young ladies of 'different religious communions' had been done of the school's achievements despite its controversial beginnings.

Conclusions

Given this failure in the majority of histories of girls' schools to explain prejudices against women's education, dangers to women's reputations, and safeguards against the dangers, it is perhaps not surprising that the reasons for the pioneers' 'double conformity' strategy are frequently misunderstood. Evans's account of the scandal at Bangor in 1892 and shows a lack of understanding of the double conformity strategy.

The double conformity strategy was designed to ensure girls' access to the higher status male subjects (classics and mathematics) while remaining ladylike. Staff and pupils not only studied the male syllabuses but also dressed and acted like perfect ladies. C.L. Maynard the founder of Westfield College argued that:

the conventionalities of the age .... were the best possible
shelter for the new aspirations, and firmly we kept to them

(1910: 189)

Sara Burstall made exactly the same point in her autobiography. What those pioneers knew has not been explained in a typical history of a girls' school - including Burstall's own account of Manchester and contemporary historians such as Evans are left puzzled by what they see as draconian or mindlessly petty rules and regulations in female education.

10. Ghettos and celibacy or, the lion, the witch and the wardrobe

Preface

This chapter is based on a paper prepared for the first University of Wales Gregynog Colloguium on Women's Studies in 1977 and a critique of feminist uses of Engel's **Origins of the Family, Private Property and the State** *published in* **The New Edinburgh Review** *in 1972.*

The latter was described by the late Maurice Blytheman as a fine piece of Scottish Marxism.

This paper attempts to disentangle the relationship between feminism and knowledge. The title is a summary of the dilemma facing the contemporary academic woman. She can be a literary and scholarly lion in her own right, or concentrate on being a bewitching seductress who maintains her academic position by consorting with famous men, or she can be a good housewife who stays in the wardrobe, close to home. This is a novel dilemma, which did not confront the nineteenth century pioneers. Indeed academic women today are different from their 19th Century foremothers in two ways.

1. The nineteenth century academic pioneers were *celibate* (Buss, Beale, Davies, Freeman Palmer, Beecher, Carey Thomas)

2. They did not challenge the male definitions of what *constituted* knowledge and scholarship, but campaigned for access to it, and then contributed to it. For example E.Constance Jones translated Frege, she did not denounce him as a male chauvinist

Today academic women are quite different.

1.   We are not celibate - many of us marry, and those who do not marry often reject celibacy as a way of life.

2.   We do, however, challenge the boundaries/foci/and standards of excellence men draw for subjects.

While at first sight these two features of life may seem quite unrelated, my argument is that they are *not*. Rather, the shift from the celibate acceptor of male definitions of knowledge boundaries to the sexually active rejector of such boundaries is, in an important way the cause and subject of the paper.

The celibacy of the nineteenth century feminists has been discussed elsewhere (Delamont (1989:b). For nineteenth century pioneers a rejection of marriage, and hence heterosexual activity, was a necessary step in establishing an alternative life style to that of Victorian *materfamilias*: the single career woman. The acceptance of male knowledge, especially classics, has also been discussed elsewhere (Delamont, 1989b). We know that the 'uncompromising' groups of feminist pioneers, who went for high-status (male) curricula and refused separate women's examinations were right - because separate women's curricula at that period would have meant second class curricula.

Thus the first generation of pioneer women were celibate scholars in "male" subjects. The second wave of feminists, however, who came to prominence after the First World War, took a different line. In this generation Dorothy L.Sayers, Vera Brittain, Naomi Mitchison, Dora Russell and Edith Summerskill and Winifred Holtby were the prominent thinkers - none of these were academics - and all rejected celibacy. They opted for heterosexual activity (and/or marriage) and started off a whole new range of feminist campaigns - birth control (irrelevant to celibate women), marriage bars, family allowances and the end of the sexual double standard.

If the first phase took from 1848 - 1918, the second occupied feminists from 1919 to 1969. Since the late sixties the third wave of feminism has been focused centrally on challenges to orthodox wisdom among intellectual women. This is because of the successes of the two previous waves. The first generation got us access to the best knowledge available, and equipped us with the tools to criticise it, remake it, and create it. The second generation success meant that we were no longer protected by celibacy from the experiences of other women. This produced a generation of women who confronted orthodox knowledge with personal experience, and found that authenticity and scholarship did not coalesce (Ann Oakley's (1979) work on childbirth is the most famous example of this).

Challenging knowledge raises two problems which can be best understood in the following series of propositions:

IF   throughout history almost all the academically respectable work has been done by male scholars.

BUT   women scholars today can see that some parts of it are seriously flawed because of sexist assumptions:

HOW can women (and men) make a 'sound' academic subject that is not flawed

WHEN just being non-sexist and/or very feminist will not, like magic, enable us to live happily ever after in thoroughly sound, flawless, objective sciences/knowledge.

Many feminist scholars have argued that grounding subjects in 'personal authenticity' is the answer. This seems to me a quite erroneous argument, as I discussed in the introduction to this volume *BECAUSE* such pleas for personal authenticity reinforce stereotypes that women are
    irrational
    ruled by their emotions
    unable to generalize
    liable to personalize everything etc.
In other words, if we use personal authenticity as a criterion, women will not be good scholars in male terms. Underdogs cannot change the rules. The modern scholar's dilemma is therefore, 'How do we do/evaluate good scholarship by any criteria other than male ones?'

If the academic woman decides to search for ideas that fit both the criterion of personal authenticity and that of academic authenticity she is faced with several kinds of problems.

One of these can be illustrated with the use of Engels's work by pioneers of "second wave feminism".. The early seventies saw the frequent use of Engels' *Origins of the Family, Private Property and the State*, as an historical account of the role of women in antiquity and the under-developed countries. Quotes from "Origins" were an obligatory part of the pamphlets and manifestos of the various Marxist women's groups. Where these quotes referred to Engel's analysis of the status of women in Victorian Britain, or his proposals for altering it, this was reasonable. Engels was perceptive both in this analysis and his remedies, and these deserve consideration.

However, there were also frequent references to his theoretical account of how women had reached their Victorian predicament, and this was and is ridiculous. This part of "*Origins*" has about as much claim to truth as The Epic of Gilgamesh, or the book of Genesis - and as much to tell us about the role of women.

Of course, the degree of confidence which is placed in the historical part of "Origins" varies from one writer to another. So too do the writers' accounts of what Engels actually said about the causes of women's oppression, which adds to the readers' confusion. Engels drew this historical and anthropological information primarily from the writings of an American contemporary, Lewis Morgan, and to this extent their work must stand or fall together.

Juliet Mitchell (1966) refers to Morgan's writings as 'fascinating, but inaccurate', and says that Engels based women's oppression on their 'physiological weakness', as well as a range of economic factors. Margaret Coulson writing in the IMG journal *International* hedges her bets by claiming that 'many contemporary anthropologists' no longer regard Morgan as 'reliable', but claims that 'At least, his analysis does not maintain that the biological characteristics of women naturally and inevitably give rise to their subordination.' Neither writer stops to explain why Morgan's theories are now in obscurity, nor discusses Engels's use of them in any detail.

This lack of reverence insensed the Maoist women in Britain, who have taken up the position that Engels and Morgan were entirely correct in every detail. They explain modern social scientists' distrust of Morgan and Engels by suggesting that the ideas are so uncomfortable for the bourgeoisie that they are 'assiduously hushed up by their lackeys the bourgeois professors and other such hacks.'

This ignores the very limited data base available to Morgan and Engels, and their misunderstandings of what they knew.

The amount of knowledge available in the human sciences was meagre in the extreme: information about the evolution of the human species, or the history and current forms of social organisation, was noticeably lacking. One might expect that this would have led those writers interested in the development and contemporary state of social systems to be tentative in their approaches to the subject. Instead, the works written in the second half of the nineteenth century are characterised by an arrogance, and a sense of omniscience, which today is only found among the contributors to the Black Papers. Obviously, the writers differed among themselves, often passionately. But writers such as Frazer, Crawley, Lang, Briffault, Clodd, MacLennan, and this includes Morgan, shared certain basic assumptions.

The chief assumption was that Victorian bourgeois, industrial society was the culmination of a developmental process: a process which was believed to be the same for the whole human race. The assumption implied that any society which was not *identical* with Victorian middle-class life was therefore un-developed - further back down the ladder of progress. The developmental process was usually held to have included three main stages - savagery, barbarism and civilisation - roughly corresponding to what we now know as the hunting and gathering cultures, the agricultural cultures with domestic animals, and urban, literate cultures.

The authors differed in their theories about what form of social organisation and religious observance accompanied the technological developments. Lang concentrated on proving that there had been a universal cult of the sun-god, Frazer that the ritual slaughter of the Corn King had been iniquitous. Morgan, and Engels, were more concerned with the development of the family, and of marriage: Briffault with proving the past existence of a universal matriarchy. All the writers had in common however, the idea of using 'survivals' as evidence for their theories, another piece of Victorian arrogance.

The doctrine of 'survivals' was directly related to the assumption that industrial society was the highest form of social organisation. This meant that only Victorian society had a reactional organisation - Frazer for example: thought that rational Science was replacing irrational religion, which had itself replaced the even more irrational magic. Because they were so confident that Victorian society was the rational way of organising human life, the scholars of the period felt free to judge other cultures as less developed, and to pick out elements from those cultures which stuck them as particularly irrational, and label them as 'survivals'.

This if another culture happened to organise its social relationships round matrilineal descent groups, that is round groups of people who shared property and claimed kinship on the basis of their common descent through women, a typical reaction from the scholar would be to claim the system as a survival from a period of matriarchy, or from the 'promiscuous horde' epoch, or whatever bizarre evolutionary scheme he happened to believe in. (There was usually a great confusion at this time between societies which had a system of matriliny-which merely means that descent is traced through women, so that you take your mother's name, and inherit property from her brother rather than her husband - and matriarchy, or mother-right, or gynaecocracy - which would be actual political rule by women. Lots of cultures have the former, while there is no evidence for any society ever having had the second, and there is no reason why one should imply the other).

As well as assuming that any form of social organisation that did not resemble the bourgeois family was a survival from the depths of antiquity, the writers of the period used myths, folk tales and customs, and accounts of rituals as equally sound evidence of the historical development of the human race. Thus if you believed that all societies had gone through a matriarchal stage, fairy stories about woodcutters' sons marrying princesses and inheriting kingdoms would be put forward as proof. The idea that it was reasonable to juxtapose survivals, myths and customs from all over the world, and all points in history, as one uses lots of scraps from different garments to make a patchwork quilt, was dignified by being classed 'the comparative method'. Apart from lacking any noticeable sense of method as we understand it, comparative system was based on wrenching isolated elements of human behaviour form their social context, without any regard from their function in that context.

Compared with the excesses of some of his contemporaries, particularly Crawley and Frazer, Morgan's theories were restrained, and based on something we might recognise as evidence. Unlike the others, Morgan had actually seen a primitive people. He spent many years studying, and living with, the Iroquois Indians - a set of tribes who inhabited forest land in what is now New York State and Delaware. He collected his other material by writing to administrators and missionaries round the world, with sets of specific questions about the social organisation of the peoples they worked with. It was left to Engels to add the classical myths, and the undigested gobbets of theory about the Celts and the Germans, and of course to give Morgan's work a new 'treatment of the economic aspects' to replace Morgan's own 'inadequate' one.

Briefly, Engels theory about human development consisted of two parallel processes, one economic, the other social. The economic development took three stages, each sub-divided into three sections, an upper, a middle and a lower. Briefly, the first stage, Savagery, begins with a vegetarian tree-dweller, and ends with the invention of the bow and arrow. The next stage, Barbarism, begins with the invention of pottery, includes the beginnings of agriculture, and ends with the discovery of iron. The final stage, Civilisation opens with the invention of writing, and continued through till Engels' own lifetime. This scheme, has not been discredited in its major features by modern research. The parallel scheme for social evolution is another matter.

Once he comes onto the discussion of sex and marriage, Engels' 'ideas become as bizarre as any of his contemporaries'. He hypothesises a developmental process which, beginning with a state of primitive promiscuity, leads through group marriage, into pairing marriage and finally to monogamy. Engels freely admits there is no evidence for the first stage: 'The primitive social stage of promiscuity, belongs to such a remote epoch that we can hardly expect to prove its existence directly by discovering its social fossils among backward savages.'

The next stage, after the complete sexual free for all, or 'spontaneous generation in the slime' era, is said to be group marriage. Group marriage involves first limiting the numbers of people who have promiscuous relations, then gradually setting up incest prohibitions, and finally forming links between separate groups, which exchange wives who are then held in common by the receiving group. Engels suggests that several cultures which were still available for study at his time of writing had group marriage at one of its points of evolution- that is, that there was proof of this stage of his theory.

Group marriage is followed by pairing marriage, at about the time when Savagery gives way to Barbarism. Pairing marriage involves the formation of short-term monogamous liaisons within the marriage group instead of promiscuous relations inside the group as a whole. These liaisons mean that the fathers of children become known, as well as the mothers. This form of marriage leads directly on to Monogamy, in which the liaisons become permanent, and man gains power over woman, both sexually and economically.

Monogamy develops with the change from Barbarism to Civilisation, and is primarily associated with the increasing efficiency of agriculture and industry. This efficiency leads to a surplus, and the surplus to slavery, profits, social classes, exploitation, the subjection of women, and most of the other things you can think of in that line. It is as if Pandora's Box had contained not devils and disease, but profit and surplus food.

Along with the change to Monogamy, Engels also suggests that the general system or organising kinship,which had been matrilineal, is changed, and becomes patrilineal. Once patrilineal kinship is established as the norm, men impose sexual faithfulness upon their wives. While they take several women, either by marrying several (polygamy) or by keeping concubines or female slaves.

The exact mechanisms by which these changes in social organisations come about is never made explicit. Changes in social structures are said to be the result of technological developments, and that is all we are told. Engels' ideas about the sequence of stages in social organisation are also unassailable, in that historical information about social life is probably always going to be a matter of conjecture. My case against 'Origins' must rest on the misconceptions within it about the nature of social behaviour in the cultures he uses as evidence: on his misinterpretation of the evidence he had. There are at least four fundamental misconceptions about social behaviour inherent in Engels' arguments, without considering the general points about his assumptions and methods made earlier in the article.

Perhaps the most important single misunderstanding involved in 'Origins' concerns groups and pairing marriage. Engels' theories that the matrilineal descent groups consisted of men and women among whom there are no restrictions about sexual relations, who had each other in common. He cites various tribes as examples of systems where this is so, and in all the cases he has muddled the way that society thinks about marriage, with the way its members actually behave. Because the Australian aborigines say that women from the fish clan become the wives of the wallabie clan does not mean that all men in the wallabie clan have equal access to them. Rather each women is monogamously married to one man within the wallabies, and by this liaison becomes a wallabie clan wife. To say she is a common wife to the whole clan makes as little sense as interpreting the phrase 'marrying into the royal family' to mean that whoever married Prince Charles also becomes the wife of Prince Edward and Prince Andrew, all the Gloucesters and Kents, and Tony Snowdon into the bargain. Many societies say that a man or woman marries into the clan, but this only means the same as the cliche about losing a daughter and gaining a son, it describes a way of thinking about kinship, not actual behaviour.

Next, Engels has misconstrued the relationship between the descent system in a society and the nature of property inheritance and political power in it. He assumes that women have at least equal property and political power in a matrilineal society, and it is only with monogamous patriliny that women becomes less privileged in these respects. This assumption is a misunderstanding of the nature of matriliny. In a patrilineal system a man passes his property to his sons, while in a matrilineal one it goes to his sister's sons. Women never actually have any rights to the property in either system, they merely form the path by which it is channelled between the generations of men.

Similarly, the political position of women is not necessarily related to their society's descent system. No-one has ever found a culture in which women wielded real political power de jure, though of course many individual women have been extremely powerful *de facto*. The political offices in matrilineal societies are held by men, and are succeeded to by their sisters' sons.

This leads directly to my final quarrel with Engels, namely his assumption that the position of women in society has something to do with the descent system and with the technology which exists in it. Women may be kept as concubines or slaves, rigidly bound in monogamy, killed when they are caught in adultery, beaten, denied any rights to property, or suffer any other form of exploitation in any type of society, irrespective of the kinship system, or the technological level of their culture. Obviously the details of the way in which women are oppressed vary according to the social system and the level of technological development, but the relationship between the overall status of women in a culture and its other aspects is so complicated that non-one has yet discovered it.

Engels' work does not stand up to critical examination. He was right in his assertion that the Victorian Bourgeois family was *not* the pinnacle of human achievement, and that it would give way to something else, and in this he differed from most of his contemporaries, who thought it would endure for ever. His historical speculations, and ideas about how other cultures function were, however, as much affected by the generally held assumptions about social structure and rationality discussed earlier. As such they are totally inadequate for use as evidence that the oppression of women is a relatively new phase of human development.

Unfortunately, the evidence from proper field-work in other cultures suggests that women are subordinated in most spheres of life in all of them. Anthropology is not a good leg for liberated women to stand on. It is true that anthropology has shown that the division of labour between the sexes, though universal, takes very different forms in different societies, which makes it difficult for anyone to claim that the particular form we have in modern Britain is in any way 'natural' or based on biological differences, for we do know it's an entirely cultural phenomenon. Beyond this, anthropology offers little comfort to those who wish to remodel the role women play in society.

Engels, though wrong, does suggest that women only became second-class citizens fairly late in human evolution. Modern anthropology, which is much sounder, suggests that women are always placed in subordinate, or separate but equal, positions in society. It would be easy, therefore, to cling to Engels, because he is more comfortable to read. This would in my opinion, be a mistake. I think we should take note of his suggestion that the bourgeois, nuclear family should be radically changed, and take up the argument about our future role on the following lines. For the very first time in the history of the race we now have a technology which can completely overcome the physiological differences between the sexes in the work sphere. This technology should be treated as revolutionary, and be used to create a new social, economic and political role for women to accompany it. It does not matter that Engels was wrong about the historic development of the status of women because we are not afraid to envisage a new role. Engels ideas are second-rate social science, and if women are to emerge from their status as second-class citizens, they cannot use second-rate ideas as a justification of the movement for Women's Liberation.

11. Old fogies and intellectual women: An episode in academic history

Preface

This paper was prepared in 1990 for a conference to celebrate the 350th Anniversary of the University of Helsinki. It was published in Finland in the proceedings of the conference (in English) and in the Finnish Journal of Women's Studies (in Finnish), and then in the UK in **Women's History Review** *in 1991.*

> Ye fusty old fogies, Professors by name,
> A deed you've been doing of sorrow and shame;
> Though placed in your chairs to spread knowledge abroad,
> Against half of mankind you would shut up the road;
> College honours and lore from the fair you withdraw
> By enforcing against them a strict Sallic Law;
> Is it fear; Is it envy; or what can it be?
> And why should a woman not get a degree?

Introduction

This poem was written by Lord Neaves as part of the campaign to get women admitted to the University of Edinburgh in the 1880's (Turner, 1933). The heroines of the story unfolded in this paper gained their university education in that same decade in the USA, and met American 'old fogies' equally opposed to their participation in scholarly activities. Lord Neaves's question could have been posed in Chicago, the location of this paper as appositely as it was in Edinburgh. 'College honours and lore' are not equally available to women even in 1992, and Lord Neaves's question 'Is it fear; Is it envy?' could still be asked.

The paper deals with an episode in intellectual history through its treatment by subsequent scholars. The perspective is structuralist. The introductory section outlines the historical episode: the involvement of women in the early years of the Sociology Department at Chicago University. The majority of histories written about that era have neglected the lives and work of the women involved: here they are reinstated.

The main body of the paper is a structuralist analysis of the intellectual worlds of the men and women in the Chicago sociology department. The purpose of this analysis is twofold: to demonstrate the power of structuralist theory for understanding women's history *and* to make historians of women more reflexive and self-conscious.

This paper is not based on original research, but is a secondary analysis. The original scholarship conducted and published by Mary Jo Deegan (1988) is reanalysed here. Deegan's research does not offer any theoretical framework, nor does she draw any general lessons for the history of women's attempts to enter and succeed in academic life. This paper therefore makes a contribution to feminist scholarship by a theorised re-interpretation of Deegan's work, and the general issues raised about scholarly women.

The central focus of this paper is the Department of Sociology at the University of Chicago between 1892 and 1942. There is an early phase 1892-1920 when women had an important place in that Department, and a subsequent period when they left (or were driven out) and their work was expunged from its history. The story of these women is worth attention from anyone interested in the careers and long term influence of women in academic disciplines. Their removal from the historical record of American sociology is a salutory lesson. Unlike most other women in academic life, there is enough published material to reconstruct them and their work.

The Chicago School has probably received more attention from subsequent generations than any other group of sociologists or set of theoretical ideas. The book by Kurtz (1984) has a 153 page bibliography of over 1000 items of literature by and about the Chicago School. In addition to the American scholarship, there are four British books about the group by Rock, (1979), Bulmer, (1984), Harvey (1987) and Smith (1988). No other American sociology department has interested British scholars to this extent. For British scholars interested in the theories, or methods or empirical concerns of the Chicago sociologists, telling and retelling the story of the ancestors is endlessly fascinating.

There is no consensus about the Chicago School, only controversy. Scholars dispute over who was and was not a true member, whose work was influential and whose was marginal, and how far qualitative and quantitative methods were central. What follows is my account drawn from a variety of sources, and is intended to provide a background for non-sociologists.

The Chicago school 1892-1920

In 1892 Chicago was a rough frontier town. Growing rapidly, with a wide range of immigrants speaking many languages, it was famous for the stockyards where millions of cattle were butchered to feed the Eastern states. Funded by Rockefeller oil money, a new University was founded with a President aged only 34, William Rainey Harper. The aim of this new University was to be different from the elite, Ivy League men's colleges of the East Coast, to be modelled on the Prussian university instead. It was also co-educational: an innovation at this period. Because Harper wanted a different kind of university (and because he had difficulty attracting classical and semitic scholars to the frontier), the new Chicago specialized in sciences and the new social sciences: especially sociology, social administration and psychology. Albion Small came to chair the sociology department in 1892 and headed it until 1924 when he was 70. He also edited *American Journal of Sociology* (*AJS*) from Volume 1 in 1895 until 1935. The men who established symbolic interactionism and sociology in that period are famous: John Dewy, W.I.Thomas, Albion Small, G.H.Mead, R.E. Park and E.W.Burgess. Chicago sociology was dominant in the USA until 1935-36, when the rest of the country's sociologists rebelled. They took control of the American Sociological Association (ASA) away from Chicago, and founded the *American Sociological Review* to challenge the *ASJ*. The later generations of Chicago-trained and Chicago-influenced men: Blumer, Hughes, Strauss, Denzin, Becker and even Goffman passed on the tradition which still exists today in the journals *Symbolic Interaction* and the *Journal of Contemporary Ethnography*.

The Chicago School is remembered and venerated for the theoretical perspective of symbolic interactionism, for pioneering participant observation in sociology, for urban sociology, for the sociology of occupations, professions and socialization into them, for medical sociology, for the sociology of crime, deviance, and social problems. The literature about the history of American sociology is dominated by Chicago, and the literature on the Chicago school is vast and apparently endless.

In the contemporary literature, one characteristic unites the disparate accounts: neglect of gender. The topic of race is also worth comment, but is quite beyond the scope of this paper. See Lissak (1989) for a discussion of the issue, and a bibliography of Chicago publications on race and immigration. (See also Lyman 1984).

In the period from 1892-1939 gender was an important theme in the research carried out in Chicago, but a modern reader of contemporary books would not be aware of the scholarship that resulted. The women who made major contributions to research and teaching, who shared the political campaigns of the men, and the research done on women, on household work and on gender, are all grossly neglected in the modern literature. Some of the women who were colleagues of Thomas, Small, Mead and Dewey and who pioneered urban sociology, are missing from the histories altogether: others are defined as irrelevant to sociology and then ignored.

The accounts of Chicago University and its Sociology Department differ from one another over emphasis and detail, but share an emphasis on men as the central actors, and revere those men as their ancestors.

Now the feminist re-appraisal of the orthodox canon has begun to appear. Mary Jo Deegan (1988) has published the first of three volumes on the women of Chicago between 1892-1918 and an edited collection of contemporary work Deegan and Hill, (1987). Rosenberg, (1982) Rossiter (1982) and Gordon (1990) provide background data on the intellectual currents of the period. Thus the sources for a secondary analysis are available.

The arrival of feminist re-tellings of the history of the Chicago sociologists can be understood at two distinct levels. It would be possible to evaluate Deegan's (1988) work as historical scholarship and dispute her interpretations compared to Bulmer's (1984) or Harvey's (1987).

Such an evaluation depends on research in the archives, and interviews with survivors from the period, and that is *not* the point of this paper. An alternative approach is to treat both the orthodox male accounts of the 1892-1920 period as accounts, as origin myths, as stories; and to treat Deegan's (1988) and Rosenberg's (1982) versions as feminist accounts, feminist origin myths or feminist stories. This parallels the treatment of published theories of primatology of Donna Haraway (1989) in which she juxtaposes analyses of feminist primatologists with examinations of how male supremacists characterised primate behaviour. Here the 'accuracy' of Deegan's and Rosenberg's account is not the point, rather their stories are analysed as a feminist myth.

The lost women of Chicago 1892-1920

The first task of feminist intellectual historians is typically establishing that women actually existed in the scholarly tradition under scrutiny. Thus the contributors to *Women of Science: Righting the Record* Kass Simon and Farnes (eds) (1990) trace forgotten women in archaeology, geology, astronomy, mathematics, engineering, physics, biology, medicine, chemistry and crystallography. Deegan, Rosenberg and Rossister have offered a list of lost women associated with the Chicago School of Sociology. There are at least ten women in the 1892-1920 period who deserve attention as contributors to the development of Chicago sociology:

Marion Talbot
Jane Addams
Florence Kelley
Edith Abbott
Sophonisba Breckinridge
Charlotte Perkins Gilman
Helen Bradford Thompson (later Woolley)
Helen Castle Mead
Alice Chipman Dewey
Dorothy Swaine Thomas

Three of these (Helen Mead, Alice Dewey and Dorothy Thomas) were married to central male figures, and therefore appear in both male and female histories. The others, lacking such achievements, are more often neglected. Brief career outlines are provided for the reader unfamiliar with them.

Marion Talbot (1936) was the first Dean of Women at Chicago, and taught in the sociology department. Her intellectual interests were in the area of overlap between urban studies, town planning and home economics, but many contemporary sociologists interested in housework, food and drink, use of space, and other aspects of everyday life would be able to recognise her as their foremother. If Talbot is remembered at all today it is as a founder of the American Association of University Women, not as a sociologist. As Dean of Women, Talbot was able to find jobs for other women, and she set the standards of ladylike behaviour for staff and students. As an East Coast lady - from Boston - she epitomized the civilised American woman who was respectable, even in the frontier town of Chicago. Talbot's rules on chaperones, dress, leisure activities and political campaigning governed the lives of Chicago women students for forty years. An account of the problems facing the women of Talbot's generation can be found in Delamont, (1989).

Jane Addams is the most famous woman in the list, but she is remembered today as a pacifist, a settlement worker, a feminist, and a social worker: her identity as a Chicago sociologist is totally forgotten or ignored.

Yet she taught sociology, was a member of the ASA, published in the *AJS*, called herself a sociologist and was, at the time, recognised as one. Addams was responsible for a major Chicago institution: Hull House. This was a settlement, modelled on Toynbee Hall in London, where many middle class intellectuals lived among the inner city poor, providing classes, a library, advice and help, and a living example of an upright, moral, worthy, American way of behaving. Hull House, guided by Addams for forty years, was three things in one. It was a home for many women (and some men) where they could eat communally and have companionship without expense and domestic chores. It was the beginnings of social work and of all the advice centres (legal, financial etc.) that characterise modern welfare.

And last, but no means least, it was the centre for data collection for the Chicago sociologists. Indeed the first empirical study done by Chicago was called the *Hull House Maps and Paper*, edited by Jane Addams (1895).

Florence Kelley was born in 1853, and came to Hull House in 1891 after a divorce which had left her with three children. She had a doctorate from Zurich, had known Engels and translated his works into English. Florence Kelley was a leading force in compiling the *Hull Maps and Papers*, the first American attempt to emulate Booth's *Life and Labour*. Initially central to the Sociology Department's work, Burgess subsequently downplayed it as a contribution to urban sociology when he wrote the history of Chicago scholarship. Deegan, (1988, p.63) traces Burgess' steady downgrading of the *Hull House Maps & Papers* from 1916 to 1964

Edith Abbott had a PhD in Political Economy from Chicago, studied with the Webbs at LSE, taught sociology at Wellesley, and was then on the staff of the sociology department in Chicago from 1908-1920. She published books on *Women in Industry* in 1910 and on school truancy in 1916. These books are not listed in Kurtz's (1984) bibliography.

Abbott was the statistician in the department, holding the title of 'Lecturer in Methods of Social Investigation'. Her sister, Grace, was also a resident of Hull House. Sophonisba Breckinridge was the first woman to qualify as a lawyer in Kentucky in 1894, but took a job as Assistant Dean of women at Chicago. She then took two Phds, one in political economy and another in law - the first woman to graduate in law at Chicago. She taught sociology in Talbot's sub-department of home economics within sociology, and published the book on truancy with Abbott, and another major work on *The Delinquent Child and the Home* 1912.

After 1904 Breckinridge, and Julia Lathrop (another neglected woman scholar) were primarily involved in what became Chicago's School of Social Service Administration (SSA) where social workers were trained. Consequently she has been dismissed from the history of sociology.

Helen Bradford Thompson Woolley grew up in Chicago and entered the university in 1893. She completed her Ph.D there in 1900. Her doctoral research on the psychology of sex differences so impressed W.I.Thomas that he changed his views, in print. He had believed that sex differences had genetic bases but after reading Thompson's findings he decided sex differences were environmentally grounded. See Rosenberg (1982)

Charlotte Perkins Gilman is not usually recognised as a pioneer sociologist. However she published in the *AJS*, spoke at the ASA, and worked with Lester Ward who is seen as a founder of American sociology. Gilman left California for Chicago in 1895 and lived in Hull House for a time. When *Women and Economics* (Gilman, 1988) was published in 1898, it was eagerly read by the Hull House women. Deegan, (1988) *Jane Addams* discusses Gillman and Hull House.

The last three women in the list of eight appear in the story as the wives of great men, although all deserve some attention as scholars in their own right. Alice Chipman Dewey was an early reader of Zola, and his fiction was an important influence on the *style* of Chicago's urban sociology. It was *possible* that Alice Dewey brought Zola's fiction to the attention of the men who later recommended him to their students. Helen Mead and Alice Dewey were both committed activists for women's suffrage. Dorothy Swaine Thomas was the second wife of W.I.Thomas, after he and Harriet had been divorced. Together they wrote *The Child in America* (1928).

This does not exhaust the women who were active in sociology in this era: Julia Lathrop, Grace Abbott and Annie Maron McLean could also be rehabilitated.

Competing mythologies about Chicago

There are two basic 'stories' about what happened to Chicago sociology after 1920. In the dominant, male versions of the story, three men of perspicacity - Faris, Park and Burgess - inherited the department, purified it, and created modern sociology there. That is, they separated academic sociology as an objective scientific discipline from social administration, social policy, social work, home economics and political activism of all kinds. (Kurtz, 1984; Rock, 1979; Bulmer, 1984; Harvey, 1987; Faris, 1967; Matthews, 1977).

The minority feminist version of the story casts Park as a villain who could not work with women and was not prepared to recognise their scholarship in his account of the period. Deegan (1988) shows in considerable detail how Mead, Dewey, Thomas and Small were all able to work with women, and shared some of the social and political concerns of Abbott, Addams, Breckinridge and Talbot. Two organizational changes, an ideological division, and the malign influence of one man (Park) explain for Deegan why these women were excluded from the historical record of sociology.

The organizational divisions were the separation of Talbot's Home Economics department, and Abbott and Breckinridge's Social Administration department from the Sociology Department. At the time, the women thought these were signs of progress, because it gave them autonomy: they got to chair their own departments where they could run courses designed particularly for women *and* geared to train people who would change society. The ideological division, Deegan argues, was between men who thought social science was best done in the university by contemplation and abstract thought, and women who wanted to apply multi-disciplinary social science to social problems.

She says that the two sexes: the men tenured in the University Department, the women identified with Hull House where they lived and focused their work: shared the same definition of the proper roles of male and female social scientists. Men belonged inside the University with the abstract; women belonged in the world collecting data. Where the sexes differed was in the value they placed on the two activities. Each sex thought that they had the better part of the bargain, that their work was more valuable. Given the way in which sociology developed as an abstract, ivory tower subject quite separate from political campaigns, social administration and charitable work, (i.e. the male view "won"),. the neglect of the work of Abbott, Addams, Talbot and the others in the standard histories is understandable, if unscholarly.

As long as Small chaired the department, relationships between the men and women seem to have stayed friendly, even after the sub-departments split away. Later in the 1920s and 1930s the relationships became extremely hostile, and none of the male historians offer any explanation for this. Some hint that women who want to teach home economics or social work would inevitably be difficult to get along with. Deegan explicitly blames Park for the rift. He had come to the department from elsewhere, was kept in a junior role for many years, but eventually became the chair and the official historian of the Chicago School. He was fanatically hostile to Addams, Talbot and Breckinridge.

Deegan argues that Park's hostility to Abbott and Breckinridge personally and his ambivalence to 'do-gooders', led him to denigrate all the women's work, and expunge their influence from the history of American sociology. His historical account has been accepted by subsequent scholars until Deegan. Park was violently anti-suffrage for women, wanted to purge sociology of 'political' taints, and wrote about Mead and Thomas stressing their academic work while ignoring their activism. Harvey (1987:31) quotes Park saying that Chicago had suffered more from 'lady reformers' than from organized crime and gangsters; and that 'reformers and do-gooders' (mostly women) were 'lower than dirt'.

Deegan's account of Park's hostility to suffrage, trade union activities and welfare rights work is not a simple list of Park's conservatism, lack of reforming zeal, and distaste for feminism. She also points out that Park was involved with the black activist Booker T.Washington, and outlines his role in the Chicago Commission of Race Relations after a race riot in 1919. Park was obviously ambivalent about social reform and political activism, and Deegan does not fall into the trap of making him a one-dimensional monster. His memory is, however, treated with great care and respect by many living sociologists, who do not wish to recognize any negative side to Park.

Deegan (1988: 154) reports that Park's quarrel with Abbott and Breckinridge is a 'no-go' area for American historians of sociology Park's biographer was told to omit it from his biography by senior figures in the discipline, Deegan (1988: 154-5) herself was threatened with blackballing from sociology if she researched it, and informants who mentioned it to her asked to remain anonymous.

British histories of the Chicago School have accepted Park's version of events at least insofar as they neglect women. British researchers should have no such inhibitions about muckraking, but appear to have accepted the male orthodoxy. Smith (1988), Harvey (1987) and Rock (1979) do not mention *Hull House Maps and Papers* at all, while Bulmer (1984) does not provide any bibliographical details of it when it is mentioned (once). An appendix to the paper shows how little attention is paid to the women of the Chicago School by the four British authors.

Here then are two competing origin myths. In one story brave men purify their discipline by separating themselves from misguided women and social reformers, in the other the feminist approach to sociology is declared a non-subject and its strengths forgotten. Although to modern eyes the women's concerns were mainstream ones, the male origin myth has become the dominant version

The next section outlines a theoretical perspective which is then used to explore the gendered worlds of Chicago sociology before 1920, and to explain the removal of the women from the intellectual record.

Structuralism and scholarship

The theoretical framework chosen to analyse the myths of the Chicago School is structuralist. This theoretical perspective stems from Durkheim and Mauss, and in post war social science has been developed by Levi-Strauss, (1966 and 1967), Leach (1969) and Douglas (1966, 1970, 1982), Bernstein (1971) and Bourdieu (1988).

Elsewhere I have used this perspective to analyse the experiences of girls at a Scottish public school in the late 1960s, the pollution control strategies of feminist educational pioneers, and the role of women in reproducing cultural capital in contemporary Britain (Delamont, 1989)

The adoption of a structuralist perspective is not a fashionable strategy for a feminist in 1992, whether one believes that post-structuralism has killed structuralism or that structuralism is based on an inherently male dualist epistemology.

It is used here because I find it compelling as an exploratory framework, whether applied to historical material on the education of women, or contemporary ethnographic material. The theoretical model has not been applied to Chicago sociology before. It helps my understanding of many aspects of women's intellectual history in Britain and the USA.

The published stories about the theories, methods and research topics associated with the Chicago School offer scope for a subsequent structuralist analysis. The issues of pure and applied, male and female, progressive and traditional, celibate and sexual, new and old, black and white, gay and straight, can all be found there, and to produce a structuralist account of any phenomenon we must start by searching for binary discriminations. As Leach (1969:11) puts it:

> In every myth system we will find a persistent sequence of binary discriminations as between human/superhuman/, mortal/immortal, male/female, legitimate/illegitimate, good/-bad... followed by a 'mediation' of the paired categories thus distinguished.

A range of binary discriminations can be seen in all the histories of the Chicago School, both the competing male stream ones and the dissident feminist alternative. Before producing the structuralist analysis of the competing myths about Chicago sociology, the variety of structuralism being proposed is briefly outlined. Delamont, (1989) provides a full exposition of the structuralist *melange* used here. It blends the work of Mary Douglas with that of Shirley and Edwin Ardener.

Shirley and Edwin Ardener (1975) developed the idea of muted groups. They argued that in all societies people have folk models of how their culture works, but that dominant groups have more power to ensure that their models are dominant. Less powerful sub-cultures may have different models, which are 'muted' by their proponents' lack of power. In many societies women form a muted group, but other subgroups or subcultures may also be 'muted'. The Ardeners argued that anthropologists had frequently collected male, dominant models of other cultures, while neglecting to study the muted models of muted groups, particularly women.

The work of Mary Douglas is also powerful as an exploratory tool. Douglas pioneered an approach to the study of pollution and contagion which showed how it was essentially matter out of place which was conceived as dirt or danger. Thus chocolate is a treat on a silver dish, but a nasty mess trodden into the carpet; lipstick is fine on lips, but not on shirt collars.

As with the physical world, so too with the moral order. The terrible shocks of the Oedipus legend turn upon what would have been relatively harmless acts (a death in a street brawl, marrying a widow) which become fundamental tragic sins once the status of the parties (son and father, son and mother) is reclassified/revealed. We have to label the world, to classify it: then we are able, in part, and in significant part, to control it. Any classification system immediately generates problems, because there are always anomalies and ambiguities. These are problematic, and hence we either revere or fear them.

Douglas went on from the seminal work on pollution and its control to develop a typology of the cosmologies of cultures: group and grid. She claimed that all human societies could be located in a two dimensional space made up by the strength or weakness of Group and of Grid. 'Group' deals with how hard it is to join something and how much commitment is demanded of members. So it is hard to get into an elite regiment and high commitment is expected. (For example, the Sacred Band of Thebes exhibited high Group). Grid refers to how much regulation is exercised over members of any culture. When grid is weak, life is free of constraint; when it is strong, there are lots of repressive controls. Douglas believes that all human cultures can be classified in the spaces that result. Each quadrant has its own 'miseries and compensations': that is there are advantages and disadvantages to each style of life. The Douglas group and grid theory has been successfully applied to academic and industrial styles in the sciences. Bloor and Bloor (1982) and Thompson (1982).

It is possible to find all four styles of life within one academic discipline: as shown in Figure 11:1.

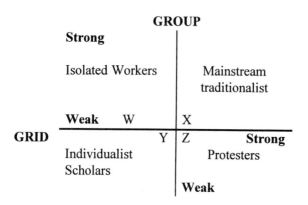

Figure 11:1   Styles within a learned discipline

In quadrant X (strong group and strong grid) the 'Grand Old Men' of any discipline are located: those who award the honours, legitimate new knowledge, award the grants, act as gatekeepers for publications, jobs, committees and so on.   Square W (Strong group, weak grid) are the majority of the workers in the discipline, teaching it and keeping it going, but not changing or developing it. Cell Y (weak group and weak grid) is the source of radical changes in the discipline, the origin of the Kuhnian paradigm shifters.   In the Z square, (strong grid, weak group) are the outsiders: those who are the rebels on the margins of the subject.

The power of such a schema is only realized if the author is clear about the level at which such a phenomenon is being analysed [a whole culture, a sub-group, a small clique, an individual], about whether the world being modelled is that of a dominant or muted group, and the vantage point of the person doing the mapping/analysis. Bearing these caveats in mind, we can explore the world of the Chicago School and the fate of the lost women.

Group, grid and the Chicago school myths

This section plots the academic world views of the men and women of the Chicago School with Douglas's model. The evidence is that male and female scholars had different perspectives. Figure 11:3 shows how the leading men saw the scholarly world of the Chicago School.

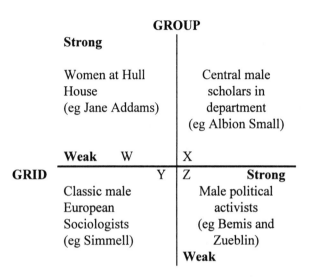

GROUP

Strong	
Women at Hull House (eg Jane Addams)	Central male scholars in department (eg Albion Small)
Weak W	X
GRID Y	Z **Strong**
Classic male European Sociologists (eg Simmell)	Male political activists (eg Bemis and Zueblin)
	Weak

Figure 11:2 Male view of Chicago scholarship

Figure 11:2 reveals the male view, in which the men of what H.M.Collins calls the 'core set' define themselves as the heart of academic sociology, excluding men such as Bemis (who was sacked for his political activities), and the women at Hull House whom they regarded as the marginal routine workers.

For the men the important polarities were pure *versus* applied, male *versus* female, theoretical *versus* empirical, university *versus* city, work *versus* home, thinkers *versus* activists, consolidation *versus* agitation, marriage *versus* celibacy, objectives *versus* political, and so on. The core set (Collins, 1985) men were concerned to build Chicago sociology as a pure, theoretical, university-based discipline carried on by married men away from their homes by theorising quite separate from political agitation.

To understand the consequences of this worldview, it is necessary to consider what type of pollution beliefs are typically associated with each quadrant, and what 'pollution' consisted of for the men of the Chicago

School at this time. Figure 11:3 shows that types of pollution fears found in each quadrant, and cell X is characterised by the strongest fears of pollution both at the boundaries of the group and between the different levels of the hierarchy. The elite men were thus at risk of pollution in two ways: both at the edges of their elite group, and between the different levels of their hierarchy. If Douglas is correct these men should show strong boundary maintenance at the edges of their group, and a strong hierarchical tendency within it.

GROUP
Strong

Pollution belief strong at group edges	Pollution beliefs at group edges, *and* surrounding hierarchy
Weak W	X
Y	Z **Strong**
Little fear of pollution	Little fear of pollution but millenarianism
	Weak

GRID

Figure 11:3   Pollution beliefs in the group/grid system

There were three 'dangers' for the elite men: radical political activity and speech; feminization of the university and the new subject; and sexual scandal. The dismissal of Bemis in 1895 because of his active support of the Pullman strikers, and the forced resignation of Zueblin in 1908 after attacks on certain university trustees' records as employers, are attempts to keep male sociology clear of political contamination. Fear of the feminization of the university and the discipline (very common in American science and social science in this period) is clear from the serious discussions of proposals to repeal co-education in the new university, a proposal supported by both Small and Vincent. Rossiter, (1982) is an excellent study of this process in biology, chemistry, geography, psychology and anthropology. The separation at faculty level, with Talbot going off to a home economics department and Breckinridge to social administration compartmentalized the women and therefore protected the men against feminization. The fear of sexual scandal is shown most vividly in the sacking of W.I.Thomas in 1918 when he was discovered in a hotel room with the wife of a serving soldier. See Bulmer (1984, pp.45-69).

If Douglas's model is correct, the elite men in quadrant X should display not only strong pollution fears at their boundaries, but also surrounding the hierarchy. Divisions between tenured full professors and more junior/temporary/part-time lecturers should - if Douglas' theory is right - have been strict and clearly marked. Park's long period as a marginal member of the department kept at arm's length by the core set can be interpreted as such a boundary maintenance measure . See Bulmer (1984: p.109-110).

The world-view of the women is rather different. Figure 11:4 plots the world of Chicago sociology as seen by the women. The women who lived in their research setting had a different set of values. They wanted to build an applied, empirical, active, political, discipline of sociology, *not* based in the university but in the city, in their home, as part of their celibate careers as agitators.

	GROUP	
	Strong	
Men supportive of women (eg Thomas, Mead)	Women at Hull House (eg Jane Addams)	
Weak W	X	
GRID Y	Z **Strong**	
Producers of radical European ideas (Marx, Tolstoy)	Anti-feminist men (eg Burgess, Park)	
	Weak	

Figure 11:4   Hull House women's view of Chicago sociology

The female view, which may have been equally clear before 1920, but has become 'muted' in the orthodox histories of the Chicago school, locates the personnel in different cells.   Jane Addams and Edith Abbott saw themselves as the core set, the pioneers of a new subject (sociology), in a new political/charitable/activist context (Hull House, Labour Unions,

Suffrage Societies). They saw the labour of the men as either supportive, or hostile, to their endeavours. (Cells W and Z). There is a major different between the men and women in the contents of Square Y, because each group sought for inspirations from different European thinkers.

For the women the important polarities were female *versus* male, celibacy *versus* marriage, morally superior *versus* morally inferior, chaste *versus* lustful, reform *versus* reaction, female emancipation *versus* female oppression, potent reform *versus* sterile academicism, empirical research *versus* theorizing, and activists *versus* thinkers. Among the women there was no simple opposition between work and home, because the women lived in their work place: they lived sociology, as they lived in the city centre.

The pollution beliefs and strategies about controlling contagion worked out rather differently for the women. If we start in Quadrant Z, the pollution beliefs of the women were even tougher (though different) from those of the men. The women were keenly protective of their status as *ladies* (respectable, celibate, properly dressed, chaperoned etc.) and of their scholarship (Breckinridge's *two* Chicago PhDs). This double conformity strategy was the common, and *essential*, feminist method of tackling entry to educational institutions, professional training and work in learned occupations see Delamont, (1993). The 'dangers' for these women were not the same as those for the elite males, with the one exception of sexual scandal which would be fatal to the feminists' educational enterprise.

Feminization was *not* a danger for women - it was their whole world, and meaningless to women as a contagion. If they had an equivalent pollution fear it was hyper-masculinity, or anti-female activities.

For these women, the danger of the men who were anti-women, and especially anti-suffrage, was best met by separation. Thus Abbott, Breckinridge and Talbot were relieved to set up their own sub-departments, where they could distance themselves from anti-suffrage men.

The issue of smoking at meetings of learned societies is a good illustration of how one sex's pollution control strategy was the other's contagion. Rossiter (1982) makes this clear in her study. Men scholars who wanted to keep women out of professional meetings had an easily available strategy: have smoking at the meeting.

> Properly bred women did not smoke or enter rooms where men were smoking before the 1920s... Thus to include smoking on the programme or to allow men to smoke... was an overt social message to the women not to attend (p.92)

154

Men could keep women out of any gathering by smoking, thus controlling the pollution they feared; for women the smoking *was* the pollution, and could only be controlled by avoiding men. Fass (1977) has an excellent discussion of the 'dangers' that smoking posed a respectable women.

For the women, the outgroup (Cell Z) was best shed/escaped from, by setting up separate departments. The men in Square W were a problem for the women. As colleagues in scholarship, or in political campaigns, they were useful allies. However, feminists could not afford to be associated with W.I. Thomas's sexual scandal, any more than the men could. The real danger to the women, however, came from elsewhere.

For both men and women, quadrant Y is the source of paradigm changes, of new ideas. One such new idea from Europe, which was unproblematic for the men, but a major danger for the women, was Freudianism. As Martha Vicinus (1985) has argued cogently, the feminists of the late nineteenth century, such as Talbot, Addams, Abbott and Kelley, were quite unable to respond to the vogue for Freud.

The women of Hull House, like counterparts in Britain, had resolved many of the contradictions of women's lives by living and working in all-female institutions. Vicinus's book deals with nurses' homes, houses for church deaconesses, schools, settlement houses and colleges and university halls of residence in Britain. These were all places where women could live with other women in quasi-domestic, quasi-familial settings. American feminists had also chosen to establish such all-female institutions, such as the women's section of Hull House. Before Freud, these institutions were seen as utterly respectable, above reproach, and economically sensible. After Freud, (or rather the dissemination of Freud into Anglo-Saxon intellectual circles) they suddenly became sinister. A theory that 'proved' all women were libidinous creatures whose 'natural' destiny was heterosexual activity and motherhood meant that the celibate spinster was dangerously suppressing her sexual urges and either subliminating them in her charitable, political or educational activities or engaging in sinister lesbian practices. The eugenicist Meyrick Booth condemned the British educational pioneers in these terms.

Meyrick Booth, writing in 1932, saw the pioneering girls. schools as old fashioned, because Freud had overthrown the theory behind them. Booth saw Miss Buss and Miss Beale motivated by 'the sterile rational doctrinairism of the J.S.Mill.... school' (143), guided by the 'unpsychological ideals of pre-war days' (162), which is a 'utilitarian, pseudo-masculine feminism' (164). The girls' schools were misguided because they exposed the pupils to;

the examination cramming; the tennis, hockey and other sports; the conversion of an interest in the other sex into *camaraderie*; the cult of hardiness, independence, and self-assertion....(p.174)

The celibate spinster living with other such women found herself re-defined as a sexual creature who was either a pervert or a repressed spinster sublimating her natural urges in 'good works', religion, or unhealthy domination of other women. Vicinus shows how Jane Addams was *totally* unable to comprehend Freudiansim, because she could only understand sexuality as heterosexual practice. She was left, like others of her generation, bewildered by the new social science theory. Paradigm changes are always threatening for established, core-set members. However it is easier for those who hold established university positions and act as gatekeepers of journals and the content of doctoral programmes to respond to new ideas without being personally or professionally threatened. W.I.Thomas was able to change his ideas on women's intellectual abilities when Helen Thompson did her research without losing his job or his scholarly status. The women, living and working away from the core, were more vulnerable to a new intellectual fashion: Freudianism. The core men's personal, sexual and moral integrity was not bound up with their sociological theories. The women's whole existence could be re-defined because they lived in a style that had become itself polluting.

The pioneer generation of Talbot, Addams and Breckinridge did not have successors. Subsequent generations of women did not want to live celibate lives with other women in settlement houses. The popularity of Freudian ideas made the pre-1920 feminism look old fashioned, innocent, or even sinister. For the next fifty years there was no feminist voice in Chicago sociology, and no research done on the private sphere which had interested Talbot. The elite men, in contrast, had successors, and the muted voice of the women was lost from historical record till recovered by Deegan, while the dominant male story passed into the mythology/history of American Sociology.

Lessons for women's history

There are two lessons that historians of women (and women historians) can take from this re-analysis of the lost women of Chicago sociology. These are the importance of searching out muted groups in all settings, and the need to see new intellectual movements as both dangerous and liberating

156

for women. Deegan's work on the lost women not only makes an impact as a piece of women's history: it also changes the way one conceptualizes the development of American sociology. If Talbot, Addams and Breckinridge had 'won', sociology would have been very different. The perspective of the muted group can be interesting in its own right - and it can lead to reinterpretations of the dominant cosmology.

The second lesson is that new intellectual movements can be both dangerous and liberating for women. Freudianism was dangerous for the Chicago women because it undermined their claim to respectability, but liberating for the next generation because it 'allowed' ladies to have sexual feelings. The historian of women needs to be alert to ways in which intellectual climates change, and how that interacts with generational change in the populations of women under study. The woman historian also needs to be alert to the ways in which changing intellectual climates can made her very existence as a scholar suddenly precarious. Whenever women intellectuals see their world differently from the elite men around them - as the Chicago women did - they are in danger of finding that a new theory has defined them out of existence. Paradigm shifts in dominant group ideology rarely benefit the muted group. Women intellectuals are frequently left like Gladstone and the Irish question in *1066 and All That* (Sellar and Yeatman, 1930)

When Sellar and Yeatman summarise the career of Gladstone, a Prime Minister in the second half of the nineteenth century, they relate how he:

> spent his declining years trying to guess the answer to the Irish Question: unfortunately, whenever he was getting warm, the Irish secretly changed the Question, so that as he grew older and older Gladstone grew angrier and angrier..
>
> (p.116)

The struggle of women to become, and be accepted, as intellectuals is rather like Gladstone's attempts on the Irish Question. Since 1850 women who want to be intellectual have to fight their way into academic institutions, do intellectual work, get it recognized, *and* remain constantly alert for men to change the question. By this, I mean that women regularly have to defend their abilities against new theories which purport to show that women cannot do adequate intellectual work.

In 1850 the dominant theories were that women had brains that were too small for intellectual activity, and/or that women who studied would use up too much blood in their heads and cease to menstruate, and/or that they would die of brainfever (Burstyn, 1980) and Russett (1989). The pioneers of the 1850-1890 generation demolished these theories, by their own performance and/or their research.

After 1914 when women had got access to higher education a wave of social Darwinism and eugenics swept academic life, attacking educated women for failing to breed (Dyhouse 1981). In the USA the WASPs were under siege from new Catholic immigrants, and the low reproduction rates of WASP college women was held up to discourage the intellectual woman. Gross theories about brain size were replaced with more subtle theories about menstruation making women incapable of sustained mental efforts. Alongside the eugenic and evolutionary arguments came Freudianism with its argument that men were meant for work, women for motherhood. Intellectual women were suffering from repressions, complexes or penis envy.

By the end of the second world war there were two new social science theories: Bowlby's maternal deprivation ideas and Parsonian functionalism. Women who did not stay at home to rear babies were flying in the face of sociological and psychological truths. With the discovery of chromosomes and hormones, 'science' had a new set of theories which could easily be used to prove women's inferiority. Women could not be intellectuals because they lacked a Y chromosome, or had the 'wrong' hormones.

More recently the vogue for hemisphere theories allows women to be devalued again. Moir and Jessel (1989) for example have published a popular book claiming that the embryo is doused with sex hormones in the womb, so the male brain develops fewer connections between the hemispheres than the female. Clearly women cannot be intellectuals, because the balance between the left and right hemispheres is different in women.

The women of the Chicago School 1892-1920 had proved themselves intellectuals and were living refutations of the brainsize, and brainfever, theories about female inferiority. They were quite unable to deal with the new Freudian and social-Darwinism ideas that hit them after the 1914-18 war. Their choice of an active, city-based, practical, celibate, empirical, political form of intellectual life made them *more* vulnerable to changes in theoretical fashion. The men shut the doors on their work and went away home, the women's whole existence was in Hull House, and when their lives were redefined as misguided, their work also became unimportant.

The feminist intellectual of 1992 has to be prepared for the next paradigm shift if she is to avoid the fate of the lost women in the Chicago School. Understanding the world-view of the dominate male group is an important aspect of defending a feminist identity.

Notes and acknowledgements

Jennifer Platt pointed out some problems with an early draft of the text of which I am grateful. An earlier version of this paper was given to the OASIS summer school in Cardiff in July 1990, and as part of the 350th Anniversary Celebration of the University of Helsinki, September 12th-14th, at a conference on "Intellectuals, University and Society".

Appendix one

Attention to the eight women highlighted in the four British texts

Index mentions in the British texts

Chicago Women	Rock	Bulmer	Harvey	Smith
Helen Mead	Nil	Nil	Nil	Nil
Alice Dewy	Nil	Nil	Nil	Nil
Helen Thompson	Nil	Nil	Nil	Nil
Marion Talbot	Nil	3	3	1
Jane Addams	Nil	2	1	2
Florence Kelley	Nil	Nil	Nil	1
Edith Abbott	Nil	11	2	Nil
Sophonisba Breckinridge	Nil	5	3	Nil
Dorothy Thomas	Nil	1	5	Nil
Charlotte P.Gilman	Nil	Nil	Nil	Nil

12. Measuring up to the scientific elite: Rosalind Franklin and the laureate profile

The publication of Zuckerman's (1988) review essay on the state of the sociology of science reiterates her earlier (1977) conclusions about the life histories and career paths of those scientific winners of the Nobel Prize who lived and worked in the USA. She claimed that

> the Nobel prizes stand as a brooding presence over all scientific awards
>
> (1977:33)

and gives them space in the 1988 review essay accordingly. One proof of the symbolic significance of the Nobel prize is the continuing debate over the 1962 Physiology/Medicine award to Crick, Watson and Wilkins. The scholarly and popular histories of the discovery of a helical structure for DNA share a perception of the importance of the Nobel prize when they regret that Rosalind Franklin's early death prevented her nomination for a share of it. (Olby, 1974; Yoxen, 1982; Sayre, 1975; Gribben, 1985). This chapter is a contribution to that debate.

Zuckerman's interviews with forty one living laureates (out of 56 then based in the USA) and her historical research on all the American winners from 1907 to 1972 enabled her to produce a composite biographical path for a 'typical' Nobelist. There were many common features in the lives and careers of Nobel winners, and their biographies differed from less distinguished scientists in a variety of ways. It was therefore straightforward to compare the life history and scientific career of Rosalind Franklin with the laureate pattern, to test the claims of authors who argue that Franklin's early death deprived her of high scientific honours.

Zuckerman's findings can be used as a template against which to set the life of Franklin. In other words, if her posthumous champions are correct in claims that Crick Watson and Wilkins benefited from Franklin's data and

160

she should have been publicly credited with equal status in the discovery, then Franklin's biography should match Zuckerman's criteria.

Zuckerman's (1977) data were predominantly on males, for in the mid-1970s there was no living women laureate in the USA (M.G.Mayer having died in 1972). Zuckerman's *Scientific Elite* lists all the science winners from 1902-1972, at which point there had been only five women winners (Marie Curie twice, Irene Joliet Curie, Maria Goeppert Mayer, Dorothy Hodgkin and Gerty Corti). Since then Barbara McClintock and Rita Levi-Montalani have received one. Her forty one interviews were all with men, therefore, and the typical career described was a male one.

Material on Rosalind Franklin comes from the biography by Sayre (1975). At each stage in the life course, the parallels between Rosalind Franklin's biography and the Zuckerman composite are striking.

Zuckerman's composite profile starts in childhood, where she found that American nobelists were the sons of professionals rather than businessmen, and their homes are described as an: 'educational environment's' rather than being backgrounds 'opulence' (1977:81). Many of the nobelists had fathers who were scientifically literate, or even scientists. Rosalind Franklin's family were merchant bankers, but her father was a scientist, and the home atmosphere was educational *and* opulent (Sayre, 1975, 28-40) Franklin's mother was a Waley, providing a suitably scholarly pedigree to meet Zuckerman's criteria.

Zuckerman (1977:81) found that the majority of American laureates were from Protestant or Jewish backgrounds, and the latter had been to schools where the science teaching was good. Rosalind Franklin's family were Jews, and she attended St.Paul School for Girls' where the science teaching was well above average for British girls' schools for the 1930s (Layton, 1984). The majority of women scientists in Britain studied by Burrage (1983) were educated at single sex fee paying or academically selective schools. The majority of American-educated laureates attended an elite university as undergraduates, for their PhDs they were:

> concentrated not only in a few places, but in elite places
> (Zuckerman, 1977:83. 88-89)

Rosalind Franklin went to Newnham College, Cambridge, and also did her PhD there, (Sayre (1975:57-59). Her PhD supervisor was Professor Norrish, who became a Nobel prize winner for Chemistry in 1967. In this she fits the pattern Zuckerman found whereby nobelists are frequently ex-pupils or junior colleagues of other nobelists, often before the older person has received the prize. Thus, 48 of 92 American laureates had worked with another nobelist as an apprentice, and ten nobelists have produced 30 prize winning pupils. Some of the apprenticeship lineages now cover five generations. The most touching facet of this has to be the three members of the radiation laboratory at Berkeley who wore the same white waistcoat at the Nobel ceremony when receiving their prizes, like family members passing down their ancestral christening gown.

Zuckerman (1977:111) found that laureates are particularly adept at spotting talented young researchers:

> they are successful scientific truffle dogs

Being trained by a laureate is correlated with receiving one's prize younger than average, a point Zuckerman (1988:530) has stressed again recently.

Zuckerman (1977:61) found that future laureates got their careers off to a flying start, so that are found:

> getting ahead initially and moving farther and farther out in frontof their equals.

The young high-flyers start to publish earlier than their contemporaries, and publish a great deal: they average 13.1 papers in their 20s, 7.9 jointly authored and 5.2 single authored. A matched sample of less successful scientists produced an average of 2.9 joint papers and 4.3 single authored ones. Rosalind Franklin was 22 in 1943, and in the next four years published five papers, 2 jointly and 3 alone even though it was war time (Sayre 1975:63). This suggests that Franklin had started her publishing career in the same prolific style as Zuckerman's laureates.

Zuckerman (1977:151) found that nearly all the future nobelists got their first job in the 16 elite institutions which had already educated many of them at doctoral level she summarises these data by saying that the elite universities 'breed' and 'keep' the future laureates. Once in their first jobs, the nobelists were promoted rapidly, reaching full professorships at a younger age than matched samples of scientists who were not nobelists. Here the careers of the two women prize winners in Zuckerman's population are quite different from those of all but one of the men. M.G. Mayer did not have a tenured post until she was 53, while Gerty Corti was 51 and had been a lowly 'research associate' for 16 years (Zuckerman, 1988: 151). Barbara McClintock was 40 before she had a secure job, and other women scientists in the USA report similar patterns.

Evelyn Fox Keller (1985 158-160) reports that McClintock chose not to take a teaching job in a women's college which would have moved her away from research and elite, frontier science, preferring to survive on grants and fellowships until she was given a post at the Carnegie Institute of Washington at Cold Spring Harbour. McClintock's male colleagues were mostly unaware of her lack of a tenured post. A.M. Briscoe (1984:147-150) a biochemist reports a similar pattern in her own career, as I have discussed elsewhere (Delamont, 1989b).

In this respect, Rosalind Franklin's career is more similar to that of Mayer and Corti (and also McClintock whose prize had not been won when Zuckerman wrote) than that of any of the male laureates. Franklin went into a government research agency during her PhD period (in the war), then to a prestigous laboratory in Paris, then to Kings College, London, and finally to Birkbeck College, London. At no time in her life did she hold a proper tenured post, but lived on research grants. Sayre implies that Franklin had private means and so was not dependent on her salary, but wealthy men at this period held tenured posts and Franklin was being denied status even if she did not need the money.

Franklin's career has fitted Zuckerman's model as far as race, education, family ethos, and scientific training are concerned, but deviates where a tenured job is concerned. Next to be considered are the age at which the prize-winning scientific work was done, and how its producers regarded it. Zuckerman found the average age of the laureates when they did the research that was cited as the reason for their prize was 39. When Zuckerman compared this age for biologists and chemists, the average age when the Nobel-prize winning research was conducted was 41 for the biologists, 39 for the chemists. Rosalind Franklin was at King's College, London, working with Maurice Wilkins on DNA between 1951-1953 when she was 31-33. Many winners told Zuckerman (1977:211) that they did not feel their prize winning research was their best work. Franklin appears to have been more enthusiastic about her work on coal and on tobacco viruses than the DNA investigation because she published far more on those topics. She produced eleven papers on the Paris coal research, and 17 on the Birkbeck tobacco virus work after leaving Kings (Sayre, 1975: 82, 177-178).

Typical laureates had received six other awards before they got the Nobel prize and Franklin stands out, in that she had received very little recognition, and no medals or prizes. This squares with the finding of Cole (1979) that women scientists are less frequently honoured than men, but separates her from male laureates Like the men in Zuckerman's sample, she was not active in the politics, administration and committee work of science. Sayre (1975:70) says she

163

never 'ran' anything but her own career

Zuckerman said that the nobelists were notable because:
    research seems to have been not their highest priority but
    their only priority.

and that they

    confined themselves to bench and blackboard
                                                    (1977:200-201)

The only task that nobelists took on board was refereeing articles for the
journals - and there is no public evidence as to whether Franklin did this.
She did not have the blackboard to distract her for, like Barbara
McClintock, she preferred research to taking a teaching post.

On several of the criteria discovered by Zuckerman to be common to
most American laureates, Franklin has the biography of an excellent or
outstanding scientist. She failed, however, on one crucial test: longevity.
McClintock received the prize in old age at 81, as did Mayer and Corti who
were both older when they were honoured than Franklin was when she
died. Zuckerman's youngest prizewinner was 31, the oldest 87 - but most
were in their late forties - so Franklin's death at 38 was her most serious
deviation from the pattern her career was following.

Yoxen (1982:279) argues that Franklin's academic reputation has been
unjustly neglected and ignored, Olby (1974) and Gribbin (1985) that she
was deprived of her share of the credit for the DNA work. Sayre (1975)
believes that Watson stole Franklin's data and took credit for her work, and
has been trying to live with his guilt ever since . Yoxen attacks the 1981
edition of *The Double Helix* because its introduction by Stent does not cite
Sayre's biography of Franklin. He states that his omission is: 'irresponsible
on scholarly grounds, and possibily malicious'; (279).

Clearly matching her career to that of the typical laureate studied by
Zuckerman can only be of academic interest - but the exercise carried out
above does suggest that Franklin was a more creative scientist than anyone
reading *The Double Helix* would ever realise.

The çareers of Nobel prize winners show the Matthew Effect, or the
theory of accumulation of advantage, at its most extreme. Elites in science
and groups working at the frontiers of their specialty have occupied
sociologists of science from all schools of thought. The careers of women
who are members of what Collins (1985) has called 'core sets', or those
whose work turns out to be crucial in changing dominant ideas about

particular topics such as McClintock, provide sociologists of science with a mechanism for challenging the taken-for-granted nature of their accounts. The general conclusion of this note, then, is that testing general sociological theories about science against the lives of women scientists has sociological payoff. A specific conclusion about Rosalind Franklin is that her career shows marked similarities to that of male laureates, and even more striking parallels with post war Nobelists. It is time that all her scholarly work was scrutinised with the care paid to Barbara McClintock's.

Notes

Margaret Ralph typed this paper originally, and Pat Harris prepared later versions for me: I am grateful to both of them. The original research was done in the University of Sussex during a sabbatical and I acknowledge help from the library staff there.

My ideas on women and science have been rehearsed in discussion and correspondence with Paul Atkinson, Jonathan Cole, Harry Collins, David Edge, Evelyn Fox Keller, Trevor Pinch and Margaret Rossiter who all forced me to clarify my ideas, but are in no way responsible for them.

13. Murder after suffrage and other stories: Feminism and the golden age of the detective story

Preface

This paper is based on the Gillian Skirrow Memorial Lecture that I delivered at the University of Strathclyde in October 1991. A version of it appeared in the Strathclyde Alumni magazine **Interface**, *Number 8, in 1992.*

Introduction

Three apparently disparate themes are united in the first part of this paper which focuses on the period 1918-1938. There is one theme from popular culture: the best selling detective stories of Dorothy L. Sayers, Ngaio Marsh and Margery Allingham. Then there are two themes from feminist history: how women's campaigns for the right to education and jobs in the nineteenth century developed after 1919 when the Sex Disqualification (Removal) Act was passed *and* what problems faced the feminist movement after the vote was won in 1918. It first occurred to me that there was a link between these themes when I found that the American feminist, Inez Haynes Irwin, who led the national Women's Party there after the vote was won, had written a detective story (*Murder in Fancy Dress*, 1935) set in suburban Massachusetts during Prohibition. This link between feminism and the detective story in the interwar years was also a British phenomenon.

The context

When the 1914-18 war ended women (over 30 with property) got the vote in the UK, and the legal barriers against degrees at Oxford and Cambridge and against entry to law, accountancy, surveying and many other 'professional' careers were abolished by the Sex Disqualification (Removal) Act. It was not immediately clear what the feminists should do next. Some historians have said that feminism 'died', others that feminism continued, but there is no doubt that the feminists were divided into several feuding factions in the interwar years. Whichever argument one accepts about the 'death' of feminism, there is a major change in the marital and social status of the women who continued feminist struggles after 1918 compared to the pioneers of the pre-1918 period.

The nineteenth century feminists were predominantly unmarried women. They were mostly 'celibate' too, at least as far as relations with men were concerned. Hence the rhyme directed at the pioneer headmistresses in England:

> Miss Buss and Miss Beale
> Cupid's darts do not feel
> They are not like us
> Miss Beale and Miss Buss

There were exceptions - Elizabeth Garrett Anderson and Millicent Fawcett married - but most of the famous campaigners *chose* to stay single. This is explored by historian Martha Vicinus (1985) in *Independent Women*, and in fiction in Gissing's (1980) *The Odd Women*. Ladies had won the right to an academic education, to university degrees and to a professional career, but the expectation was that the jobs were for *single* women, not for married ones. The generation of women who shared the goals of education, careers and autonomy but came to adulthood during the 1914-1918 war were different. Unlike Emily Davies, Dorothea Beale, Frances Buss, and their contemporaries, the new generation of feminists: Dora Russell, Naomi Mitchison, Vera Britain, Winifred Holtby, Edith Summerskill and Dorothy L. Sayers *rejected* celibacy. They chose marriage or heterosexual activity outwith marriage, and rejected the idea that women were asexual, pure, morally superior creatures. Naomi Mitchison's (1979) autobiography is extremely lucid on this issue.

The detective story flourished between the wars - at a time when the vote had been won and the women's movement had dissipated itself into many separate campaigns. Many women wrote crime fiction between the wars, and there is a relation between the dilemmas facing feminists and the plots of the crime fiction written by some of the most popular authors of the period. Yet the two best known histories of British crime fiction totally fail to recognize the feminist dilemma which is the central theme of this chapter.

The two "standard" histories of British crime fiction are *Bloody Murder* (Symons, 1972) and Colin Watson's *Snobbery with Violence* (1971). Both books manage to suggest that all the important detective stories were written by men. But, if we try to think of other famous writers of crime fiction, apart from Conan Doyle, we come up with women - not men: Agatha Christie, Dorothy Sayers, Ngaio Marsh, Margery Allingham, Patricia Highsmith, Emma Lathen, Josephine Tey - and so on. Yet, apart from Christie, many of the women are undervalued - particularly Sayers, Marsh and Allingham. Symons and Watson suggest they write boring detective stories - I think they present three emancipated heroines whose development into independent human beings is more than the male critics can take.

Feminism went out of fashion and stayed that way till the sixties - and while it was out of fashion Dorothy Sayers, Ngaio Marsh and Margery Allingham started detective sagas with concealed feminist strains. At a time when open advocacy of feminism was sparse, a mixed audience were presented with three very interesting women - Harriet Vane, Agatha Troy and Amanda Fitton. I argue that the reasons Julian Symons and Colin Watson can appreciate Agatha Christie but not Sayers, Marsh and Allingham is precisely the presence of these heroines.

The detective stories of Sayers, Marsh and Allingham

The three women authors under scrutiny here all published their early work in what is generally known as the 'Golden Age' of the British detective story, the period from 1920-1939. This period is dated from the publication of Agatha Christie' *Mysterious Affair at Styles*, but Christie is not a feminist author and her work is not considered here. Agatha Christie writes one-off novels - the stories do not show any development in the characters even if they appear in several books. They get older, and their arthritis gets worse - but that is all. Agatha Christie's female detective (Miss Marple) is a classic old maid - dependent and fluffy. Women in the books rarely have careers - and if they do they are unhappy in them, and rush into marriage at the first opportunity, dropping any gainful employment. In *Evil Under the Sun*, for example, a successful dress designer happily abandons her business to marry a hopeless drip. Only in her *Cat Among the Pigeons*, set in a girls' school, are there any women who have choosen a career rather than marriage. In short, Christie's women are womanly - and easily acceptable to men. This analysis focuses on Dorothy L.Sayers, Ngaio Marsh and Margery Allingham, three contemporaries of Christie's who have sold well since the 1920s, have all their books still in print, and whose work has been filmed, televised and "done" on radio and audio cassette.

The detective novels of Sayers, Marsh and Allingham have several features in common, although Sayers and Allingham were British and Marsh a New Zealander. Most of Marsh's books are set in the UK and her hero and heroine are British. All three writers had a set of characters who appear in a long series of books, including a detective hero, his faithful friend, his loyal servant, eccentric relatives and a heroine. The relationship between hero and heroine is the focus here, and the similarities are striking.

The three heroes are aristocratic Englishmen. Sayers's Lord Peter Wimsey is the younger son of a duke, Marsh's Roderick Alleyn the younger brother of a baronet, and Allingham's Albert Campion has been disinherited and/or disowned by a family who are at least ducal and might be a minor branch of royalty. Wimsey and Campion are 'private' detectives, although Wimsey is so rich he takes no fees while Campion, because disinherited, does work for clients and gets paid. Alleyn is actually employed at Scotland Yard, but Wimsey and Campion both have best friends at Scotland Yard and so can call up police facilities and manpower, so all three can be cerebral rather than do actual legwork. As aristocratic, wealthy men they get to attend balls and embassy parties; are invited to country houses, and travel across the world freely. Wimsey, Alleyn and Campion are as 'unreal' as most of the other fictional detectives of the 1920s and 1930s.

The three heroes differ, in one very important respect, from the many other detectives of the 1920s and 1930s. They eventually marry very unusual wives. Wimsey marries Harriet Vane, Alleyn marries Agatha Troy and Campion marries Amanda Fitton. The Wimseys have three sons, the other couples one son each. Harriet Vane, Agatha Troy and Amanda Fitton are very unusual heroines for the 1920s and 1930s, and the marriages are one reason why the books have sold steadily ever since. Harriet Vane is the daughter of a poor doctor, an Oxford graduate and has earned her own living as a detective story writer since she graduated. Troy (she is never called Agatha) is the daughter of a successful artist, who is herself a successful painter and supports herself by painting and teaching. Amanda Fitton is an impoverished aristocrat who serves an engineering apprenticeship in an aircraft factory and becomes an aircraft designer.

All three are, therefore, career women, who have no need to marry in order to live. Harriet is shown employing a secretary, runs a car and buys silk shirts for herself. Troy has a house with several servants, runs a car, supports proteges and travels round the Pacific. Amanda is shown designing planes for Alan Dell - a leading UK manufacturer - and has a cottage by a river. None of the women is eager to marry the hero - even though Wimsey, Alleyn and Campion are intelligent, rich, amusing, and thoroughly 'good catches'. Once married the three women become mothers, but all three *go on working*. Harriet is shown writing more books, Troy paints, and Campion actually turns down a job as Governor of a colony because Amanda could not work at her trade in the tropics. These heroines are not only unusual before marriage, their partners recognise their careers and support them in continuing at work even after motherhood.

Sayers, Marsh and Allingham each created an emancipated woman with a life of her own. Each heroine is at worst threatening to the social worlds of male literary critics and at best seen as irrelevant to the plots.

Dorothy Sayers's detective stories are set entirely in the prewar period - and her heroine attended University in the twenties when women students were rare. Harriet Vane is an orphan, who gets a first class degree at Oxford, writes detective stories to make a living, and lives in sin with a poet, before finally agreeing to marry Sayers's detective - Lord Peter Wimsey. When she does marry, we are left knowing her career is to go on as she tells Salcombe Hardy, a journalist who interrupts her honeymoon:

Hardy:	'Oh by the way, ...do you intend to go on writing now you are married'
Vane:	'yes, of course'
Hardy:	'Under the same name?'
Vane:	'Naturally'
Hardy:	[.....] 'Your husband eager you should continue your professional career -?'
	[............]
Vane:	'He certainly doesn't object - in fact, I think he entirely approves'

(Sayers, 1937 p.274)

Harriet has already discovered her poet was a male chauvinist and left him - and negotiated a new kind of relationship with Lord Peter. We have already learnt earlier in this book, *Busman's Honeymoon* that:

'Peter is insistent his wife's work must not be interrupted'
(p.30)

by housework or domestic duties of any kind. Indeed when they first met, in *Strong Poison*, Peter Wimsey outlined why he wanted Harriet as a wife.

I'd like somebody I could talk sensibly, to, who would make life interesting. *And* I could give you a lot of plots for your books...

But you wouldn't want a wife who wrote books, would you?

But I should, it would be great fun.

(Sayers, 1930 p.37)

171

Ngaio Marsh's books span the war. We meet Agatha Troy in 1938 and she was still appearing in Marsh's books in the 1970s. Troy is a painter - a serious, internationally famous painter, whose career is not affected by her eventual marriage to Marsh's detective, Roderick Alleyn.

Troy is careless of her appearance - we meet her first wearing

> exceedingly grubby flannel trousers and a short grey overall... Her face was disfigured by a smudge of green paint and her short hair stood up in a worried shock.
>
> (Marsh, 1938a p.11)

She is desperately trying to finish a painting of the wharf at Suva before the ship leaves, and it is clear her work is far more important to her than her appearance, as she even smells of turpentine and paint (p.14)

Alleyn writes to a friend that

> her voice is 'gruff and stand-offish' (p.23)

We are asked to believe that Troy is

> the best living English painter

Her one-man shows occur at regular intervals throughout the books and are taken to Paris and New York. Troy is reluctant to marry - although she is not short of men friends. She admits to finding the loss of individuality attendant on marriage frightening

> The whole business. The breaking down of all one's reserves. The mental as well as the physical intimacy
>
> (1938b p.230).

For the Alleyns the war brings separation. Her war work at home is demanding. Alleyn goes overseas hunting spies Troy spends

> Four years of intensive work at pictorial surveys for the army, followed by similar and even more exacting work for the U.N.R.A.A. Four years work with little painting and no husband.

After the war, they have their son, and all three figured in further adventures, but Troy's painting is central. In 1962, for example, Troy is doing a society portrait and taking promising pupils (*Hand in Glove*).

The Allingham books also span the Second World War, like Marsh's, although they stop earlier because of the author's death. Margery Allingham's hero Albert Campion meets and eventually marries Lady Amanda Fitton who appears as an enterprising seventeen year old in 1933, and matures into an aircraft designer of international repute by 1949.

Amanda at seventeen is running a business charging people's batteries so they can listen to the radio, and exercising her mechanical ingenuity in the domestic sphere. When we next meet her, she is 24 and is working in the aircraft industry. She explains:

> It took me three and a half years to do it, but I'm a pretty good engineer, you know. I went straight into the shops when I got some money. I hadn't a sufficiently decent education to take an ordinary degree, so I had to go the back way
>
> (1938: 70)

She too spends the war in vital work, separated from Albert, they have their son, and in 1949 he turns down the colonial governor's job. because Amanda's

> Work is not unimportant (1949: 22)

and she could not carry on with it as a governor's wife.

These three relationships are not, of course, 'realistic' in modern terms. The men are rich, there are servants, and, by avoiding the creation of daughters, the three authors ducked the problem of the next generation. However, all three couples are shown working at establishing a new type of marriage, in which new kinds of egalitarianism are struggled for. Perhaps most unusually Harriet Vane is not a virgin before marriage, and Wimsey explicitly repudiates the idea of a sexual double standard, stating that he is not a virgin so there is no reason he should expect Harriet to be one either.

| Harriet: | You're bearing in mind... that I've had a lover? |
| Peter: | So have I,.... In fact, several |

(Sayer, 1930 p38)

Harriet had lived in sin, believing that it was the modern alternative to the Victorian marriage, only to discover she was 'on probation' as a potential wife. When offered marriage she had left the poet, Philip, immediately.

> Philip wasn't the sort of man to make a friend of a woman. He wanted devotion. I gave him that... But I couldn't stand being made a fool of. I couldn't stand being put on probation like an office-boy, to see if I was good enough.... I quite thought he was honest when he said he didn't believe in marriage - and then it turned out that it was a test, to see whether my devotion was abject enough. Well it wasn't. I didn't like having matrimony offered as a bad-conduct prize.
>
> (Sayers, 1930 p.36)

To previous generations of feminists, this would have been unthinkable, to the post 1918 women it was desirable and modern.

The three authors - Sayers, Marsh and Allingham - were young adult women when feminism was facing a novel dilemma : how to live with men but not abandon autonomy. In their detective stories they created three men who valued autonomous, independent, career women as wives, three heroines who *chose* marriage but did not submerge themselves in their husband's identities, and three marriages in which new ways of relating as men and women were depicted. In these novels, the feminist dilemmas of the post-suffrage era were rehearsed and, to some extent resolved.

The existence of Harriet Vane, Agatha Troy and Amanda Fitton in the detective fiction of the Golden Age is not entirely unparalleled in the writing of other authors. There are some parallels with Marta Hallard, the actress in Josephine Tey's Alan Grant books although Marta and Allan do not marry. Harriet, Troy and Amanda would recongnize Clare Massinger, the sculpter, and Georgia Cavendish, the explorer, the two women attached to Nigel Strangeways in the crime novels by Nicholas Blake as spiritual sisters. Gladys Mitchell's Beatrice Adela Lestrange Bradley could also be seen as a varient of the model. All these women with their careers and autonomy are in striking contrast to the female characters in the 'serious' fiction of the same period.

C.P.Snow is a useful comparator because he dabbled with crime fiction, as many 'serious' authors did in the Golden Age. *The Search* (1934) is an insider's view of science, in that the narrator is himself a crystallographer, rather than the lawyer watching science used as narrator in *The Affair* (1960). *The Search* is interesting for its portrayal of laboratory life in the 1930s, and women are completely absent from that life. None of the scientists is a woman: the women are scientists' wives and mistresses. The possibility of a woman being a scientist is only raised twice in the whole book. At one point, two of the bright young men are discussing what arguments an older man, who is past his own research peak and an idiot, might use to block a career. One possible argument is: 'Probably he'll say that the women on the staff would dislike you' (254). This is clearly intended to be a stupid point, not worth serious consideration. Later in the book a man who has a reputation for flirting is being groomed to become a professor at Leeds. His friends make him promise not to make passes at any women there: 'not a scientist's wife. Not one. Not even a woman scientist' (325). As this character is not an ethical scientist, but falsifies experimental results, the feeling that he might seduce women scientists is presumably all part of his defective character.

The scientific world described in Snow's novel is, then entirely male - even though the actual scientists working on crystallography in the 1930s included several women. The hero is portrayed facing a choice between science (an all-male world) and people (life with his wife) in a simplistic way. The omission of women from the London and Cambridge laboratories of the 1930s is particularly odd when one of the central characters in *The Search* - Constantine - is modelled on J.D. Bernal, according to Philip Snow (1982). Bernal was notoriously pro-women in his laboratories:

> he held to the rather old-fashioned communist notions
> about the equality of male and female workers, and was
> well-known for his willingness to accept women students,

to encourage them, to promote their careers, to find opportunities for them.

(Sayer 1975: 174)

No hint of this comes through in *The Search*.

Snow returned to non-military science for *The Affair*, set in the 1950s. This book is a reworking of the Dreyfus Affair, with communist beliefs replacing Jewishness, and scientific fraud instead of espionage. Everyday laboratory life is only mentioned in passing, and the scientific action has taken place in 'a Scottish university' before the story begins. The Dreyfus figure, Howard, is accused of fraud but claims that his deceased supervisor, Palairet, actually carried out the falsification of results. Among the parallels to the Howard/Palairet fraud drawn by the characters in Snow's fiction is the work of Barkla, a physics profession at Edinburgh from 1924-44. Barkla believed he had discovered a 'J-phenomenon' and fourteen research students successfully got Ph.Ds for work on this, non-existent, phenomenon (Wynne, 1979). Snow may well have had the Barkla department in mind but if so he did not represent it faithfully, for Barkla had women students, and no scientific women appear in *The Affair*. Despite the footnote to the 'Two Cultures' lecture, this omission probably reflects Snow's views of women - common in scientists of his age - captured when his niece was born in the immediate post-war period. He wrote to his brother: 'one advantage of a girl is that you don't have to bother about her education' (Snow, 1982:93).

Conclusions

While the two standard histories of the British chime novel see no merit in the novels of Sayers, Marsh and Allingham, their work has lasted for over fifty years. The argument of this chapter is that this is partly because at the heart of the books are serious attempts at developing marriages between equals.

References

Abbott, E. and Breckinridge, S. (1916) *Truancy and Non-Attendance in the Chicago Schools*. Chicago, Chicago University Press.

Abir-Am, P. (1987) 'Synergy or Clash'. In P.G. Abir-Am and D. Outram (Eds) *Uneasy careers and Intimate Lives*. London, Rutgers University Press.

Abir-am, P.G. and Outram, D. (Eds) (1987) *Uneasy Careers and Intimate Lives*. London, Rutgers University Press.

Abraham, J. (1989a) 'Teacher ideology and sex roles in curriculum texts', *British Journal of Sociology of Education*. Vol.10, No.1, pp.33-52.

Abraham, J. (1989b) 'Gender differences and anti-school boys', *Sociological Review*. Vol.37, No.1, pp.65-88.

Acker, S. (1978) *Sex Differences in Graduate Student Ambition*. Unpublished Ph.D. thesis, University of Chicago.

Acker, S. (1980) 'Women: the other academics'. *British Journal of the Sociology of Education*. Vol.1, No.1, pp.81-91.

Acker, S. (1981) 'No woman's land', *Sociological Review*. Vol.29, No.1, pp.65088.

Acker, S. (1982) 'Women and Education'. In A. Harnett (Ed) *The Social Sciences in Education Studies*. London, Heinemann.

Acker, S., Megarry, J., Nisbett, S. and Hoyle, E. (Eds) (1984) *World Yearbook of Education 1984: Women and Education*. London, Kogan Page.

Addams, J. (1895) *Hull House Maps and Papers*. Boston, Cravell.

Adelman, C. (Ed) (1981) *Uttering, Muttering*. London, Grant MacIntyre.

Aggleton, P., Homans, H. and Warwick, I. (1988) 'Young people's health beliefs about AIDS'. In P. Aggleton and H. Homans (Eds) *Social Aspects of AIDS*. London, Falmer.

Allingham, M. (1938) *The Fashion in Shrouds*. Harmondsworth, Penguin.

Allingham, M. (1949) *More Work for the Undertaker*. Harmondsworth, Penguin.

Alsiss, (1987) *The Social Science Ph.D. since Winfield: The ALSISS response to the Winfield Report and subsequent developments*. London, ALSISS.

Anon (1930) *The Park School, Glasgow 1880-1930*. Glasgow and Edinburgh, William Hodge and Co. Ltd.

Ardener, E. (1972) 'Belief and the problem of women'. In J. Lafontaine (Ed) *The Interpretation of Ritual*. London, Tavistock.

Ardener, E. (1975) 'The "Problem" Revisited'. In S. Ardener (Ed) *Perceiving Women*. London, Dent.

Ardener, S. (Ed) (1975) *Perceiving Women*. London, Dent.

Ardener, S. (Ed) (1978) *Defining Females*. London, Croom Helm.

Ardener, S. (Ed) (1981) *Women and Space*. London, Croom Helm.

Ardener, S. (1985) 'The social anthropology of women and feminist anthropology'. *Anthropology Today*. Vol.1, No.5, pp.24-6.

Arnot, M. (Ed) (1985) *Race and Gender: Equal Opportunities Policies in Education*. Oxford, Pergamon Press for the Open University.

Askew, S. and Ross, C. (1988) *Boys Don't Cry*. Milton Keynes, Open University Press.

Atkinson, P. (1981) *The Clinical Experience: The Construction and Reconstruction of Medical Reality*. Farnborough, Gower.

Atkinson, P. (1984a) 'Wards and deeds: taking knowledge and control seriously'. In R. Burgess (Ed) *The Research Process in Educational Settings: Ten Case Studies* pp.163-185. Lewes, Falmer.

Atkinson, P. (1984b) 'Training for certainty'. *Social Science and Medicine* pp.949-56.

Atkinson, P. (1985a) *Language, Structure and Reproduction*. London, Methuen.

Atkinson, P. (1985b) 'Strong minds and weak bodies'. *British Journal of the History of Sport*. Vol.2, No.1, pp.62-71.

Atkinson, P. (1987) 'Man's best hospital and the Mug and Muffin: An innocent ethnographer meets American medicine'. In N.P. McKeganey and S. Cunningham-Burley (Eds) *Enter the Sociologist* pp.174-193. Aldershot, Avebury.

Atkinson, P. (1988) 'Discourse, descriptions and diagnoses: The reproduction of normal medicine'. In M. Lock and D. Gordon (Eds) *Biomedicine Observed* pp.179-204. Boston and Dordrecht, Reidel.

Atkinson, P. (1990) *The Ethnographic Imagination: Textual Constructions of Reality*. London, Routledge.

Atkinson, P. (1991) 'Supervising the text'. *International Journal of Qualitative Studies in Education*, Vol.4, pp.161-174.

Atkinson, P. and Delamont, S. (1980) 'The two traditions in educational ethnography' *British Journal of Sociology of Education*. Vol.1, No.2, pp.139-152.

Atkinson, P. and Delamont, S. (1985a) 'Socialisation into Teaching'. *British Journal of Sociology of Education.* Vol.6, No.3, pp.307-322.

Atkinson, P. and Delamont, S. (1985b) 'Bread and Dreams or Bread and Circuses?' In M. Shipman (Ed) *Educational Research*. London, Falmer.

Atkinson, P. and Delamont, S. (1990) 'Writing about teachers'. *Teaching and Teacher Education.* Vol.6, No.2, pp.111-125.

Atkinson, P.A., Reid, M.E., and Sheldrake, P.F. (1977) 'Medical mystique'. *Sociology of Work and Occupations.* Vol.4, pp.243-80.

Atkinson, P.A., Delamont, S. and Hammersley, M. (1988) 'Qualitative research traditions'. *Review of Educational Research.* Vol.38, No.2, pp.231-250.

Atkinson, P.A. and Hammersley, M. (1983) *Ethnography: Principles in Practice.* London, Tavistock.

Bamford, C. (1988) *Gender and Education in Scotland.* Edinburgh, SIACE.

Bannister, D. and Fransella, F. (1971) *Inquiring Man.* Harmondsworth: Penguin.

Bauman, R. (1982) 'Ethnography of children's folklore'. In P. Gilmore and A.A. Glatthorn (Eds) *Children in and out of School.* Washington, D.T. Cal.

Becker, H.S. (1971) Footnote. Added to the paper by Wax, M. and Wax, R. (1971) 'Great Tradition, little tradition, and formal education'. In M. Wax *et al* (Eds) *Anthropological Perspectives on Education* pp.3-27. New York, Basic Books.

Becker, H.S. (1972) 'School is a lousy place to learn anything'. In B. Geer (Ed) *Learning to Work.* Beverley Hills, Sage.

Becker, H.S., Geer, B., Hughes, E.C. and Strauss, A.L. (1961) *Boys in White.* Chicago, Chicago University Press.

Becker, H.S., Geer, B. and Hughes, E.C. (1968) *Making the Grade.* New York, Wiley.

Bell, R. (1983) 'The Education departments in the Scottish Universities'. In W.M. Humes and H.M. Paterson (Eds) *Scottish Culture and Scottish Education 1800-1980.* Edinburgh, John Donald.

Bennett, S.N. (1976) *Teaching Styles and Pupil Progress.* London, Open Books.

Bernstein, B. (1971) 'On the classification and framing of educational knowledge'. In M.F.D. Young (Ed) *Knowledge and Control*. London, Macmillan.

Bernstein, B. (1974) *Class and pedagogies: visible and invisible*. Paris, OECD.

Best, R. (1983) *We've All Got Scars*. Bloomington, Indiana University Press.

Beynon, J. (1985) *Initial Encounters in the Secondary School*. London, Falmer.

Beynon, J. (1987) 'Miss Floral mends her ways'. In L. Tickle (Ed) *The Arts in Education*. London, Croom Helm.

Beynon, J. and Atkinson, P. (1984). 'Pupils as data-gatherers'. In S. Delamont (Ed) *Readings on Interaction in the Classroom*. London, Methuen.

Blackburn, R. and Mann, M. (1979) *The Working Class in the Labour Market*. London, Macmillan.

Blatchford, P. *et al* (1982) *The First Transition*. Windsor, NFER-Nelson.

Bloor, D. and Bloor, C. (1982) 'Twenty Industrial Scientists'. In M. Douglas (Ed) *In the Active Voice*. London, Routledge.

Bone, A. (1983) *Girls and Girls-only Schools: A Review of the Evidence*. Manchester, EOC.

Booth, C. 1892-1897 *Life and Labour of the People in London*. 9 vols. London, Macmillan.

Booth, M. (1927) 'The present day education of girls'. *The Nineteenth Century and After*. 102 (August) pp.259-269.

Booth, M. (1932) *Youth and Sex*. London, Allen and Unwin.

Borer, M.C. (1976) *Willingly to School*. London, Lutterworth.

Bossert, S.T. (1982) 'Understanding sex differences in children's classroom experiences'. In W. Doyle and T.L. Good (Eds) *Focus on Teaching*. Chicago, The University Press.

Bourdieu, P. (1988) *Homo Academicus*. Oxford, Polity Press.

Bourdieu, P. and Passeron, J.C. (1977) *Reproduction in Education, Society and Culture*. London, Sage.

Breckinridge, Sophonisba and Abbott, E. (1912) *The Delinquent Child and the Home*. New York, Charities Publication Committee.

Briscoe, A.M. (1987) 'Scientific Sexism: The World of Chemistry'. In V. Haas and C.C. Perrucci (Eds) *Women and Scientific Engineering Professions*. Ann Arbor, University of Michigan Press.

Broadbent, D. (1987) 'Psychology'. In G. Winfield (Ed) *The Social Science Ph.D.* 2 vols. London, ESRC.

Brown, G. (1973) *The effects of training upon performance in teaching situations.* Unpublished D.Phil. Coleraine, University of Ulster.

Brown, G. (1975) 'Microteaching'. In G. Chanan and S. Delamont (Eds) *Frontiers of Classroom Research.* Slough, NFER.

Brown, S. and Riddell, S. (Eds) (1992) *Class, Race and Gender in Schools: A New Agenda for Policy and Practice in Scottish Education.* Edinburgh, SCRE.

Brunvand, J. (1983) *The Vanishing Hitchhiker.* London, Picador.

Brunvand, J. (1984) *The Choking Doberman.* New York, W. Norton.

Brunvand, J. (1985) *The Mexican Pet.* New York, W. Norton.

Bryan, K.A. (1980) 'Pupil perception of transfer'. In A. Hargreaves and L. Tickle (Eds) *Middle School.* London, Harper and Row.

Bryant, M. (1979) *The Unexpected Revolution.* London, University of London Institute of Education.

Bullivant, B.M. (1978) *The Way of Tradition.* Victoria, Australian Council for Educational Research.

Bulmer, M. (1984) *The Chicago School of Sociology.* Chicago, Chicago University Press.

Burchell, H. and Millman, V. (1989) (Eds) *Changing Perspectives on Gender.* Milton Keynes, The Open University Press.

Burgess, E.W. (1916) 'The Social Survey' in *American Journal of Sociology,* 21 January 1916, pp.492-500.

Burgess, R.G. (1983) *Experiencing comprehensive education.* London and New York, Methuen.

Burgess, R.G. (1984) (Ed) *The Research Process in Educational Settings.* London, Falmer.

Burgess, R.G. (1985) (Ed) *Field Methods in the Study of Education.* London, Falmer.

Burgess, R.G. (1994) (Ed) *PostGraduate Education and training in the social sciences: processes and products.* London, Jessica Kingsley Publishers.

Burrage, H.F. (1983) 'Women University Teachers of Natural Science, 1971-72'. *Social Studies of Science,* Vol.13, pp.147-60.

Burstall, S. (1933) *Retrospect and Prospect.* London, Longmans.

Burstyn, J. (1980) *Victorian Education and the Ideal of Womanhood.* London, Croom Helm.

Buswell, C. (1981) 'Sexism in school routines and classroom practice'. *Durham and Newcastle Research Review.* Vol.9, No.4/6, pp.195-200.

Buswell, C. (1984) 'Sponsoring and stereotyping in a working-class English Secondary School'. In S. Acker *et al* (Eds) *World Year Book of Education*. London, Kogan Page.

Buswell, C. (1988) 'Flexible workers for flexible firms?' In A. Pollard *et al* (Eds) *Education Training and the New Vocationalism*. Milton Keynes, Open University Press.

Butt, R. (1990) 'Boys will be Boys'. *The Times* August 23rd.

Canaan, J. (1986) 'Why a 'slut' is a 'slut''. In H. Varenne (Ed) *Symbolizing America*. Lincoln, Nebraska, The University of Nebraska Press.

Cazden, C. (1986) 'Classroom discourse'. In M. Wittrock (Ed) *Handbook of Research on Teaching*. (3rd edition). pp.432-463. New York, Collier-Macmillan.

Chanan, G. and Delamont, S. (1975) (Eds) *Frontiers of Classroom Research*. Slough, NFER.

Clarricoates,K.(1980) 'The importance of being Ernest...Emma...Tom...Jane'. In R. Deem (Ed) *Schooling for Women's Work*. London, Routledge.

Clarricoates, K. (1983) 'The experience of patriarchal schooling'. *Interchange*. Vol.12, No.2/3, pp.185-206.

Clarricoates, K. (1987) 'Child culture at school'. In A. Pollard (Ed) *Children and their Primary Schools*. London, Falmer.

Cleave, S. *et al* (1982) *And So To School*. Windsor, NFER, Nelson.

Clegg, S. (1985) 'Feminist Methodology'. *Quality and Quantity*. Vol.19, No.1, pp.83-97.

CNAA (1987) *Annual Report 1986/87*. London, CNAA.

Coats, M. (1983) 'Gender, class and education: a teaching bibliography of European Studies'. In L. Barton and S. Walker (Eds) *Gender, Class and Education*. Lewes, Falmer.

Cockburn, C. (1987) *Two Track Training*. London, Macmillan.

Coffield, F. *et al.* (1986) *Growing up at the Margins*. Milton Keynes, The Open University Press.

Cohen, P. (1973) *The Gospel According to the Harvard Business School*. New York, Penguin.

Cohen, L. and Manion, L. (1981) *Research Methods in Education*. London, Croom Helm.

Cohen, L. and Manion, L. (1985) *Research Methods in Education*. London, Croom Helm. (Second edition).

Cole, J. (1979) *Fair Science: Women in the Scientific Community*. New York, The Free Press.

182

Cole, J.R. and Cole, S. (1973) *Social Stratification in Science.* Chicago, The University Press.

Collins, H.M. (1985) *Changing Order.* London, Sage.

Colombo, R. and Morrison, D. (1987) *Blacklisting social science departments with poor submission rates.* Unpublished paper. Marketing Department, New York University.

Courtney, J.E. (1934) *The Women of My Time.* London, Lovat Dickson.

Cowell, A., Rees, T.L. and Read, M. (1981) 'Occupational aspirations and rising unemployment in a South Wales valley'. *Education for Development.* Vol.6, pp.14-24.

Coxon, A.P.M. (1983) 'A cookery class for men'. In A. Murcott (Ed) *The Sociology of Food and Eating.* Farnborough, Gower.

Croll, P. (1980) 'Data presentation, analysis and statistical methods'. In M. Galton *et al. Inside the Primary Classroom.* London, Routledge and Kegan Paul.

Croll, P. and Moses, D. (1990) 'Sex roles in the primary classroom'. In C. Rogers and P. Kutnick (Eds) *The Social Psychology of the Primary School.* London, Routledge.

Crossman, M. (1987) 'Teachers' interactions with girls and boys in science lessons'. In A. Kelly (Ed) *Science for Girls.* Milton Keynes, The Open University Press.

Dale, R. (1978) *The Tumour in the Whale.* London, W.H. Allen.

Deegan, M.J. (1988) *Jane Addams and the Men of the Chicago School.* New Brunswick, Transaction Books.

Deegan, M.J. and Hill, M. (1987) (Eds) *Women and Symbolic Interactionism.* Boston, Allen and Unwin.

Deem, R. (1978) *Women and Schooling.* London, Routledge.

Deem, R. (1984) (Ed) *Co-education Reconsidered.* London, Methuen.

Delamont, S. (1973) *Academic Conformity Observed.* Unpublished Ph.D. thesis, University of Edinburgh.

Delamont, S. (1975a) 'Participant observation and educational anthropology'. *Research Intelligence.* Vol. 1, pp.13-22.

Delamont, S. (1975b) 'Introduction'. In G. Chanan and S. Delamont (Eds) *Frontiers of classroom research.* pp.5-12. Slough, National Foundation for Education Research.

Delamont, S. (1976a) *Interaction in the Classroom.* London, Methuen.

Delamont, S. (1976b) 'Beyond Flanders Fields'. In M. Stubbs and S. Delamont (Eds) *Explorations in Classroom Observation.* Chichester, Wiley.

Delamont, S. (1976c) 'The girls most likely to'. *Scottish Journal of Sociology.* Vol.1, No.1, pp.29-43: reprinted in R. Parsler (1980)

(Ed) *Capitalism, Class and Politics in Scotland.* Farnborough, Gower.

Delamont, S. (1978a) 'The Contradictions in Ladies' Education'. In S. Delamont and L. Duffin (Eds) *The Nineteenth Century Woman.* London, Croom Helm.

Delamont, S. (1978b) 'The Domestic Ideology and Women's Education'. In S. Delamont and L. Duffin (Eds) *The Nineteenth Century Woman.* London, Croom Helm pp.134-187.

Delamont, S. (1980) *Sex Roles and the School.* London, Methuen.

Delamont, S. (1981) 'All too familiar? A decade of classroom research'. *Educational Analysis.* Vol.3, No.1, pp.69-84.

Delamont, S. (1983a) 'The Conservative School'. In S. Walker and L. Barton (Eds) *Gender, Class and Education.* Brighton, Falmer.

Delamont, S. (1983b) 'A Woman's Place in Education'. *Research Intelligence.* Vol.13, pp.2-4.

Delamont, S. (1983c) 'The Ethnography of Transfer'. In M. Galton and J. Willcocks (Eds) *Moving from the Primary Classroom.* London, Routledge.

Delamont, S. (1983d) *Interaction in the Classroom* (2nd edition). London, Routledge.

Delamont, S. (1984a) (Ed) *Readings on Interaction in the Classroom.* London, Routledge.

Delamont, S. (1984b) 'The Old Girl Network'. In R.G. Burgess (Ed) *Fieldwork in Educational Settings.* London, Falmer.

Delamont, S. (1984c) 'Debs, Dollies, Swots and Weeds: Classroom Styles at St. Lucke's'. In G. Walford (Ed) *British Public Schools.* London, Falmer.

Delamont, S. (1987) 'Three Blind Spots?' *Social Studies of Science.* Vol.17, No.1, pp.163-170.

Delamont, S. (1989) 'The Nun in the toilet'. *Qualitative Studies in Education.* Vol.2, No.3, pp.191-202.

Delamont, S. (1989b) *Knowledgeable Women.* London, Routledge.

Delamont, S. (1990) *Sex Roles and the School.* (2nd edition). London, Routledge.

Delamont, S. (1991) 'The Hit List and other horror stories' *Sociological Review.* Vol.39, No.2, pp.238-259.

Delamont, S. (1992) *Fieldwork in Educational Settings.* London, Falmer.

Delamont, S. (1993a) 'The Beech-Covered Hill Side'. In G. Walford (Ed) *The Private Schooling of Girls.* London, Woburn Press pp.79-100.

Delamont, S. (1993b) 'Distant Dangers and forgotten standards'. *Women's History Review.* Vol.2, No.2, pp.233-252.

Delamont, S. and How, J.A.M. (1973) 'Pupils' answer to computer language' *Education in the North.* Vol.10, pp.73-78.

Delamont, S. and Duffin, L. (1978) (Eds) *The Nineteenth Century Woman.* London, Croom Helm.

Delamont, S. and Galton, M. (1986) *Inside the Secondary Classroom.* London, Routledge.

Delamont, S. and Galton, M. (1987) 'Anxieties and anticipations'. In A. Pollard (Ed) *Children and their Primary Schools.* London, Falmer.

Denham, C. and Leiberman, A. (1980) (Eds) *Time to Learn.* Washington D.C., NIE/DHEW.

Dingwall, R., Reid, M., Heath, C., and Stacey, M. (1977) (Eds) *Health Care and Medical Knowledge.* London, Croom Helm.

Douglas, M. (1966) *Purity and Danger.* London, Routledge.

Douglas, M. (1970) *Natural Symbols.* London, Barnes and Rockliff.

Douglas, M. (1975a) 'Social and religious symbolism of the Lele'. In M. Douglas (Ed) *Implicit Meanings.* London, Routledge.

Douglas, M. (1975b) 'Animals in Lele religious symbolism'. In M. Douglas (Ed) *Implicit Meanings.* London, Routledge.

Douglas, M. (1982) (Ed) *In the Active Voice.* London, Routledge.

Driver, R. (1983) *The Pupil as Scientist.* Milton Keynes, The Open University Press.

Duffin, L. (1978) 'The Conspicuous consumptive'. In S. Delamont and L. Duffin (Eds) *The Nineteenth Century Woman.* London, Croom Helm.

Duthie, J. (1970) *Primary School Survey.* Edinburgh, HMSO.

Dyhouse, C. (1976) 'Social-Darwinist ideas and the development of women's education in England 1880-1920' *History of Education.* Vol.5, No.1, pp.41-58.

Dyhouse, C. (1977) 'Good wives and little mothers' *Oxford Review of Education.* Vol.3, No.1, pp.21-35.

Dyhouse, C. (1981) *Girls Growing up in late Victorian and Edwardian England.* London, Routledge.

Edwards, A.E. (1980) 'Perspectives on classroom language'. *Educational Analysis.* Vol.3, No.1, pp.21-35.

Eggleston, J.F. and Delamont, S. (1983) *Supervision of Students for Research Degrees.* Kendal, Dixon Printing Co. for BERA.

Eickelman, D.F. (1978) 'The Art of Memory' *Comparative Studies in Society and History.* Vol.20, No.3, pp.485-516.

Elliot, J. and Powell, C. (1987) 'Young women and science' *British Journal of Sociology of Education.* Vol.8, No.3, pp.277-286.

Engels, F. (1972) 'The Origins of the Family'. *The New Edinburgh Review*

ESRC (1987) *Newletter 60*. London, ESRC.

Evans, G.W. (1990) *Education and Female Emancipation.* Cardiff, University of Wales Press.

Faris, R.E.L. (1967) *Chicago Sociology 1920-1932.* Chicago, University Press.

Fass, P.S. (1977) *The Damned and the Beautiful.* Oxford, The University Press.

Feldman, S.D. (1974) *Escape from the Doll's House.* New York, McGraw-Hill.

Fine, G.A. (1981) 'Rude Words' *Maledicta*. Vol.5 pp.51-68.

Fine, G.A. (1987) *With the Boys.* Chicago, The University Press.

Fine, G.A. (1988) 'Good children and dirty play'. *Play and Culture* Vol.1, No.1, pp.43-56.

Flanders, N.A. (1970) *Analysing Teaching Behaviour.* New York, Adison-Welsey.

Fletcher, S. (1980) *Feminists and Bureaucrats.* Cambridge, The University Press.

Fox Keller, E. (1983) *A Feeling for the Organism.* San Francisco, Freeman.

Fox Keller, E. (1985) *Reflections on Gender and Science.* Newhaven and London, Yale University Press.

Fox, I. (1985) *Private school and public issues.* London, Macmillan.

French, J. and French, P. (1984) 'Sociolinguistics and gender divisions'. In S. Acker (Ed) *Women and Education.* London, Kogan Paul.

Fuller, M. (1980) 'Black girls in school'. In R. Deem (Ed) *Schooling for Women's Work.* London, Routledge.

Furlong, V.J. (1976) 'Interaction sets in the Classroom'. In M. Stubbs and S. Delamont (Eds) *Explorations in Classroom Observation.* Chichester, Wiley.

Gadesden, F. (1901) 'Secondary education of girls'. In R.D. Roberts (Ed) *Education in the Nineteenth Century.* Cambridge, The University Press.

Galloway, H.M. (1973) *Female Students and their Aspirations.* Unpublished M.Phil thesis, University of Edinburgh.

Galton, M. (1978) *British Mirrors.* Leicester, The School of Education.

Galton, M. and Delamont, S. (1976) *An evaluation of Ph.D/PGCE Chemistry Courses.* Leicester, The School of Education.

Galton, M., Simon, B. and Croll, P. (1980) *Progress and Performance in the Primary Classroom.* London, Routledge.

Galton, M. and Willcocks, J. (1983) *Moving from the Primary Classroom.* London, Routledge and Kegan Paul.

Galton, M. and Delamont, S. (1985) 'Speaking with forked tongue'. In R.G. Burgess (Ed) *Field Methods in the Study of Education.* London, Falmer.

Geer, B. (1964) 'First days in the field'. In P. Hammond (Ed) *Sociologists at Work.* New York, Basic Books.

Geer, B. (1972) (Ed) *Learning to Work.* Beverley Hills, Sage.

Gilbert, J. and Watts, M. (1983) 'Concepts, misconceptions and alternative conceptions'. *Studies in Science Education.* Vol.10, pp.61-98.

Gilman, C.P. (1898) *Women and Economics.* New York, Harper Torchbooks (originally 1898).

Gissing, G. (1980) *The Odd Women.* London, Virago. (originally published 1893).

Glaser, B. (1992) *Basics of Grounded Theory Analysis.* Mill Valley, Sociology Press.

Glaser, B. and Strauss, A. (1967) *The Discovery of Grounded Theory.* Chicago, Aldine.

Godber, J. and Hutchins, I. (1982) (Eds) *A Century of Challenge: Bedford High school 1882-1982.* Bedford, The School.

Gordon, L.O. (1979) 'Co-education on two campuses'. In M. Kelly (Ed) *Woman's Being, Woman's Place.* Boston, G.K. Hall.

Gordon, L.D. (1990) *Gender and Higher Education in the Progressive Years.* New Haven, Yale University Press.

Gornick, V. (1984) *Women in Science.* New York: Simon and Schuster.

Grant, C. and Sleeter, C. (1986) *After the School Bell Rings.* London, Falmer.

Gray, J. (1981) 'A biological basis for sex differences in achievement in science?'. In A. Kelly (Ed) *The Missing Half?* Manchester, The University Press.

Gray, J., McPherson, A.F. and Raffe, D. (1983) *Reconstructions of Secondary Education.* London, Routledge.

Green, J. and Wallat, C. (1981) (Eds) *Ethnography and Language in Educational Settings.* New Jersey, Norwood.

Gribbin, J. (1985) *In Search of the Double Helix.* London, Corgi.

Grugeon, E. (1988) 'Underground knowledge'. *English in Education* Vol.22 p.2.

Grylls, R.G. (1948) *Queen's College 1848-1948.* London, Routledge.

Guttentag, M. and Bray, H. (1976) (Eds) *Undoing Sex Stereotypes.* New York, McGraw-Hill.

Halsey, A.H., Heath, A. and Ridge, J.M. (1980) *Origins and Destinations.* Oxford, Clarendon Press.

Hamilton, D. (1974) *Project PHI: The Fieldwork.* Glasgow, The Education Department University of Glasgow.

Hamilton, D. (1975) 'Handling innovations in the classroom: two Scottish examples'. In W.A. Reid and D.F. Walker (Eds) *Case Studies in Curriculum Change.* London, Routledge and Kegan Paul.

Hamilton, D. (1976) 'The advent of curriculum integration'. In M. Stubbs and S. Delamont (Eds) *Explorations in Classroom Observation.* Chichester, Wiley.

Hamilton, D. (1977) *In Search of Structure.* Edinburgh, SCRE.

Hamilton, D. and Delamont, S. (1974) 'Classroom Research: A Cautionary Tale?'. *Research in Education* Vol.11, pp.1-15.

Hamilton, D. and Delamont, S. (1984) 'Classroom research: a continuing cautionary tale?' In S. Delamont (Ed) *Readings on Interaction in the Classroom.* London, Methuen.

Hammersley, M. (1976) 'The Mobilisation of Pupil Attention'. In M. Hammersley and P. Woods (Eds) *The Process of Schooling.* London, Routledge.

Hammersley, M. (1980) 'Classroom ethnography'. *Educational Analysis.* Vol.2., pp.47-74.

Hammersley, M. (1982) 'The sociology of classrooms'. In A. Harnett (Ed) *The social sciences in educational studies.* pp.227-242. London, Heinemann.

Hammersley, M. (1984) 'Staffroom News'. In A. Hargreaves and P. Woods (Eds) *Classrooms and Staffrooms.* Milton Keynes, The Open University Press.

Hammersley, M. (1990) 'An evaluation of two studies of gender imbalances in primary classrooms' *British Educational Research Journal.* Vol.16, No.2, pp.125-144.

Hanna, J. (1982) 'Social policy and children's worlds'. In G. Spindler (Ed) *Doing the Ethnography of Schooling.* New York, Holt, Rinehart and Winston.

Haraway, D. (1989) *Primate Visions.* London, Routledge.

Harding, J. (1986) (Ed) *Perspectives on Gender and Science.* London, Falmer Press.

Hargreaves, D. (1967) *Social Relations in a Secondary School.* London, Routledge and Kegan Paul.

Hargreaves, D. (1978) 'Whatever happened to Symbolic Interactionism?' In L. Barton and R. Meighan (Eds) *Sociological Interpretations of Schooling and Classrooms.* Driffield, Yorkshire, Nafferton Books.

Hargreaves, D. (1980) 'The occupational culture of teaching'. In P. Woods (Ed) *Teacher Strategies*. London, Croom Helm.

Hargreaves, D., Hestor, S., and Mellor, F. (1975) *Deviance in Classrooms*. London, Routledge.

Hargreaves, A. and Hammersley, M. (1982) 'CCS Gas'. *Oxford Review of Education*.

Hartnett, A. (1982) (Ed) *The Social Sciences in Educational Studies*. London, Heinemann.

Harvey, L. (1987) *Myths of the Chicago School*. Farnborough, Avebury

Hass, V. and Pierucci, C.C. (1987) (Eds) *Women and Scientific and Engineering Professions*. Ann Arbor, University of Michigan Press.

Haynes-Irwin, I. (1935) *Murder in Fancy Dress*. London, Heinemann.

Herbert, C. (1989) *Talking of Silence*. London, Falmer.

Hicklin, S. (1978) *Polished Corners*. Hatfield, Stellar Press.

Hilton, G.L.S. (1991) 'Boys will be boys - won't they?' *Gender and Education*. Vol.3, No.3, pp.311-314.

Holmwood, J. (1987) 'The Winfield Report and its implications' *Network 38* May, pp.3-4.

Hovey, R. (1931) *Penrhos 1880-1930*. Colwyn Bay, The College.

Hudson, L. (1966) *Contrary Imaginations*. London, Methuen.

Hudson, L. (1968a) *Frames of Mind*. London, Methuen.

Hudson, L. (1968b) 'Student style and teaching style', *British Journal of Medical Education*. Vol.2, pp.28-32.

Hudson, L. (1977) 'Picking winners: A case study of the recruitment of research students', *New Universities Quarterly*. Vol.32, No.1, pp.88-106.

Humes, W.A. and Paterson, H. (1983) (Ed) *Scottish Culture and Scottish Education 1800-1980*. Edinburgh, John Donald.

ILEA (1988a) Secondary Transfer Project Bulletin 2. 'The views of primary school pupils'. London, ILEA.

ILEA (1988b) Secondary Transfer Project Bulletin 5. 'My first day at school'. London, ILEA.

ILEA (1988c) Secondary Transfer Project Bulletin 6. 'Pupils' early experiences of secondary school'. London, ILEA.

Jackson, B. (1964) *Streaming*. London, Routledge.

Jackson, P.W. (1968) *Life in Classrooms*. New York, Holt, Rhinehart and Winston.

Jayaratne, T.N. (1983) 'The value of quantitative methodology for feminist research'. In G. Bowles and R. Duelli-Klein (Eds) *Theories of Women's Studies*.

Jewel, H.M. (1976) *A School of unusual excellence.* Leeds, The School.

Joffe, C. (1974) 'As the twig is bent'. In J. Stacey *et al* (Eds) *And Jill Came Tumbling After.* New York, Dell.

Jones, G.E. (1982) *Controls and Conflicts in Welsh Secondary Education 1889-1944.* Cardiff, University of Wales Press.

Jones, P.E. (1989) 'Some trends in Welsh secondary education 1967-1987', *Contemporary Wales,* Vol.2, pp.99-117.

Julian, M.M. (1990) 'Women in Crystallography'. In G. Kass-Simon and R. Farnes (Eds) *Women of Science Righting the Record.* Bloomington, Indiana University Press.

Kamm, J. (1965) *Hope Deferred.* London, Methuen.

Kass Simon, G. and Farnes, R. (1990) (Eds) *Women of Science Righting the Record.* Bloomington, Indiana University Press.

Keillor, G. (1986) *Lake Wobegon Days.* London, Faber and Faber.

Keller, E.F. (1983) *A feeling for the Organism.* New York, W.E. Freeman.

Kelly, A. (1981) (Ed) *The Missing Half.* Manchester, The University Press.

Kelly, A. (1985) 'The Construction of Masculine Science' *British Journal of the Sociology of Education.* Vol.6, No.2, pp.133-154.

Kelly, A. (1987) *Science for Girls.* Milton Keynes, The Open University Press.

Kenealy, A. (1920) *Feminism and Sex Extinction.* London, Fisher-Unwin.

Kenna, M.E. (1985) *History of Religious Icons in Theory and Practice: An Orthodox Christian Example.* Chicago, Chicago University Press.

Kidwell, P.A. (1987) Celia Payne-Gaposchkin. In P.G. Abir-Am and D. Outram (Eds) *Uneasy Careers and Intimate Lives.* London, Rutgers University Press.

King, R. (1978) *All Things Bright and Beautiful.* Chichester, Wiley.

Kleinberg, S. (1975) (note in margin) - In G. Chanan and S. Delamont (Eds) *Frontiers of Classroom Research.* Slough, NFER.

Kleinfeld, J.S. (1979) *Eskimo School on the Andreafsky.* New York, Praeger.

Knapp, M. and Knapp, H. (1976) *One Potato.* New York, W. Norton.

Komorovsky, M. (1946) 'Cultural Contradictions and Sex Roles'. *American Journal of Sociology.* Vol.52, pp.182-89.

Komorovsky, M. (1972) 'Cultural Contradictions and Sex Roles: The Masculine Case'. In J. Huber (Ed) *Changing Women in a Changing Society.* Chicago: The University Press.

Kurtz, L.R. (1984) *Evaluating Chicago Sociology.* Chicago, Chicago University Press.

190

Kuvlesky, W.P. and Bealer, R.C. (1972) 'A Clarification of the concept of "Occupational Choice"'. In R.M. Pavalko (Ed) *Sociological Perspectives on Occupations.* Itasca, Illinois: Peacock Press.

Lacey, C. (1970) *Hightown Grammar.* Manchester, The University Press.

Lambart, A. (1977) 'The Sisterhood'. In M. Hammersley and P. Woods (Eds) *The Process of Schooling.* London, Routledge and Kegan Paul.

Lambart, A. (1982) 'Expulsion in Context'. In R. Frankenberg (Ed) *Custom and Conflict in British Society.* Manchester, The University Press.

Larkin, R.W. (1979) *Suburban youth in cultural crisis.* New York and London, Oxford University Press.

Lawton, D. (1975) *Class, Culture and the Curriculum.* London, Routledge and Kegan Paul.

Layton, D. (1984) *Interpreters of Science.* London, John Murray.

Leach, E.R. (1958) 'Magical hair'. *Journal of the Royal Anthropological Institute.* Vol.88, No. 2, pp.147-64, reprinted in J. Middleton (1976) (Ed) *Myth and Cosmos.* New York, The Natural History Press.

Leach, E.R. (1969) *Genesis as Myth and Other Essays.* London, Cape.

Leacock, S. and Leacock, R. (1975) *Spirits of the Deep.* New York, Doubledale Anchor.

Lees, S. (1986) *Losing Out.* London, Hutchinson.

Liebow, E. (1967) *Tally's Corner, Washington, DC.* London, Routledge.

Levi-Montalcini, R. (1988) *In Praise of Imperfection.* New York, Basic Books.

Levi-Strauss, C. (1966) *The Savage Mind.* London, Weidenfeld and Nicolson.

Levi-Strauss, C. (1967) 'The Story of Asdival'. In E.R. Leach (Ed) *The Structural Study of Myth and Totemisim.* London, Tavistock.

Lightfoot, S.L. and Carew, J. (1979) *Beyond Bias.* Cambridge, Mass: Harvard University Press.

Lissak, R.S. (1989) *Pluralism and Progressives.* Chicago, Chicago University Press.

Llewellyn, M. (1980) 'Studying girls at school'. In R. Deem (Ed) *Schooling for Women's Work.* London, Routledge.

Lloyd, B. (1989) 'Rules of the gender game'. *New Scientist.* December 2nd, pp.66-70.

Lyman, S. (1984) 'Interactionism and the study of race relations'. *Symbolic Interactionism.* Vol.7, No.1, pp.107-120.

191

Mac an Ghaill, M. (1988) *Young, Gifted and Black*. Milton Keynes, The Open University Press.

Mac an Ghaill, M. (1991) 'Schooling sexuality and male power'. *Gender and Education* Vol.3, No.3, pp.291-310.

Macdonald, G. (1981) *Once a Week is Ample or The Intelligent Victorian's Guide to Sexuality and the Physical Passions: Quotations from Victorian Experts on Sex and Marriage*. London, Hutchinson.

Macintyre, S. (1977) *Single and Pregnant*. London, Croom Helm.

Mahoney, P. (1985) *Schools for the Boys*. London, Hutchinson.

Malim, M.C. and Escreet, E.C. (1927) *The book of the Blackheath High School*. Blackheath, The Blackheath Press.

Manthorpe, C. (1982) 'Men's science, women's science or science?' *Studies in Science Education* Vol.9, pp.65-80.

Manthorpe, C. (1985) Socio-historical perspectives on the scientific education of girls in 19th and 20th Century England. Unpublished Ph.D. thesis, University of Leeds.

Marsland, D. (1982) 'The sociology of adolescence and youth'. In A. Hartnett (Ed) *The Social Sciences in Educational Studies*. London, Heinemann.

Marsh, N. (1938a) *Artists in Crime*. Glasgow, Collins.

Marsh, N. (1938b) *Death in a White Tie*. Glasgow, Collins.

Marsh, N. (1962) *Hand in Glove*. London, Fontana.

Martin, W.B. (1976) *The Negotiated order of the School*. New York, Maclean-Hunter.

Martin, J.R. (1984) 'Philosophy, Gender and Education'. In S. Acker *et al* (Eds) *Women and Education*. London, Kogan Page.

Matthews, F.H. (1977) *Quest for an American Sociology*. Montreal, McGill-Queen's University Press.

Maynard, C.L. (1910) *Between College Terms*. London, The University Press.

McIntyre, D. and McLeod, G. (1978) 'The characteristics and uses of Systematic Classroom Observation' in R. McAleese and D. Hamilton (Eds) *Understanding Classroom Life*. Windsor, NFER Publishing Co. Ltd.

McPherson, G. (1972) *Small Town Teacher*. Cambridge, Mass: Harvard University Press.

McPherson, A.F. and Neave, G. (1976) *Scottish Sixth*. Slough: NFER.

McPherson, A.F. and Willms, D. (1987) 'Equalisation and Improvement' *Sociology*. Vol.21, No.4, pp.509-540.

McWilliams-Tulberg (1975) *The Women at Cambridge*. Cambridge, Cambridge University Press.

Measor, L. (1984) 'Gender and the Sciences'. In M. Hammersley and P. Woods (Eds) *Life in School*. Milton Keynes, The Open University Press.

Measor, L. (1989) 'Are you coming to see some dirty films today?'. In L. Holly (Ed) *Girls and Sexuality*. Milton Keynes, Open University Press.

Measor, L. and Woods, P. (1983) 'The Interpretation of pupil myths'. In M. Hammersley (Ed) *The Ethnography of Schooling*. Driffield, Yorkshire, Nafferton Books.

Measor, L. and Woods, P. (1984) *Changing Schools*. Milton Keynes, Open University Press.

Medley, D. and Mitzel, H. (1963) 'Measuring classroom behaviour by systematic observation'. In N. Gage (Ed) *Handbook of Research on Teaching*. Chicago, Rand McNally.

Mehan, H. (1978) 'Structuring school structure'. *Harvard Educational Review*. Vol.48, pp.32-64.

Mehan, H. (1979) *Learning Lessons*. Cambridge, M.A, Harvary University Press.

Mehan, H., Hertweck, A. and Meihls, J.L. (1986) *Handicapping the handicapped*. Stanford, Stanford University Press.

Meyenn, R.J. (1980) 'School girls' peer groups'. In P. Woods (ed) *Pupil Strategies*. London, Croom Helm.

Middleton, J. (1965) *The Lugbara of Uganda*. New York, Rinehart and Winston.

Miller, R. (1990) (Ed) *Doing Science*. London, Falmer.

Millman, M. and Kantor, R.M. (1974) (Eds) *Another Voice*. New York, Anchor Books.

Mitchell, J. (1966) 'Women: The Longest Revolution?' *New Left Review*. Vol. 40, pp.17-28.

Mitchinson, N. (1979) *You May Well Ask*. London, Gollancz.

Moir, A. and Jessel, D. (1989) *Brain Sex*. London, Michael Joseph.

Morgan, D. (1981) 'Men, masculinity and the process of sociological enquiry'. In H. Roberts (Ed) *Doing Feminist Research*. London, Routledge.

Morin, E. (1971) *Rumour in Orleans*. London, Weidenfeld and Nicholson.

Morris, J.G. (1981) 'The Research and Intelligence Unit of the SED', *Scottish Educational Review*. Vol.1, No.2, pp.162-166.

Morrison, A. (1973) 'The teaching of international affairs in secondary schools in Scotland'. *MOST*. No.2, (May).

Murcott, A. (1983) 'Cooking and the cooked'. In A. Murcott (Ed) *The Sociology of Food and Eating*. Aldershot, Gower.

Murcott, A. (1988) 'Sociological and social anthropological approaches to food and eating'. *World Review of Nutrition and Dietetics*. Vol.55, pp.1-40.

Murdock, G. and Phelps, G. (1973) *Mass Media and the Secondary School*. London, Macmillan.

Nash, R. (1973) *Classrooms Observed*. London, Routledge.

Nash, R. (1977) *Schooling in rural societies*. London and New York, Methuen.

Newby, H. (1977) *The Deferential Worker*. London, Allen Lane.

The Newport High School for Girls Jubilee Book 1896-1931. Newport, Johns Ltd. 1946.

Nilan, P. (1991) 'Exclusion, Inclusion and Moral Ordering in Two Girls' Friendship Groups'. *Gender and Education*. Vol.3, No.2, pp.163-183.

Niven, B.S. (1988) 'On what is known: personal viewpoint'. *Philosophy and Social Action*. Vol.14, No.2 pp.7-12.

Noblit, G. and Hare, R.E. (1988) *Meta-Ethnography*. Newbury Park, Sage.

Oakley, A. (1979) *Becoming a Mother*. Oxford, Martin Robertson.

Olby, R. (1974) *The Path to the Double Helix*. London, Macmillan.

Opie, I. and Opie, I. (1959) *The lore and language of schoolchildren*. Oxford, Clarendon Press.

Ott, S. (1986) *The Circle of the Mountains*. Oxford, Clarendon Press.

Overfield, K. (1981) 'Dirty fingers, grime and slag heaps'. In D. Spender (Ed) *Men's Studies Modified*. Oxford, Pergamon.

Paley, V.G. (1984) *Boys and Girls: Superheroes in the Doll Corner*. Chicago, The University Press.

The Park School (1930) *The Park School 1880-1930*. Glasgow, Hodge and Co.

Parker, H. (1974) *View from the Boys*. Newton Abbot, David and Charles.

Parsler, R. (1980) (Ed) *Capitalism, Class and Politics in Scotland*. Farnborough, Gower.

Parlett, M. (1967) *Classroom and Beyond*. Boston, Mass: Education Research Center. MIT.

Parlett, M. (1970) 'The syllabus-bound student'. In L. Hudson, (Ed) *The Ecology of Human Intelligence*. Harmondsworth, Penguin.

Parlett, M. and Hamilton, D. (1972) 'Evaluation as Illumination'. Reprinted in D. Hamilton *et al*. (1977) (Eds) *Beyond the Numbers Game*. London, Macmillan.

Paterson, F.M.S. and Fewell, J. (1990) (Eds) *Girls in their Prime*. Edinburgh, Scottish Academic Press.

Phillips, N. (1986) 'Sean is Sean'. *Times Educational Supplement.* 9.7.1986 p.32.

Phillips, P. (1990) *Scientific Ladies.* London, Weidenfeld and Nicholson.

Pilcher, J., Delamont, S., Powell, G., Rees, T. and Read, M. (1989a) 'Evaluating a women's careers convention'. *Research Papers in Education* Vol.4, No.1, pp.57-76.

Pilcher, J., Delamont, S., Powell, G., and Rees, T. (1989b) 'Challenging occupational stereotypes', *British Journal of Guidance and Counselling.* Vol.17, No.1, pp.59-67.

Pilcher, J., Delamont, S., Powell, G. and Rees, T. (1989c) *Career Choices for Schoolgirls: An Evaluative Study of the Cardiff Women's Training Roadshow.* (bilingual), Cardiff, Welsh Office.

Pollert, A. (1981) *Girls, Wives, Factory Lives.* London, Hutchinson.

Porter, M. (1984) 'The Modification of Method in researching postgraduate education'. In R.G. Burgess (Ed) *The Research Process in Educational Settings.* London, Falmer.

Powell, R.C. (1979) 'Sex differences and language learning'. *Audio-Visual Language Journal.* Vol.17, No.1, pp.19-24.

Powell, R.C. (1984) 'Where have all the young men gone?' *Times Educational Supplement.* 4 February 1984.

Powell, R.C. (1986) *Boys, Girls and Language.* Bristol, Multilingual Matters.

Powell, R.C. and Littlewood, P. (1982) 'Foreign Languages, The avoidable options'. *British Journal for Language Teaching.* Vol.20, No.3, pp.153-159.

Powell, R.C. and Littlewood, P. (1983) 'Why Choose French?' *British Journal for Language Teaching.* Vol.21, No.1, p101.

Price, D.T.W. (1990) *A History of Saint David's University College Lampeter. Volume Two 1898-1971.* Cardiff, University of Wales Press.

Purvis, J. (1981) 'Separate Spheres and Inequality in the Education of Working Class Women 1854-1900'. *History of Education.* Vol.10, No.4, pp.227-243.

Raine, K. (1975) *The Land Unknown.* London, Hamish Hamilton.

Rauschenbush, W. (1979) *Robert E. Park: Biography of a Sociologist.* Durham NC, Duke University Press.

Rees, G., Williamson, H. and Winkler, V. (1989) 'The New Vocationalism'. *Journal of Educational Policy.* Vol.4, No.3, pp.227-244.

Reskin, B.F. (1978). 'Sex differentiation and the social organisation of science'. In J. Gaston (Ed) *The Sociology of Science.* San Francisco, Jossey-Bass.

Riddell, S. (1984). 'Bibliography and biographical notes'. In S. Acker, J. Megarry, S. Nisbett and E. Hoyle (Eds) *Women and Education.* London, Kogan Page.

Riddell, S. (1989) 'It's nothing to do with me'. In S. Acker (Ed) *Teachers, Gender and Careers.* London, Falmer.

Riddell, S. (1992) *Gender and the Politics of Curriculum.* London, Routledge.

Riesman, D. (1967) 'Preface' to A. Millar (Ed) *A College in Dispersion.* Boulder Colorado, Westview Press.

Rock, P. (1979) *The Making of Symbolic Interactionism.* London, Macmillan.

Rosenberg, R. (1982) *Beyond Separate Spheres.* New Haven, Yale University Press.

Rosenshine, B. (1971) *Teaching Behaviours and Student Achievement.* Slough, NFER.

Rosenshine, B. (1978) Letter to the editors of the *British Journal of Teacher Education* Vol.4, No.1, p.4.

Rosenshine, B. and Berliner, D.C. (1978). 'Academic engaged time'. *British Journal of Teacher Education.* Vol.4, No.1, p.4-16.

Rossiter, M. (1982) *An Enquiry into the Social Science Research Council.* London, HMSO.

Rothschild, Lord (1982) *An Enquiry into the Social Science Research Council.* London, HMSO.

Rubashow, N. (1986) *Survey of Ph.D. Completion Rates.* London, Makotest.

Russett, C. (1989) *Sexual Science.* Harvard, Harvard University Press.

Rutter, M. *et al* (1979) *1500 Hours.* London, Open Books.

Sayers, D.L. (1930) *Strong Poison.* London, Gollancz.

Sayers, D.L. (1937) *Busman's Honeymoon.* London, Gollancz.

Sayers, J. (1984) 'Psychology and gender divisions'. In S. Acker *et al* (Eds) *Women and Education.* London, Kogan Page.

Sayre, A. (1975) *Rosalind Franklin and DNA.* New York, Norton and Co.

Scharlieb, M. (1924) *Reminiscences.* London, Williams and Norgate.

Scheibinger, L. (1989) *The Mind has no Sex?* Harvard, Harvard University Press.

Scott, J.F. (1980) 'Sororities and the husband game'. In J.P. Spradley and D.W. McCurdy (Eds) *Conformity and Conflict.* Boston, Little, Brown and Co.

Scott, J.P. (1979) *Corporations, Classes and Capitalism*. London, Hutchinson.

Scott, J.P. (1982) *The Upper Classes*. London, Macmillan.

Scott, J.P. and Hughes, M.D. (1980) *The Anatomy of Scottish Capital*. London, Croom Helm.

Scott, S. (1984) 'The personable and the powerful'. In C. Bell and H. Roberts (Eds) *Social Researching*. London, Routledge and Kegan Paul.

Scott, S. (1985) 'Working through the contradictions in researching postgraduate education'. In R.G. Burgess (Ed) *Field Methods in the Study of Education*. London, Falmer.

Scott, S. and Porter, M. (1980) 'Postgraduates, sociology and cuts'. In P. Abrams and P. Leuthwaite (Eds) *Transactions of the BSA*. London, BSA.

Scott, S. and Porter, M. (1983) 'On the bottom rung'. *Women's Studies International Forum* Vol.6, No.2.

Scott, S. and Porter, M. (1984) 'Women in research'. In S. Acker and D. Warren-Piper (Eds) *Is Higher Education Fair to Women*. London, SRHE.

Sellar, W.C. and Yeatman, R.J. (1930) *1066 and All That*. London, Methuen.

Serbin, L. (1978) 'Teachers, peers and play preferences'. In B. Sprung (Ed) *Perspectives on Non-Sexist Early Childhood Education*. New York, Teachers College Press.

Sharp, E. (1926) *Hertha Ayrton*. London, Edward Arnold.

Sharp, R. and Green, A.G. (1976) *Education and Social Control*. London, Routledge.

Shaw, J. (1976) 'Finishing School'. In D.L. Barker and S. Allen (Eds) *Sexual Division and Society*. London, Tavistock.

Shibutani, T. (1966) *Improvised News*. Indianapolis, Bobbs-Merrill Co.

Shone, D. and Atkinson, P. (1981) *Everyday Life in the Merthyr Tydfil Industrial Training Unit an observational study*. Cardiff, Sociological Research Unit, University College, Cardiff.

Sikes, P.J. (1991) 'Nature took its course?' *Gender and Education*. Vol.3, No.2, pp.145-162.

Simon, B. (1965) *Education and the Labour Movement 1870-1920*. London, lawrence and Wishart.

Simon, B. (1974a) *The Two Nations and the Educational Structure 1780-1870*. London, Lawrence and Wishart.

Simon, B. (1974b) *The Politics of Educational Reform 1920-1940*. London, Lawrence and Wishart.

Simon, B. (1990) (Ed) *The Search For Enlightenment*. London, Lawrence and Wishart.

Singleton, J. (1971) *Nichu*. New York, Rinehart and Winston.

Smail, B. *et al* (1982) GIST: the first 2 years *School Science Review* Vol.63 pp.620-630.

Smith, D. (1988) *The Chicago School*. London, Macmillan.

Smith, D.L. (1976) 'Some Implications for a sociology for women'. In N. Glazer and H.Y. Waehrer (Eds) *Woman in a Man-made World* pp.15-39. Chicago, Rand McNally.

Smith, D.L. (1977) 'Women, the family and corporate capitalism'. Reprinted in M. Stephenson *Women in Canada*. Ontario, General Publishing Co. Ltd. revised edition.

Smith, J.V. and Hamilton, D. (1980) (Eds) *The Meritocratic Intellect*. Aberdeen, University Press.

Smith, L.M. (1978) 'An evolving logic of participant observation: education ethnography and other case studies'. In L. Shulman (Ed) *Review of Research in Education 6*. pp.86-101. Itasca, Illinois, Peacock Press.

Smith, L.M. (1982) 'Ethnography'. In H. Mitzel (Ed) *The Encyclopedia of Educational Research*. (Fifth edition) New York, Macmillan.

Smith, L.M. (1990) 'Critical Introduction: Whither Classroom Ethnography?' In M. Hammersley *Classroom Ethnography*. Bristol, PA: The Open University Press.

Smith, L.M. and Geoffrey, W. (1968) *Complexities of an Urban Classroom*. New York, Holt, Rinehart and Winston.

Smith, L.M. and Keith, P. (1971) *Anatomy of Educational Innovation*. New York, Wiley.

Smith, L.S. (1978) 'Sexist assumptions and female delinquency'. In C. Smart and B. Smart (Eds) *Women, Sexuality and Social Control*. London, Routledge.

Smithers, A. and Zientek, P. (1991) *Gender, Primary Schools and the National Curriculum*. Manchester, The University.

Snow, C.P. (1934) *The Search*. London, Gollancz.

Snow, C.P. (1960) *The Affair*. London, Macmillan.

Snow, P. (1980) *Stranger and Brother*. London, Macmillan.

Soloman, J. (1991) 'School laboratory life'. In B.E. Woolnough (Ed) *Practical Science*. Milton Keynes, Open University Press.

Spear, M. (1987) 'Teachers' views about the importance of science for boys and girls'. In A. Kelly (Ed) *Science for Girls*. Milton Keynes, The Open University Press.

Spender, D. (1982) *Invisible Women*. London, Writers and Readers Publishing Co-operative.

Spindler, G. (1974) 'Schooling in Schonhausen'. In G. Spindler (Ed) *Education and Cultural Process*. New York, Holt, Rinehart and Winston.

Stack, V.E. (1963) (Ed) *Oxford High School*. Oxford, Privately Printed.

Stanworth, M. (1981) *Gender and Schooling*. London, WRRC.

Steedman, J. (1983) *Examination results in mixed and single sex schools*. Manchester, EOC.

Stubbs, M. (1975) 'Teaching and talking: a sociolinguistic approach to classroom interaction'. In G. Chanan and S. Delamont (Eds) *Frontiers of Classroom Research*. Slough, National Foundation of Educational Research.

Stubbs, M. and Delamont, S. (1976) (Eds) *Explorations in Classroom Observation*. Chichester, Wiley.

Sussman, L. (1977) *Tales Out of School*. Philadelphia, Temple University Press.

Sutherland, M. (1981) *Sex Bias in Education*. Oxford, Basil Blackwell.

Sutherland, M. (1985a) *Women who teach in Universities*. Stoke on Trent, Trentham Books.

Sutherland, M. (1985b) 'Whatever happened about co-education?' *British Journal of Educational Studies*. Vol.xxviii, pp.155-63.

Swinnerton-Dyer, P. (1982) *Report of the Working Party on Postgraduate Education*. London, HMSO.

Symons, J. (1972) *Bloody Murder*. London, Faber and Faber.

Talbot, M. (1936) *More than Lore* Chicago, Chicago University Press.

Taylorson, D. (1984) 'The professional socialization integration, and identity of women Ph.D. candidates'. In S. Acker and D. Warren Piper (Eds) *Is Higher Education Fair to Women?* London, SRHE.

T.H.E.S. 19.8.77

T.H.E.S. 1.10.92

Thomas, W.I. and Thomas, D.S. (1928) *The Child in America*. New York, Knopf.

Thompson, M. (1982) 'A Three dimensional model'. In M. Douglas (1982) (Ed) *In The Active Voice*. London, Routledge.

Tickle, L. (1987) (Ed) *The Arts in Education*. London, Croom Helm.

Tobias, S. (1990) *They're not Dumb, They're Different*. Tucson, Arizona, Research Corporation.

Torode, B. (1976) 'Teacher's Talk'. In M. Stubbs and S. Delamont (Eds) *Explorations in Classroom observation*. Chichester, Wiley.

199

Traweek, S. (1984) *Beamtimes and Lifetimes*. Cambridge, MA: Harvard University Press.

Turner, B. (1974) *Equality for Some*. London, Ward Lock.

Turner, L. (1933) *Edinburgh University 1883-1933*. Edinburgh, Edinburgh University Press.

Tylecote, M. (1933) *The education of women at Manchester University*. Manchester, Manchester University Press.

U.C.C. (1980/82) 'Prospectus'. Cardiff, University Press.

UGC (1981) *University Statistics 1980* Vol.1. *Students and Staff*. Cheltenham, USR.

UGC (1987) *University Statistics 1987*. Vol.

Valli, L. (1986) *Becoming Clerical Workers*. London, Routledge.

Vartuli, S. (1982) (Ed) *The Ph.D. Experience*. New York, Praeger.

Vicinus, M. (1985) *Independent Women*. London, Virago.

Wakeford, J. (1985) 'A director's dilemmas'. In R.G. Burgess (Ed) *Field Methods in the Study of Education*. London, Falmer.

Walford, G. (1989) 'Shouts of joy and cries of pain'. In D. Raffe (Ed) *Education and the Youth Labour Market*. Basingstoke, Falmer.

Walker, S. and Barton, L. (1983) (Eds) *Gender, Class and Education*. Brighton, Falmer.

Watson, C. (1971) *Snobbery with Violence*. London, Eyre and Spottiswoode.

Watson, J. (1968) *The Double Helix*. London, Weidenfeld and Nicholson.

Watts, D.M. and Gilbert, J.K. (1989) The "new learning" *Studies in Science Education* Vol.16, p.75-121.

Weiner, G. (1985) (Ed) *Just a Bunch of Girls*. Milton-Keynes, The Open University Press.

White, J.P. (1973) *Towards a Compulsory Curriculum*. London, Routledge and Kegan Paul.

Whyte, J. (1985) *Gender, Science and Technology: Inservice Handbook*. York, Longman.

Whyte, J. (1986) *Girls into Science and Technology*. London, Routledge and Kegan Paul.

Wilcox, K. (1982) 'Ethnography as a methodology and its applications to the study of schooling: A review'. In G. Spindler (Ed) *Doing the ethnography of schooling*. pp.456-488. New York, Holt, Rinehart and Winston.

Wilkins, K.S. (1979) *Women's Education in the United States*. Detroit, Gale Research Co.

Willis, P. (1977) *Learning to Labour*. Farnborough, Saxon House.

Wilson, D. (1978) 'Sexual codes and conduct'. In C. Smart and B. Smart (Eds) *Women, Sexuality and Social Control*. London, Routledge and Kegan Paul.

Wilson, E. (1980) *Only Halfway to Paradise* London, Tavistock.

Winfield, G. (1987) *The Social Science Ph.D.* Two Volumes. London, ESRC.

Wober, J.M. (1971) *English girls' boarding schools*. London, Allen Lane.

Wolcott, H.F. (1971) *A Kwakiutl Village and School*. New York, Holt, Rinehart and Winston.

Wolcott, H.F. (1977) *Teachers versus Technocrats*. Eugene, Oregon: Centre for Educational Policy and Management, University of Oregon.

Wolcott, H.F. (1981) 'Confessions of a "trained" observer'. In T.S. Popkewitz and B.R. Tabachnick (Eds) *The Study of Schooling*. New York, Praeger.

Wolcott, H.F. (1982) 'Mirrors, models and monitors'. In G. Spindler (Ed) *Doing the Ethnography of Schooling*. New York, Holt, Rinehart and Winston.

Wolcott, H.F. (1987) 'On Ethnographic intent'. In G. Spindler and L. Spindler (Eds) *Interpretive ethnography of education* pp.37-5. Hillsdale, NJ, Erlbaum.

Wolpe, A.M. (1977) *Some Processes in Sexist Education*. London, WRRC.

Woods, P. (1975) '"Showing them up" in Secondary School'. In G. Chanan and S. Delamont (Eds) *Frontiers of Classroom Research*. Windsor, NFER Publishing Company.

Woods, P. (1979) *The Divided School*. London, Routledge.

Woods, P. and Hammersley, M. (1977) (Eds) *School experience*. London, Routledge.

Woods, P. and Hammersley, M. (1984) (Eds) *Life in School*. Milton Keynes, Open University Press.

Wragg, E.C. (1975). 'The first generation of British interaction studies'. In G. Chanan and S. Delamont (Eds) *Frontiers of Classroom Research*. Slough, NFER.

Wynne, B. (1979) 'Barkla's Ph.D. students and the J-phenomenon'. In R. Wallis (Ed) *On the Margins of Science*. Keele, Sociological Review Monograph.

Young, K. *et al* (1987) *The Management of Doctoral Studies in the Social Sciences*. London, PSI.

Young, M.F.D. (1971) (Ed) 'Introduction'. In M.F.D. Young (Ed) *Knowledge and Control*. London, Collier-Macmillan.

Young, R.E. (1981) 'The epistemic discourse of teachers: an ethnographic study'. *Anthropology and Education Quarterly*, Vol.12, No.2, pp.122-44.

Yoxen, E. Review of the 1981 edition of *The Double Helix* edited by G.S. Stent. *Studies in the History and Philosophy of Science* Vol.14 (1982) pp.279.

Zuckerman, H. (1977) *Scientific Elite: Nobel Laureates in the United States*. New York, Free Press.

Zuckerman, H. (1988) 'The Sociology of Science'. In N.J. Smelser (Ed) *Handbook of Sociology*. London, Sage, pp.511-574.